THE DEATH OF DOCTOR STRANGE

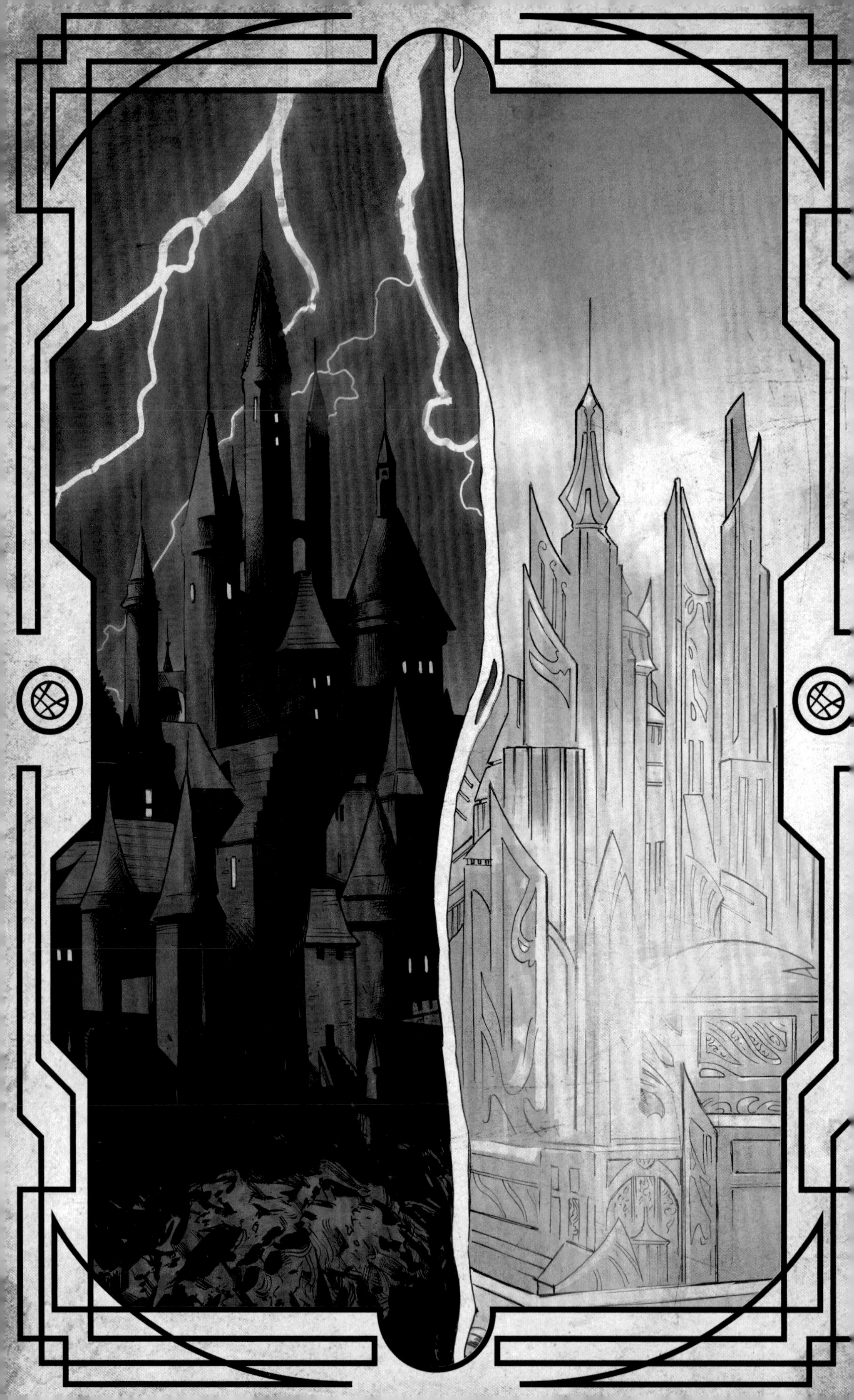

THE DEATH OF DOCTOR STRANGE

Jed MacKay
WRITER

Lee Garbett
ARTIST

Antonio Fabela
COLORIST

VC's Cory Petit
LETTERING

Kaare Andrews
COVER

Kat Gregorowicz
ASSISTANT EDITOR

Darren Shan
EDITOR

SPECIAL THANKS TO TOM BREVOORT

DOCTOR STRANGE CREATED BY STAN LEE & STEVE DITKO

COLLECTION EDITOR JENNIFER GRÜNWALD
ASSISTANT EDITOR DANIEL KIRCHHOFFER
ASSISTANT MANAGING EDITOR MAIA LOY
ASSOCIATE MANAGER, TALENT RELATIONS LISA MONTALBANO
VP PRODUCTION & SPECIAL PROJECTS JEFF YOUNGQUIST
BOOK DESIGNER JAY BOWEN
SVP PRINT, SALES & MARKETING DAVID GABRIEL
EDITOR IN CHIEF C.B. CEBULSKI

DEATH OF DOCTOR STRANGE. Contains material originally published in magazine form as DEATH OF DOCTOR STRANGE (2021) #1-5. First printing 2021. ISBN 978-1-302-93022-6. Published by MARVEL WORLDWIDE, INC., a subsidiary of MARVEL ENTERTAINMENT, LLC. OFFICE OF PUBLICATION: 1290 Avenue of the Americas, New York, NY 10104.

Printed in Canada. KEVIN FEIGE, Chief Creative Officer; DAN BUCKLEY, President, Marvel Entertainment; JOE QUESADA, EVP & Creative Director; DAVID BOGART, Associate Publisher & SVP of Talent Affairs; TOM BREVOORT, VP, Executive Editor; NICK LOWE, Executive Editor, VP of Content, Digital Publishing; DAVID GABRIEL, VP of Print & Digital Publishing; JEFF YOUNGQUIST, VP of Production & Special Projects; ALEX MORALES, Director of Publishing Operations; DAN EDINGTON, Managing Editor; RICKEY PURDIN, Director of Talent Relations; JENNIFER GRÜNWALD, Senior Editor, Special Projects; SUSAN CRESPI, Production Manager; STAN LEE, Chairman Emeritus. For information regarding advertising in Marvel Comics or on Marvel.com, please contact Vit DeBellis, Custom Solutions & Integrated Advertising Manager, at vdebellis@marvel.com. For Marvel subscription inquiries, please call 888-511-5480. **Manufactured between 12/31/2021 and 2/1/2022 by SOLISCO PRINTERS, SCOTT, QC, CANADA.**

10 9 8 7 6 5 4 3 2 1

CHAPTER ONE

The Strange Day

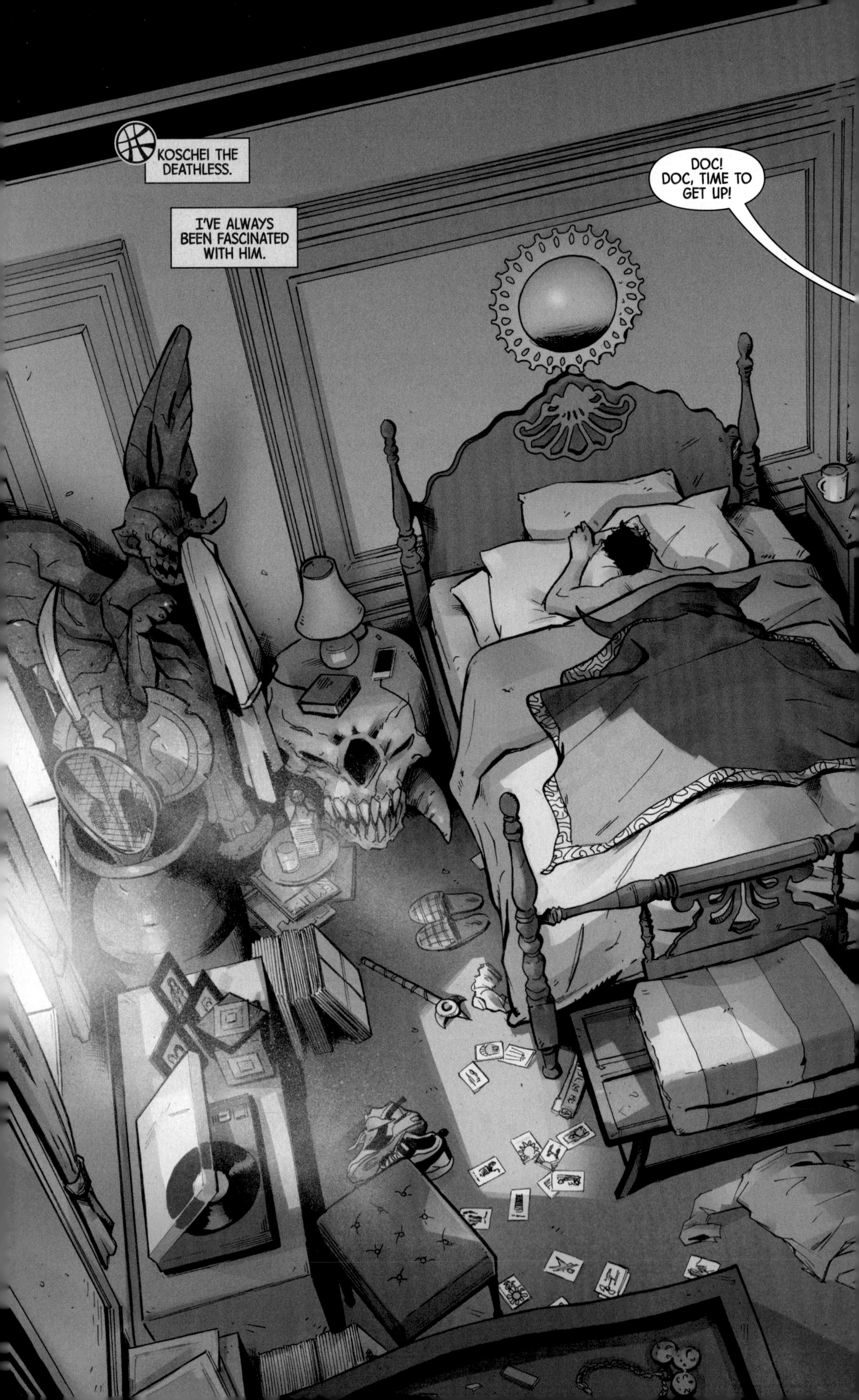
KOSCHEI THE DEATHLESS.
I'VE ALWAYS BEEN FASCINATED WITH HIM.
DOC! DOC, TIME TO GET UP!

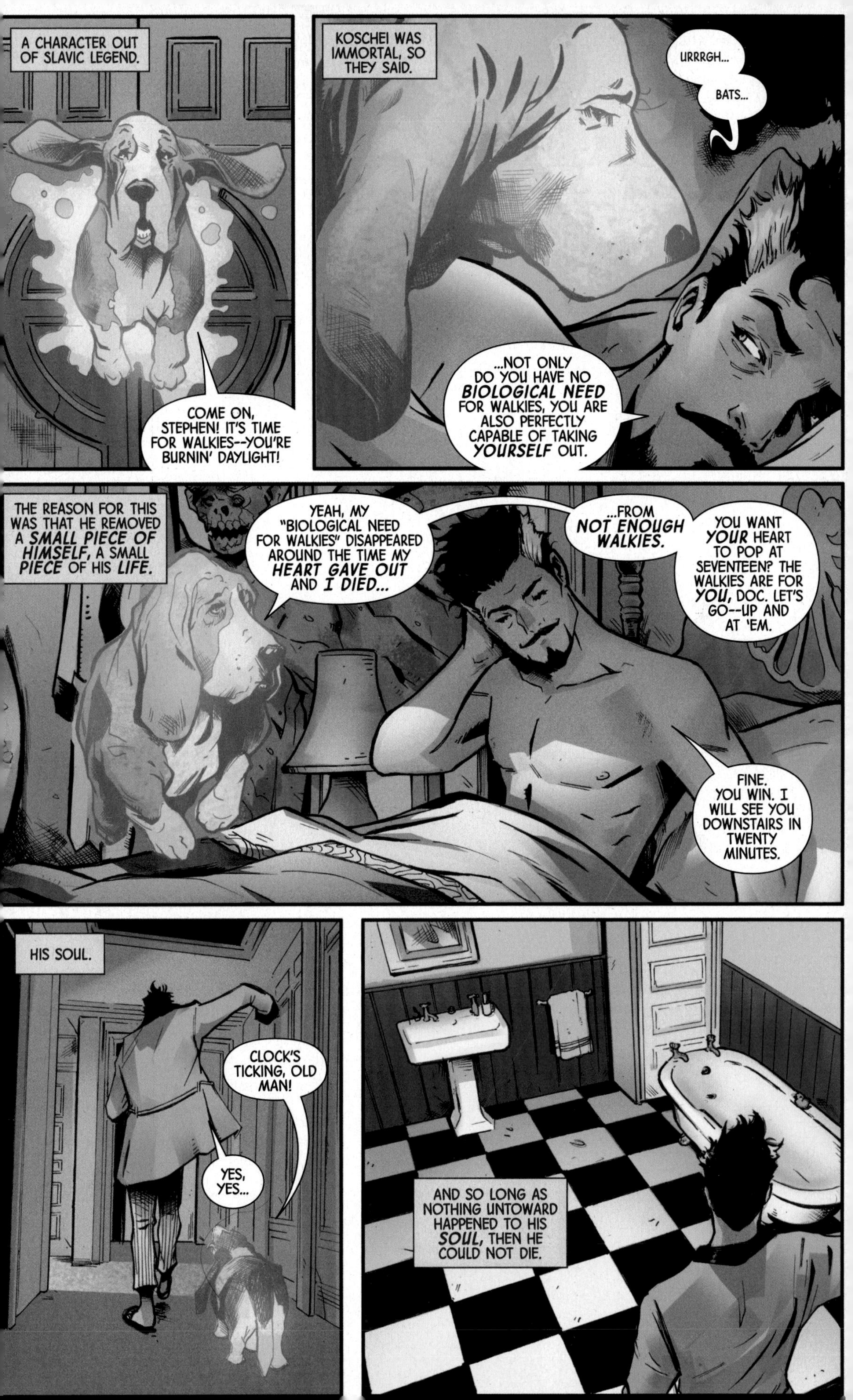
A CHARACTER OUT OF SLAVIC LEGEND.
COME ON, STEPHEN! IT'S TIME FOR WALKIES--YOU'RE BURNIN' DAYLIGHT!
KOSCHEI WAS IMMORTAL, SO THEY SAID.
URRRGH...
BATS...
...NOT ONLY DO YOU HAVE NO BIOLOGICAL NEED FOR WALKIES, YOU ARE ALSO PERFECTLY CAPABLE OF TAKING YOURSELF OUT.
THE REASON FOR THIS WAS THAT HE REMOVED A SMALL PIECE OF HIMSELF, A SMALL PIECE OF HIS LIFE.
YEAH, MY "BIOLOGICAL NEED FOR WALKIES" DISAPPEARED AROUND THE TIME MY HEART GAVE OUT AND I DIED...
...FROM NOT ENOUGH WALKIES.
YOU WANT YOUR HEART TO POP AT SEVENTEEN? THE WALKIES ARE FOR YOU, DOC. LET'S GO--UP AND AT 'EM.
FINE. YOU WIN. I WILL SEE YOU DOWNSTAIRS IN TWENTY MINUTES.
HIS SOUL.
CLOCK'S TICKING, OLD MAN!
YES, YES...
AND SO LONG AS NOTHING UNTOWARD HAPPENED TO HIS SOUL, THEN HE COULD NOT DIE.

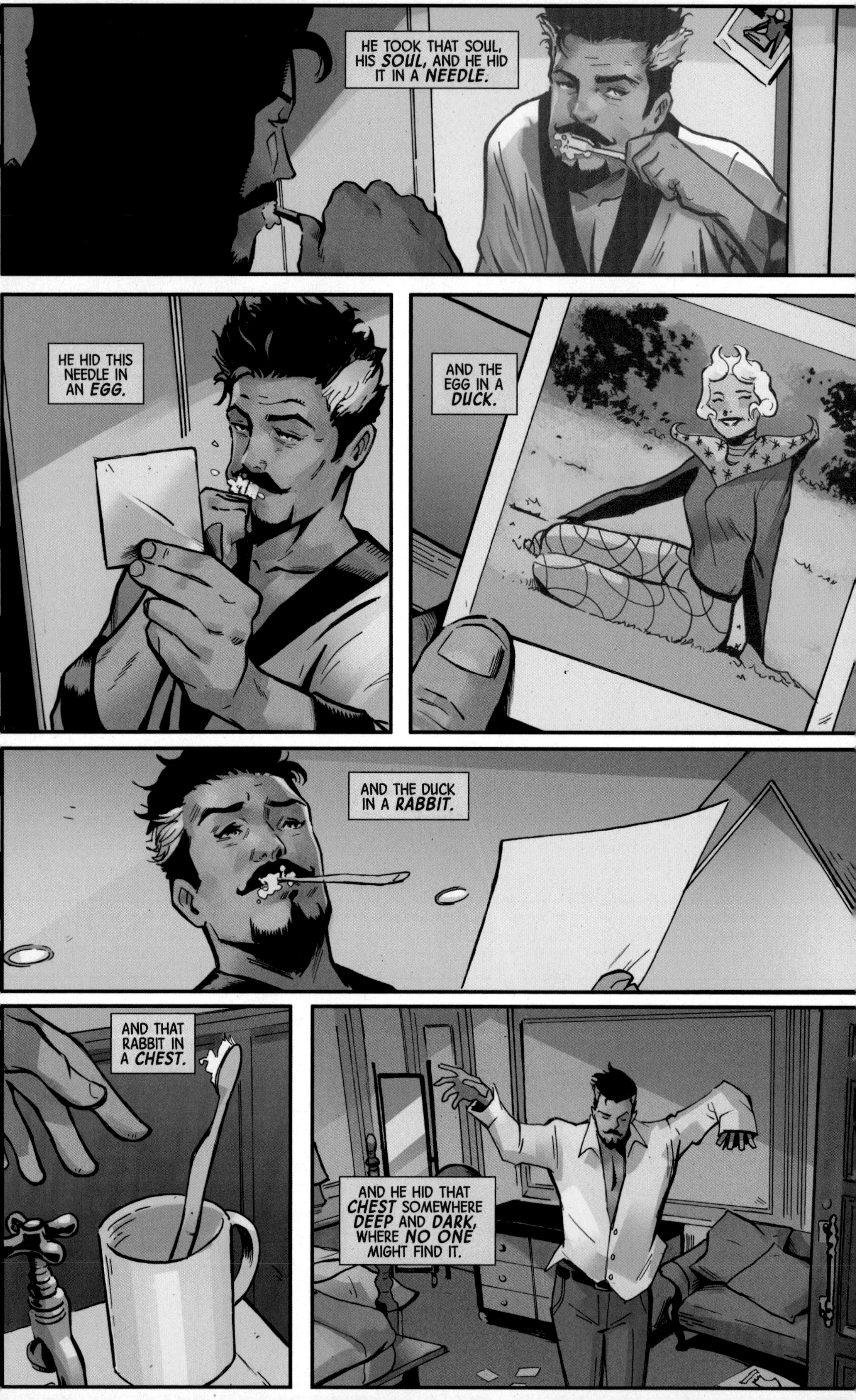
HE TOOK THAT SOUL, HIS SOUL, AND HE HID IT IN A NEEDLE.
HE HID THIS NEEDLE IN AN EGG.
AND THE EGG IN A DUCK.
AND THE DUCK IN A RABBIT.
AND THAT RABBIT IN A CHEST.
AND HE HID THAT CHEST SOMEWHERE DEEP AND DARK, WHERE NO ONE MIGHT FIND IT.

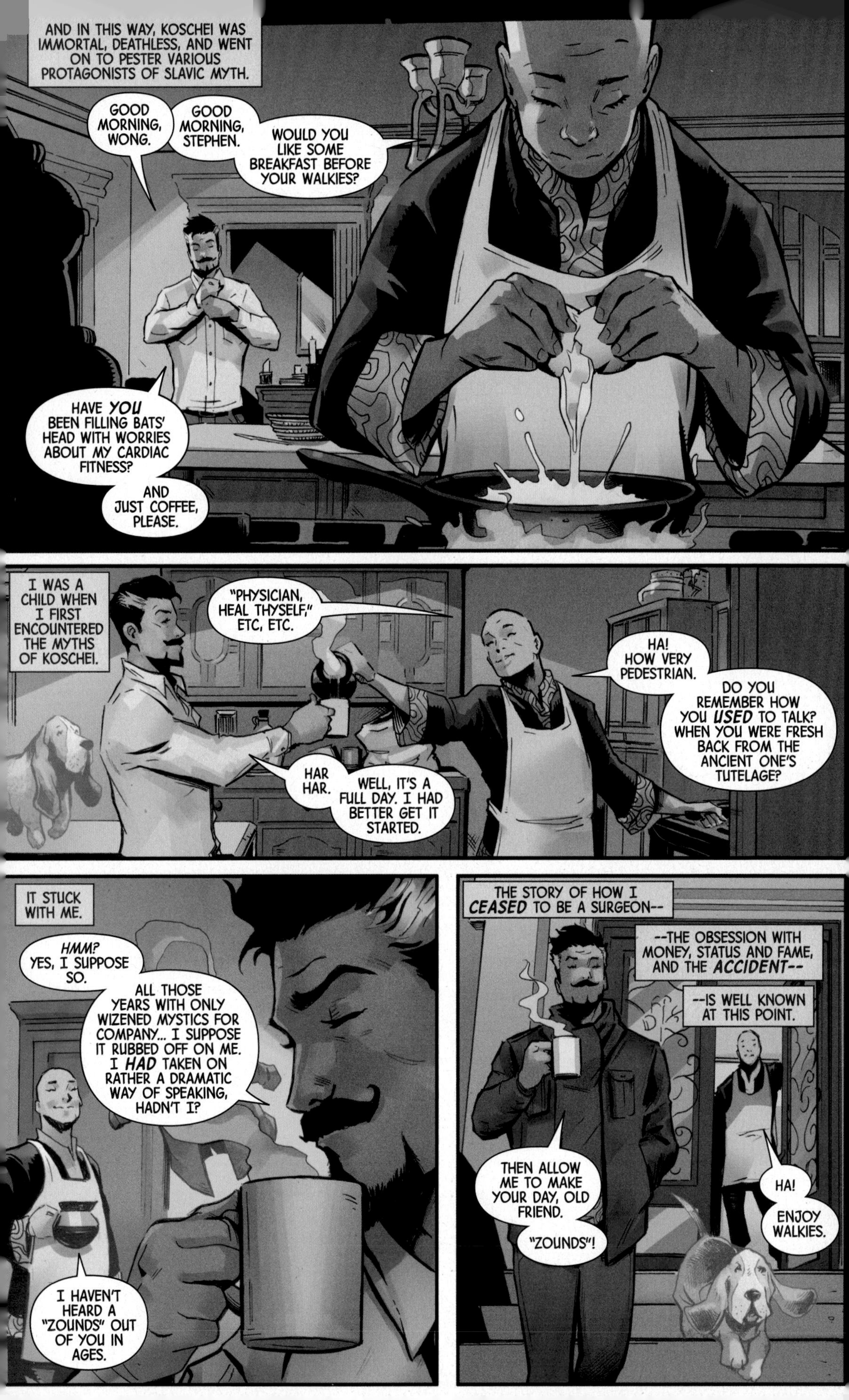

AND IN THIS WAY, KOSCHEI WAS IMMORTAL, DEATHLESS, AND WENT ON TO PESTER VARIOUS PROTAGONISTS OF SLAVIC MYTH.
GOOD MORNING, WONG.
GOOD MORNING, STEPHEN.
WOULD YOU LIKE SOME BREAKFAST BEFORE YOUR WALKIES?
HAVE *YOU* BEEN FILLING BATS' HEAD WITH WORRIES ABOUT MY CARDIAC FITNESS?
AND JUST COFFEE, PLEASE.
I WAS A CHILD WHEN I FIRST ENCOUNTERED THE MYTHS OF KOSCHEI.
"PHYSICIAN, HEAL THYSELF," ETC, ETC.
HA! HOW VERY PEDESTRIAN.
DO YOU REMEMBER HOW YOU *USED* TO TALK? WHEN YOU WERE FRESH BACK FROM THE ANCIENT ONE'S TUTELAGE?
HAR HAR.
WELL, IT'S A FULL DAY. I HAD BETTER GET IT STARTED.
IT STUCK WITH ME.
HMM? YES, I SUPPOSE SO.
ALL THOSE YEARS WITH ONLY WIZENED MYSTICS FOR COMPANY... I SUPPOSE IT RUBBED OFF ON ME. I *HAD* TAKEN ON RATHER A DRAMATIC WAY OF SPEAKING, HADN'T I?
I HAVEN'T HEARD A "ZOUNDS" OUT OF YOU IN AGES.
THE STORY OF HOW I *CEASED* TO BE A SURGEON--
--THE OBSESSION WITH MONEY, STATUS AND FAME, AND THE *ACCIDENT*--
--IS WELL KNOWN AT THIS POINT.
THEN ALLOW ME TO MAKE YOUR DAY, OLD FRIEND.
"ZOUNDS"!
HA!
ENJOY WALKIES.

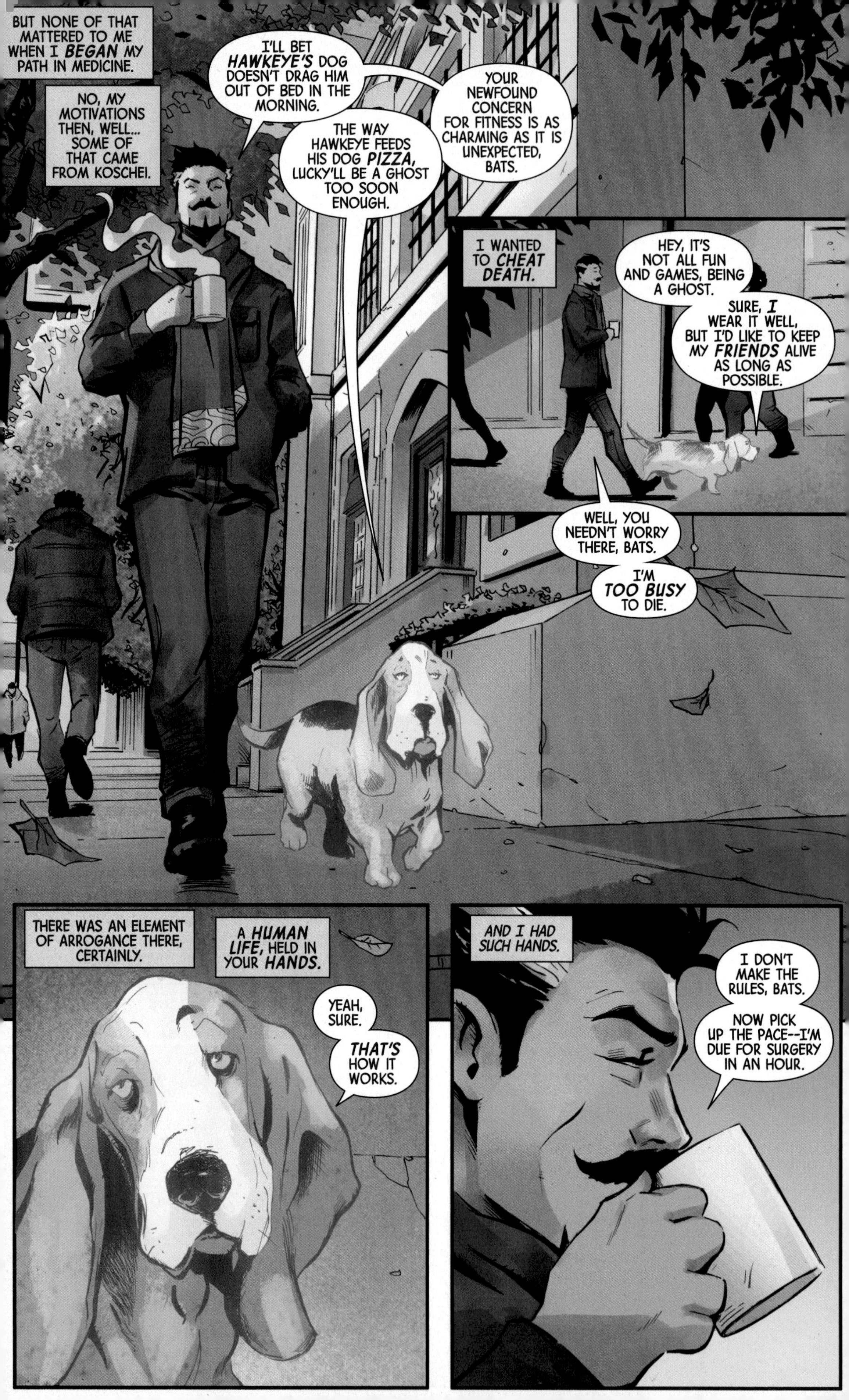
BUT NONE OF THAT MATTERED TO ME WHEN I BEGAN MY PATH IN MEDICINE.
NO, MY MOTIVATIONS THEN, WELL... SOME OF THAT CAME FROM KOSCHEI.
I'LL BET HAWKEYE'S DOG DOESN'T DRAG HIM OUT OF BED IN THE MORNING.
YOUR NEWFOUND CONCERN FOR FITNESS IS AS CHARMING AS IT IS UNEXPECTED, BATS.
THE WAY HAWKEYE FEEDS HIS DOG PIZZA, LUCKY'LL BE A GHOST TOO SOON ENOUGH.
I WANTED TO CHEAT DEATH.
HEY, IT'S NOT ALL FUN AND GAMES, BEING A GHOST.
SURE, I WEAR IT WELL, BUT I'D LIKE TO KEEP MY FRIENDS ALIVE AS LONG AS POSSIBLE.
WELL, YOU NEEDN'T WORRY THERE, BATS.
I'M TOO BUSY TO DIE.
THERE WAS AN ELEMENT OF ARROGANCE THERE, CERTAINLY.
A HUMAN LIFE, HELD IN YOUR HANDS.
YEAH, SURE.
THAT'S HOW IT WORKS.
AND I HAD SUCH HANDS.
I DON'T MAKE THE RULES, BATS.
NOW PICK UP THE PACE--I'M DUE FOR SURGERY IN AN HOUR.

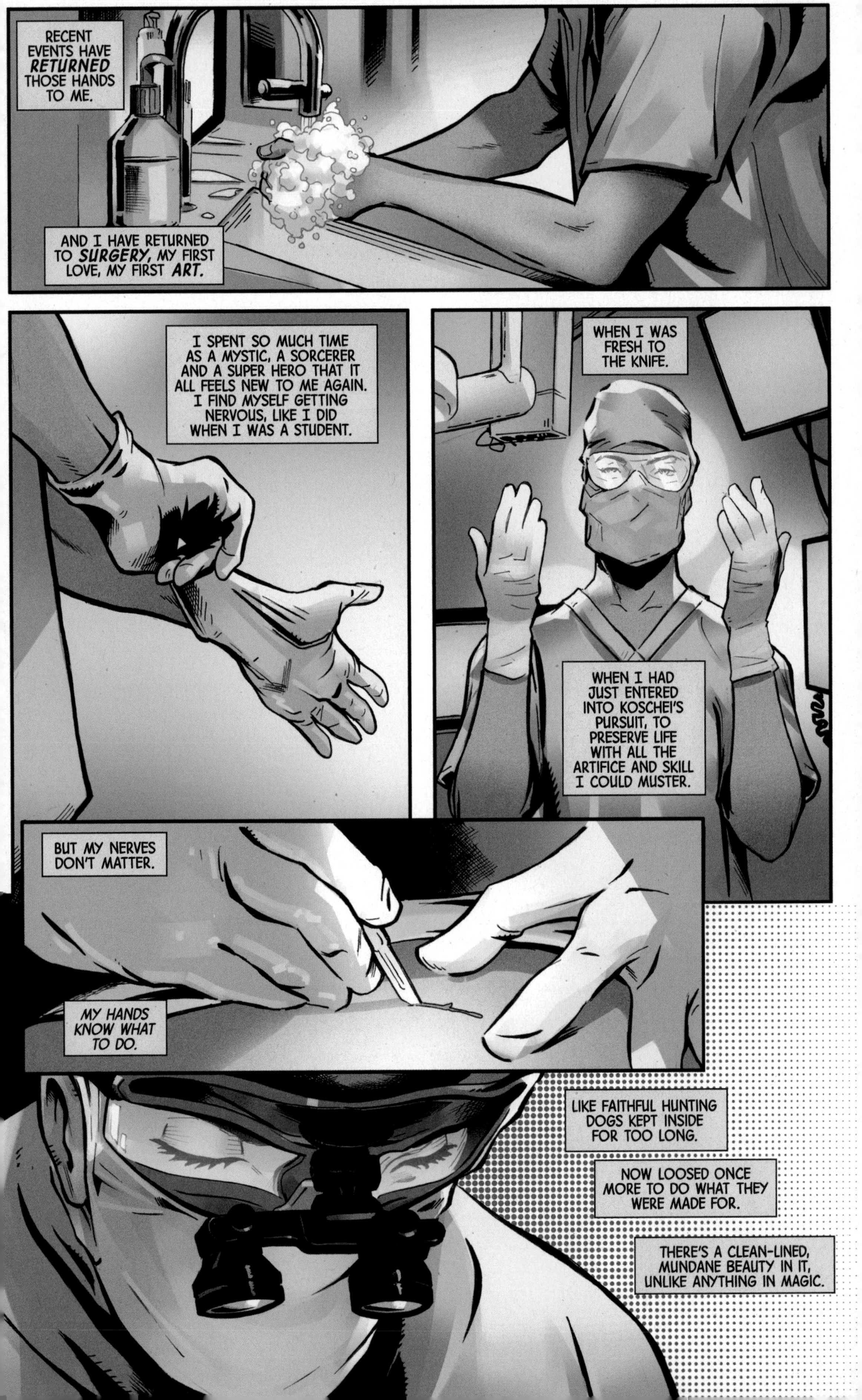
RECENT EVENTS HAVE RETURNED THOSE HANDS TO ME.
AND I HAVE RETURNED TO SURGERY, MY FIRST LOVE, MY FIRST ART.
I SPENT SO MUCH TIME AS A MYSTIC, A SORCERER AND A SUPER HERO THAT IT ALL FEELS NEW TO ME AGAIN. I FIND MYSELF GETTING NERVOUS, LIKE I DID WHEN I WAS A STUDENT.
WHEN I WAS FRESH TO THE KNIFE.
WHEN I HAD JUST ENTERED INTO KOSCHEI'S PURSUIT, TO PRESERVE LIFE WITH ALL THE ARTIFICE AND SKILL I COULD MUSTER.
BUT MY NERVES DON'T MATTER.
MY HANDS KNOW WHAT TO DO.
LIKE FAITHFUL HUNTING DOGS KEPT INSIDE FOR TOO LONG.
NOW LOOSED ONCE MORE TO DO WHAT THEY WERE MADE FOR.
THERE'S A CLEAN-LINED, MUNDANE BEAUTY IN IT, UNLIKE ANYTHING IN MAGIC.

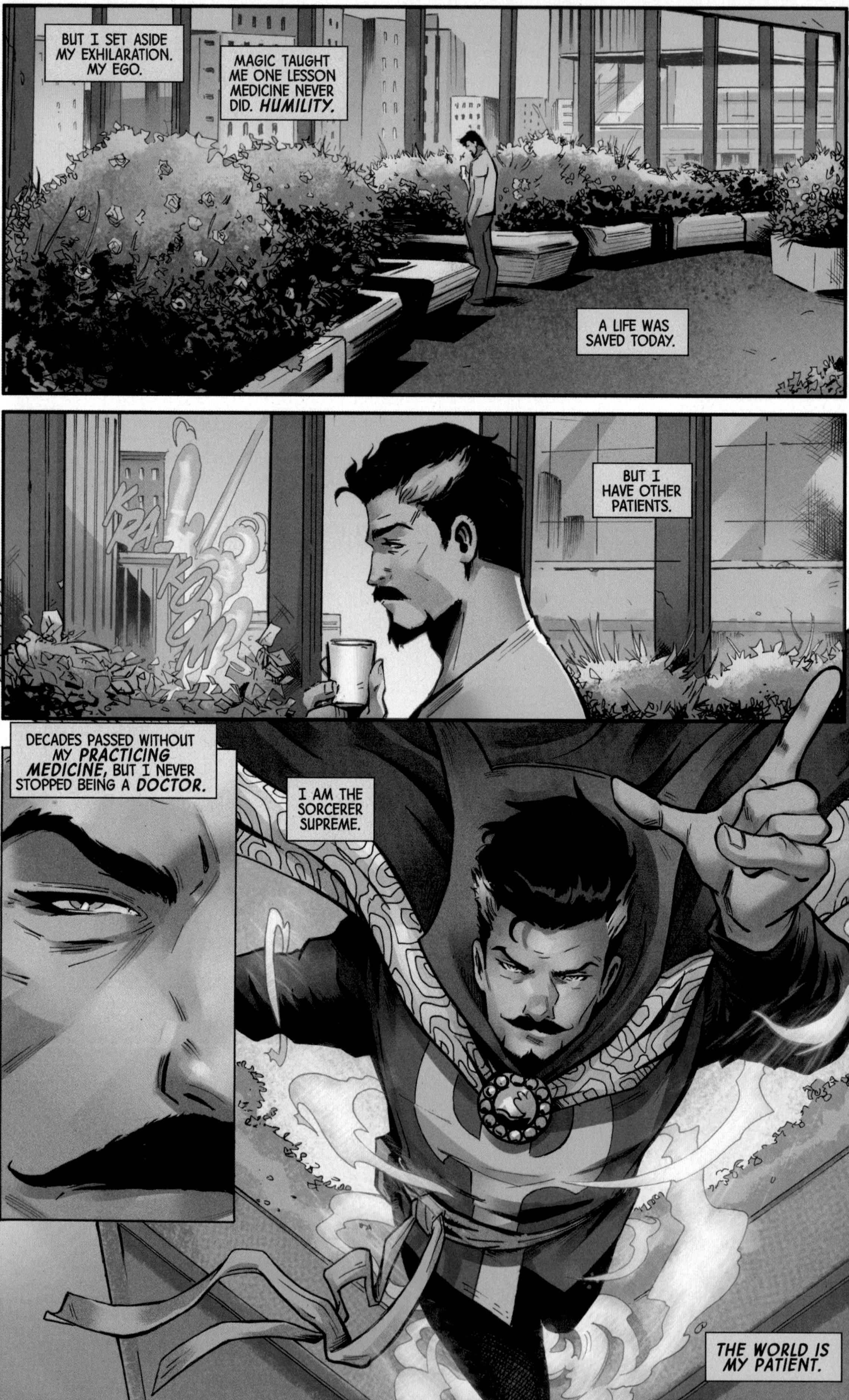

BUT I SET ASIDE MY EXHILARATION. MY EGO.
MAGIC TAUGHT ME ONE LESSON MEDICINE NEVER DID. HUMILITY.
A LIFE WAS SAVED TODAY.
KRA-KOOM
BUT I HAVE OTHER PATIENTS.
DECADES PASSED WITHOUT MY PRACTICING MEDICINE, BUT I NEVER STOPPED BEING A DOCTOR.
I AM THE SORCERER SUPREME.
THE WORLD IS MY PATIENT.

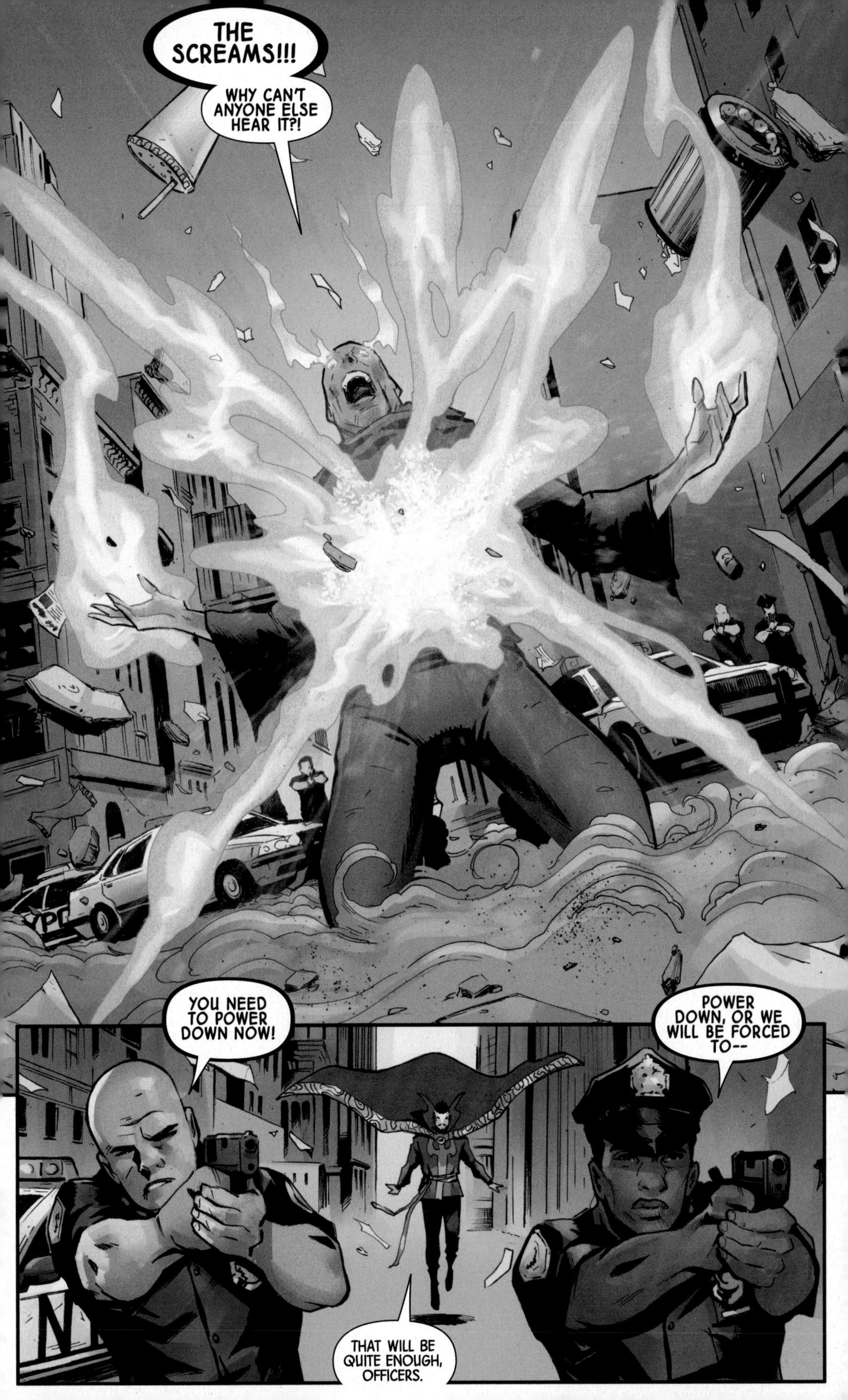
THE SCREAMS!!!
WHY CAN'T ANYONE ELSE HEAR IT?!
YOU NEED TO POWER DOWN NOW!
POWER DOWN, OR WE WILL BE FORCED TO--
THAT WILL BE QUITE ENOUGH, OFFICERS.

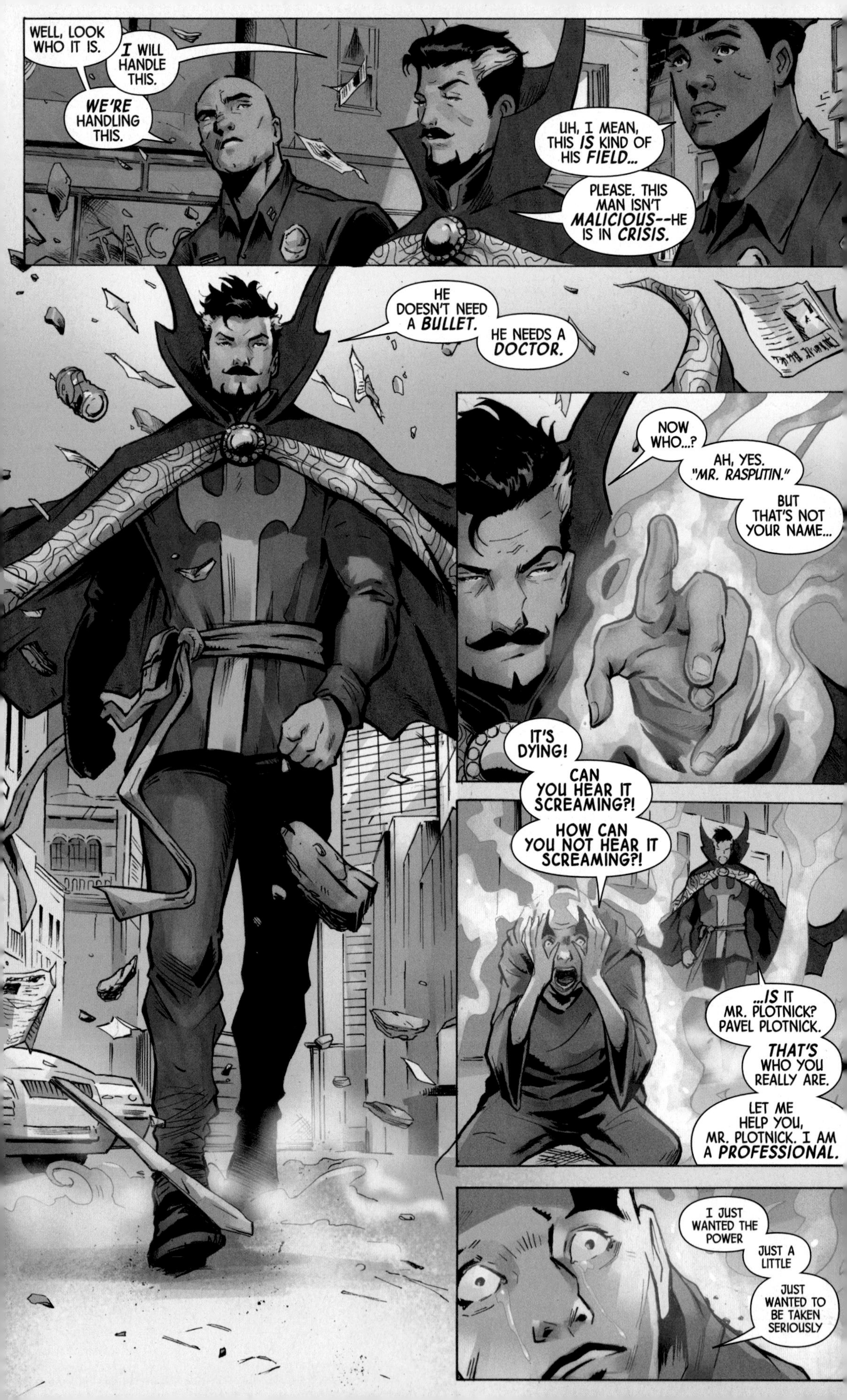
WELL, LOOK WHO IT IS.
I WILL HANDLE THIS.
WE'RE HANDLING THIS.
UH, I MEAN, THIS IS KIND OF HIS FIELD...
PLEASE. THIS MAN ISN'T MALICIOUS--HE IS IN CRISIS.
HE DOESN'T NEED A BULLET.
HE NEEDS A DOCTOR.
NOW WHO...?
AH, YES. "MR. RASPUTIN."
BUT THAT'S NOT YOUR NAME...
IT'S DYING!
CAN YOU HEAR IT SCREAMING?!
HOW CAN YOU NOT HEAR IT SCREAMING?!
...IS IT MR. PLOTNICK? PAVEL PLOTNICK.
THAT'S WHO YOU REALLY ARE.
LET ME HELP YOU, MR. PLOTNICK. I AM A PROFESSIONAL.
I JUST WANTED THE POWER
JUST A LITTLE
JUST WANTED TO BE TAKEN SERIOUSLY

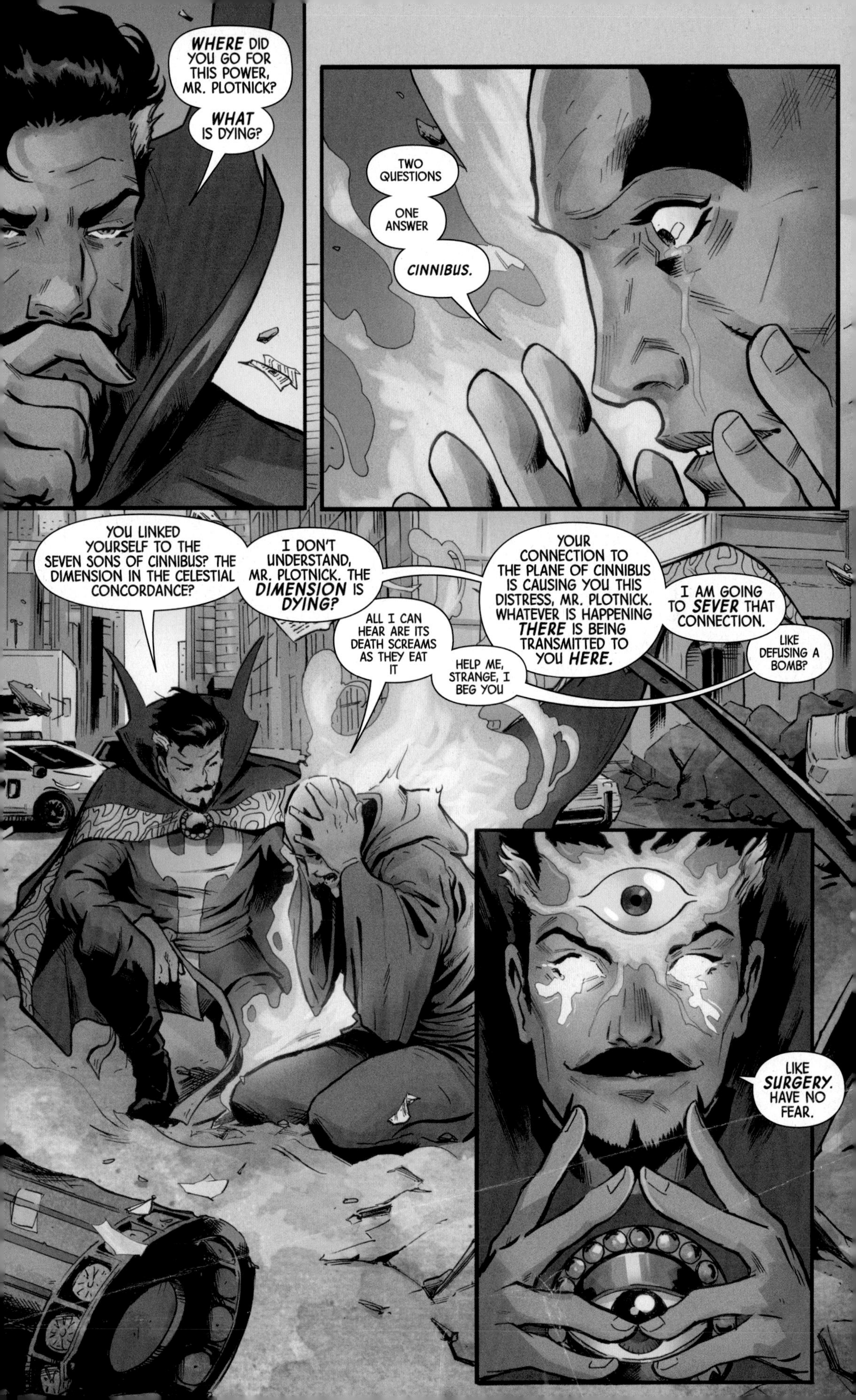
WHERE DID YOU GO FOR THIS POWER, MR. PLOTNICK?
WHAT IS DYING?
TWO QUESTIONS
ONE ANSWER
CINNIBUS.
YOU LINKED YOURSELF TO THE SEVEN SONS OF CINNIBUS? THE DIMENSION IN THE CELESTIAL CONCORDANCE?
I DON'T UNDERSTAND, MR. PLOTNICK. THE DIMENSION IS DYING?
ALL I CAN HEAR ARE ITS DEATH SCREAMS AS THEY EAT IT
HELP ME, STRANGE, I BEG YOU
YOUR CONNECTION TO THE PLANE OF CINNIBUS IS CAUSING YOU THIS DISTRESS, MR. PLOTNICK. WHATEVER IS HAPPENING THERE IS BEING TRANSMITTED TO YOU HERE.
I AM GOING TO SEVER THAT CONNECTION.
LIKE DEFUSING A BOMB?
LIKE SURGERY. HAVE NO FEAR.

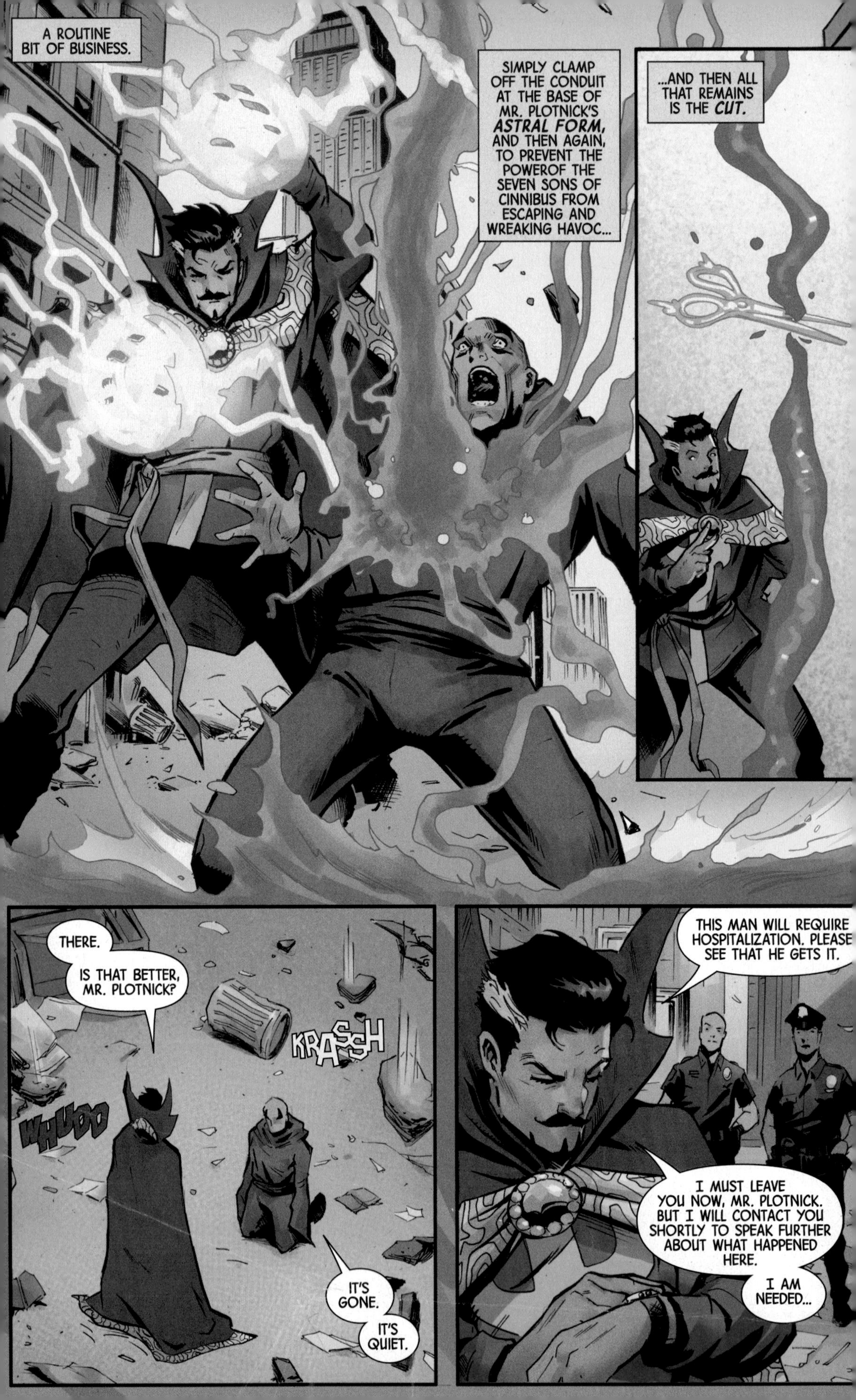
A ROUTINE BIT OF BUSINESS.
SIMPLY CLAMP OFF THE CONDUIT AT THE BASE OF MR. PLOTNICK'S *ASTRAL FORM,* AND THEN AGAIN, TO PREVENT THE POWEROF THE SEVEN SONS OF CINNIBUS FROM ESCAPING AND WREAKING HAVOC...
...AND THEN ALL THAT REMAINS IS THE *CUT.*
THERE.
IS THAT BETTER, MR. PLOTNICK?
KRASSH
WHUDD
IT'S GONE.
IT'S QUIET.
THIS MAN WILL REQUIRE HOSPITALIZATION. PLEASE SEE THAT HE GETS IT.
I MUST LEAVE YOU NOW, MR. PLOTNICK. BUT I WILL CONTACT YOU SHORTLY TO SPEAK FURTHER ABOUT WHAT HAPPENED HERE.
I AM NEEDED...

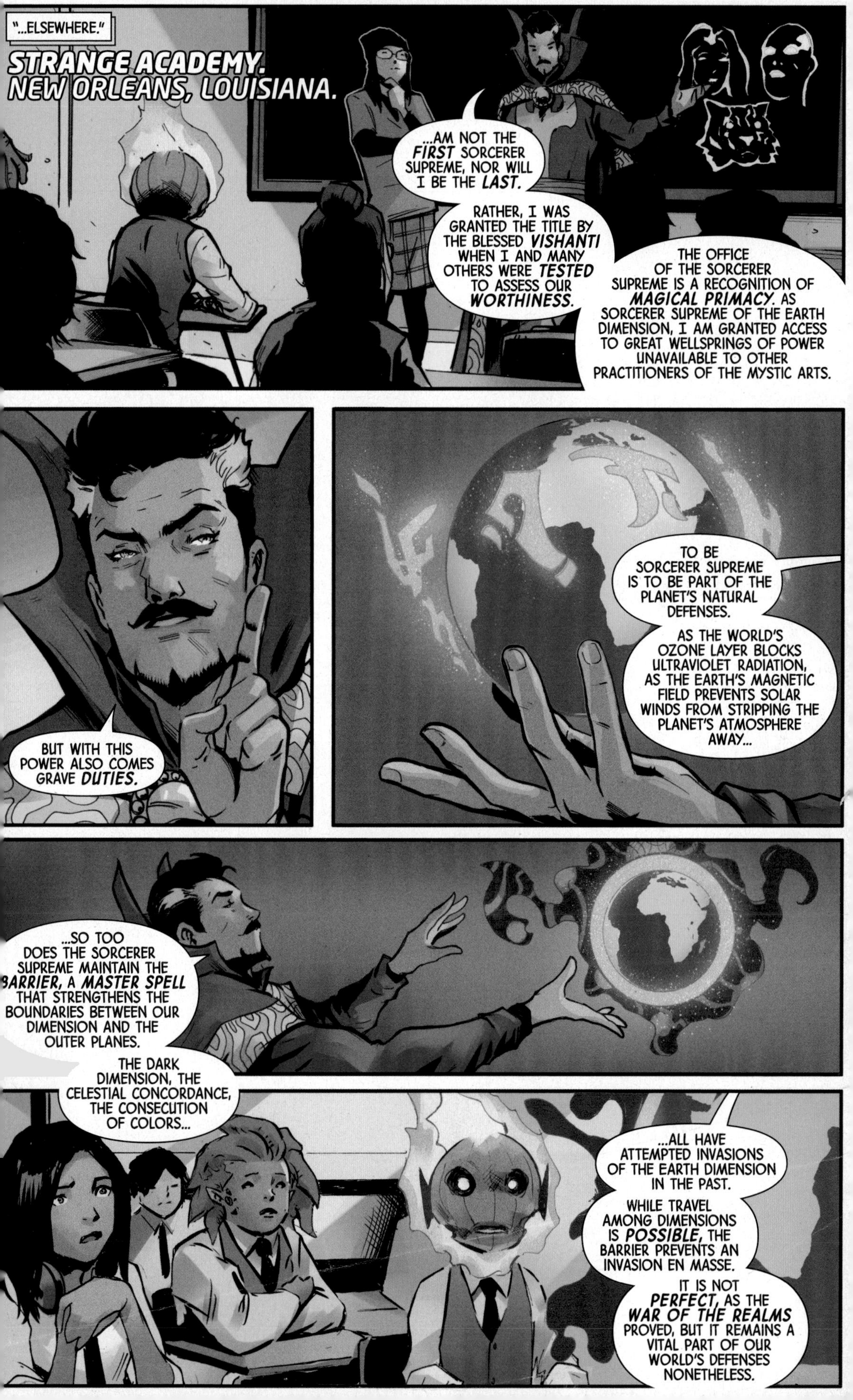
"...ELSEWHERE."
STRANGE ACADEMY. NEW ORLEANS, LOUISIANA.
...AM NOT THE FIRST SORCERER SUPREME, NOR WILL I BE THE LAST.
RATHER, I WAS GRANTED THE TITLE BY THE BLESSED VISHANTI WHEN I AND MANY OTHERS WERE TESTED TO ASSESS OUR WORTHINESS.
THE OFFICE OF THE SORCERER SUPREME IS A RECOGNITION OF MAGICAL PRIMACY. AS SORCERER SUPREME OF THE EARTH DIMENSION, I AM GRANTED ACCESS TO GREAT WELLSPRINGS OF POWER UNAVAILABLE TO OTHER PRACTITIONERS OF THE MYSTIC ARTS.
BUT WITH THIS POWER ALSO COMES GRAVE DUTIES.
TO BE SORCERER SUPREME IS TO BE PART OF THE PLANET'S NATURAL DEFENSES.
AS THE WORLD'S OZONE LAYER BLOCKS ULTRAVIOLET RADIATION, AS THE EARTH'S MAGNETIC FIELD PREVENTS SOLAR WINDS FROM STRIPPING THE PLANET'S ATMOSPHERE AWAY...
...SO TOO DOES THE SORCERER SUPREME MAINTAIN THE BARRIER, A MASTER SPELL THAT STRENGTHENS THE BOUNDARIES BETWEEN OUR DIMENSION AND THE OUTER PLANES.
THE DARK DIMENSION, THE CELESTIAL CONCORDANCE, THE CONSECUTION OF COLORS...
...ALL HAVE ATTEMPTED INVASIONS OF THE EARTH DIMENSION IN THE PAST.
WHILE TRAVEL AMONG DIMENSIONS IS POSSIBLE, THE BARRIER PREVENTS AN INVASION EN MASSE.
IT IS NOT PERFECT, AS THE WAR OF THE REALMS PROVED, BUT IT REMAINS A VITAL PART OF OUR WORLD'S DEFENSES NONETHELESS.

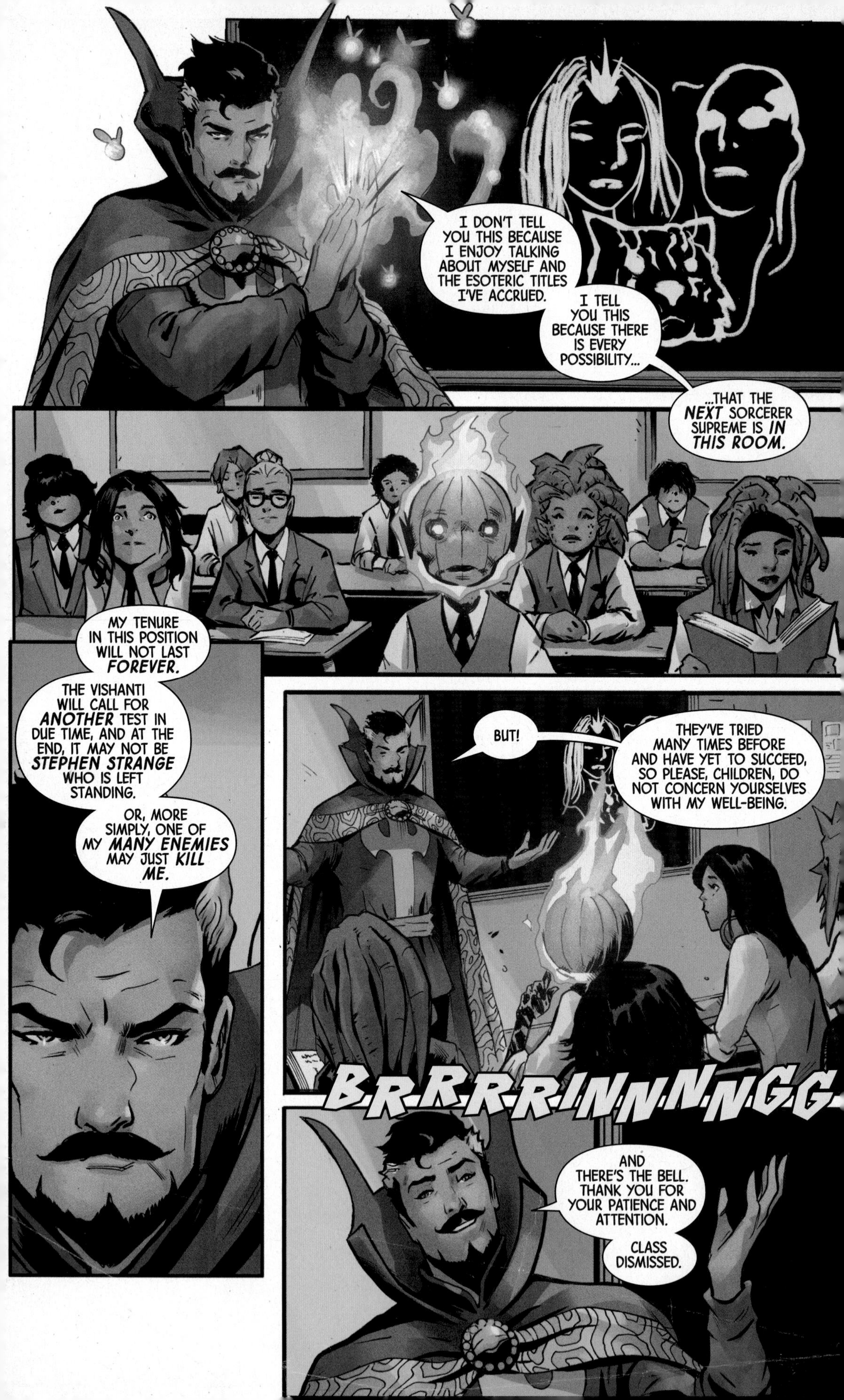
I DON'T TELL YOU THIS BECAUSE I ENJOY TALKING ABOUT MYSELF AND THE ESOTERIC TITLES I'VE ACCRUED.
I TELL YOU THIS BECAUSE THERE IS EVERY POSSIBILITY...
...THAT THE NEXT SORCERER SUPREME IS IN THIS ROOM.
MY TENURE IN THIS POSITION WILL NOT LAST FOREVER.
THE VISHANTI WILL CALL FOR ANOTHER TEST IN DUE TIME, AND AT THE END, IT MAY NOT BE STEPHEN STRANGE WHO IS LEFT STANDING.
OR, MORE SIMPLY, ONE OF MY MANY ENEMIES MAY JUST KILL ME.
BUT!
THEY'VE TRIED MANY TIMES BEFORE AND HAVE YET TO SUCCEED, SO PLEASE, CHILDREN, DO NOT CONCERN YOURSELVES WITH MY WELL-BEING.
B.R.R.R.R.I.N.N.N.N.G.G.
AND THERE'S THE BELL. THANK YOU FOR YOUR PATIENCE AND ATTENTION.
CLASS DISMISSED.

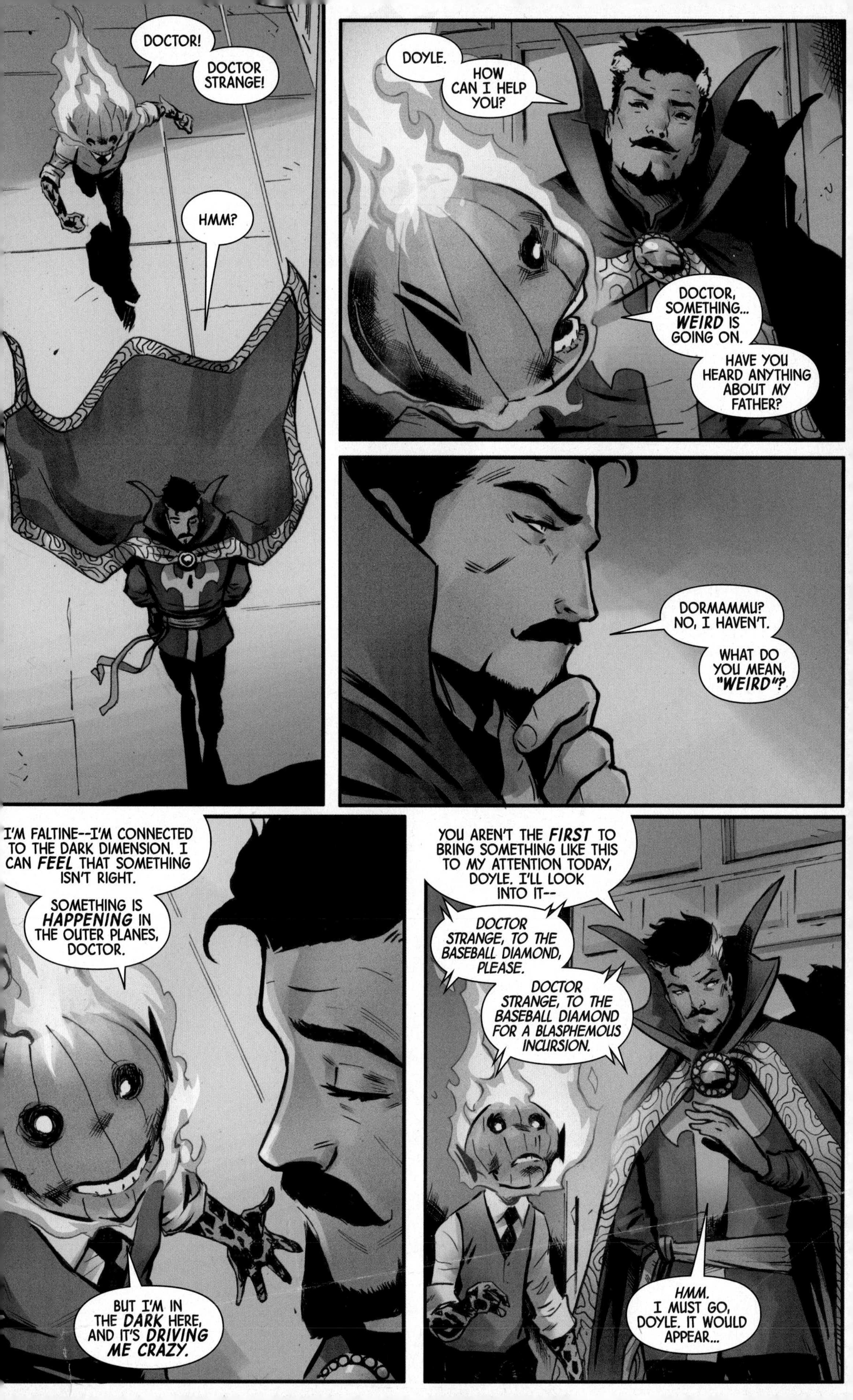
DOCTOR!
DOCTOR STRANGE!
HMM?
DOYLE.
HOW CAN I HELP YOU?
DOCTOR, SOMETHING... WEIRD IS GOING ON.
HAVE YOU HEARD ANYTHING ABOUT MY FATHER?
DORMAMMU? NO, I HAVEN'T.
WHAT DO YOU MEAN, "WEIRD"?
I'M FALTINE--I'M CONNECTED TO THE DARK DIMENSION. I CAN FEEL THAT SOMETHING ISN'T RIGHT.
SOMETHING IS HAPPENING IN THE OUTER PLANES, DOCTOR.
BUT I'M IN THE DARK HERE, AND IT'S DRIVING ME CRAZY.
YOU AREN'T THE FIRST TO BRING SOMETHING LIKE THIS TO MY ATTENTION TODAY, DOYLE. I'LL LOOK INTO IT--
DOCTOR STRANGE, TO THE BASEBALL DIAMOND, PLEASE.
DOCTOR STRANGE, TO THE BASEBALL DIAMOND FOR A BLASPHEMOUS INCURSION.
HMM. I MUST GO, DOYLE. IT WOULD APPEAR...

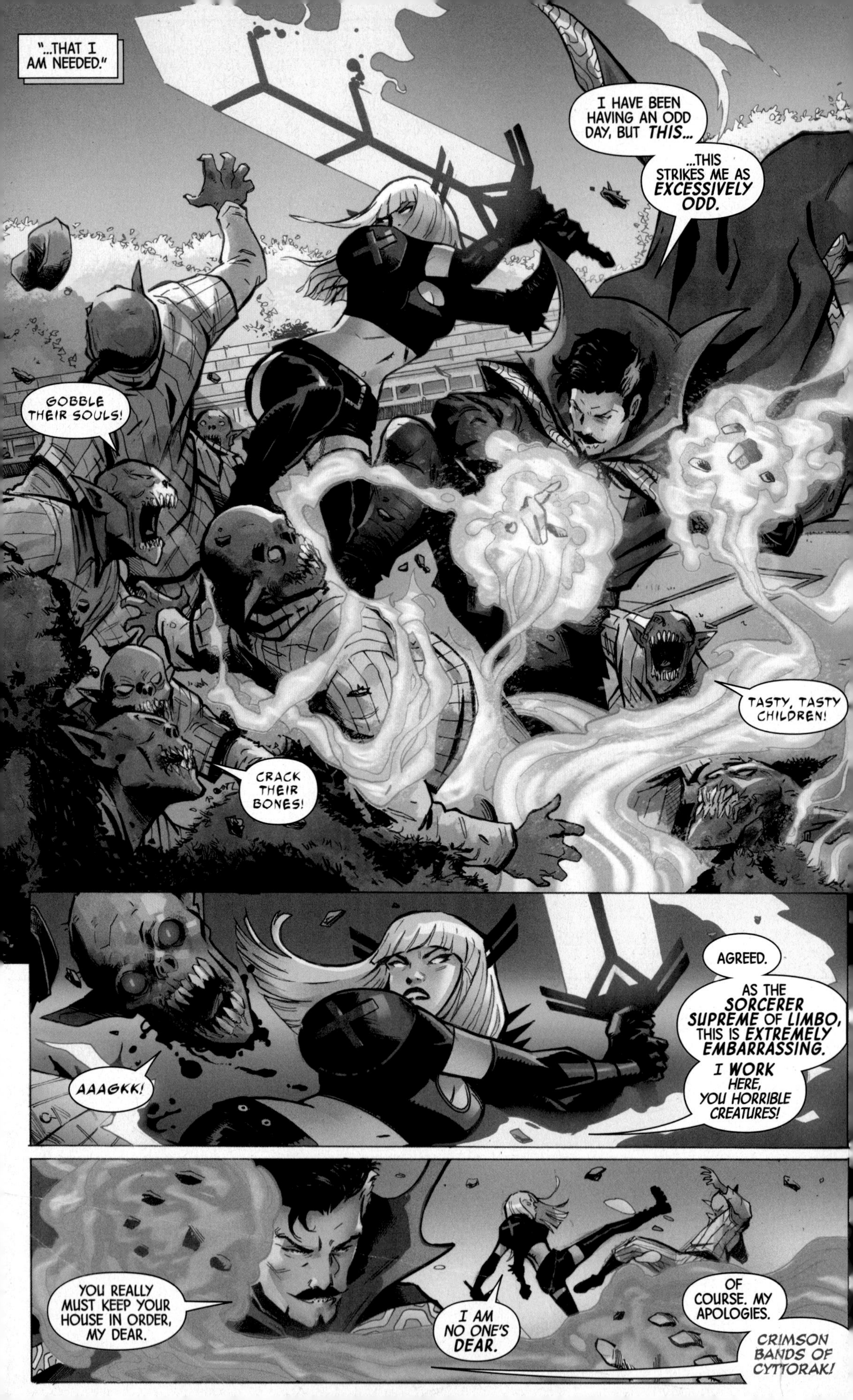
"...THAT I AM NEEDED."
I HAVE BEEN HAVING AN ODD DAY, BUT THIS...
...THIS STRIKES ME AS EXCESSIVELY ODD.
GOBBLE THEIR SOULS!
TASTY, TASTY CHILDREN!
CRACK THEIR BONES!
AGREED.
AS THE SORCERER SUPREME OF LIMBO, THIS IS EXTREMELY EMBARRASSING.
I WORK HERE, YOU HORRIBLE CREATURES!
AAAGKK!
YOU REALLY MUST KEEP YOUR HOUSE IN ORDER, MY DEAR.
I AM NO ONE'S DEAR.
OF COURSE. MY APOLOGIES.
CRIMSON BANDS OF CYTTORAK!

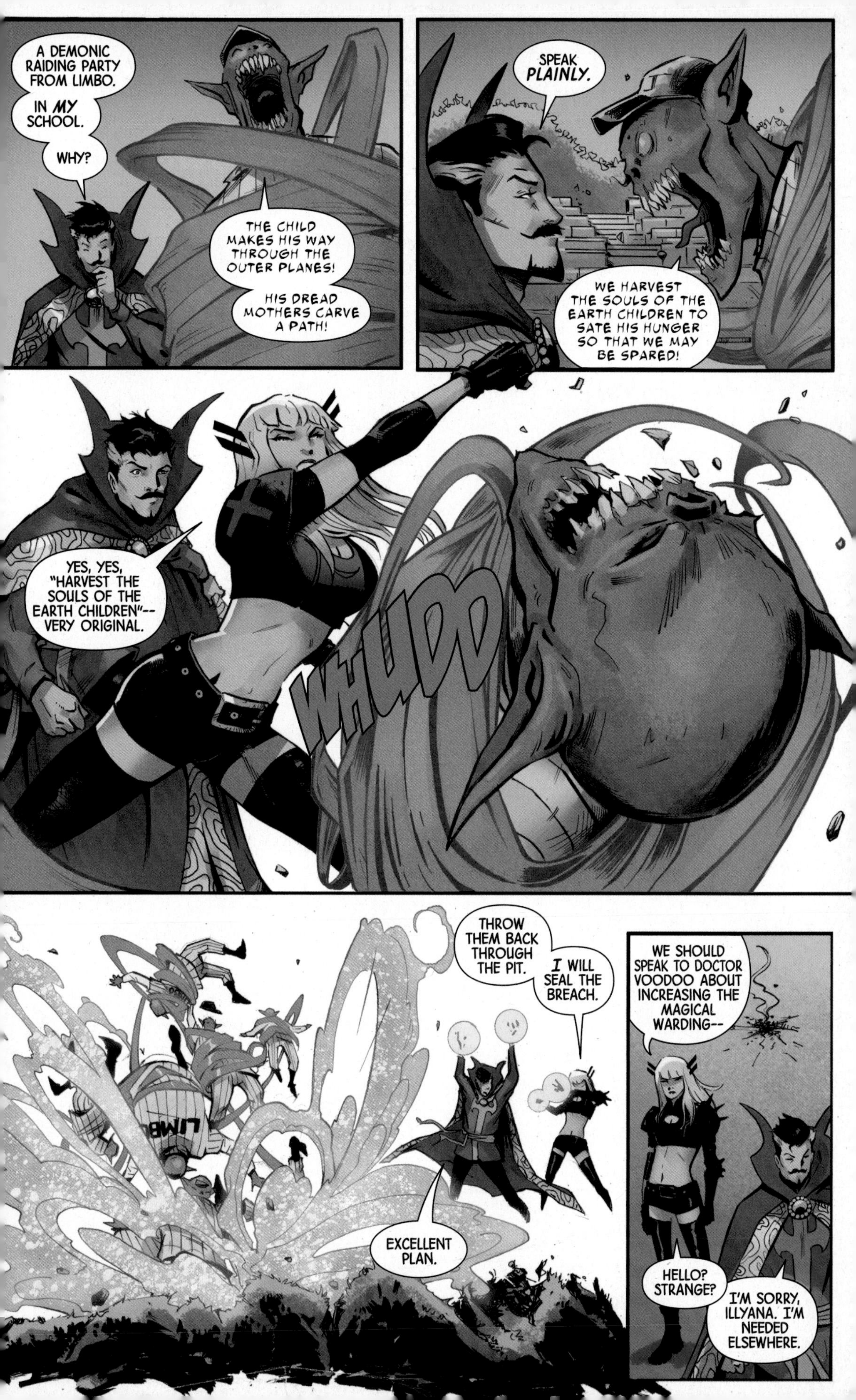

A DEMONIC RAIDING PARTY FROM LIMBO.
IN MY SCHOOL.
WHY?
THE CHILD MAKES HIS WAY THROUGH THE OUTER PLANES!
HIS DREAD MOTHERS CARVE A PATH!
SPEAK PLAINLY.
WE HARVEST THE SOULS OF THE EARTH CHILDREN TO SATE HIS HUNGER SO THAT WE MAY BE SPARED!
YES, YES, "HARVEST THE SOULS OF THE EARTH CHILDREN"-- VERY ORIGINAL.
WHUDD
THROW THEM BACK THROUGH THE PIT.
I WILL SEAL THE BREACH.
EXCELLENT PLAN.
WE SHOULD SPEAK TO DOCTOR VOODOO ABOUT INCREASING THE MAGICAL WARDING--
HELLO? STRANGE?
I'M SORRY, ILLYANA. I'M NEEDED ELSEWHERE.

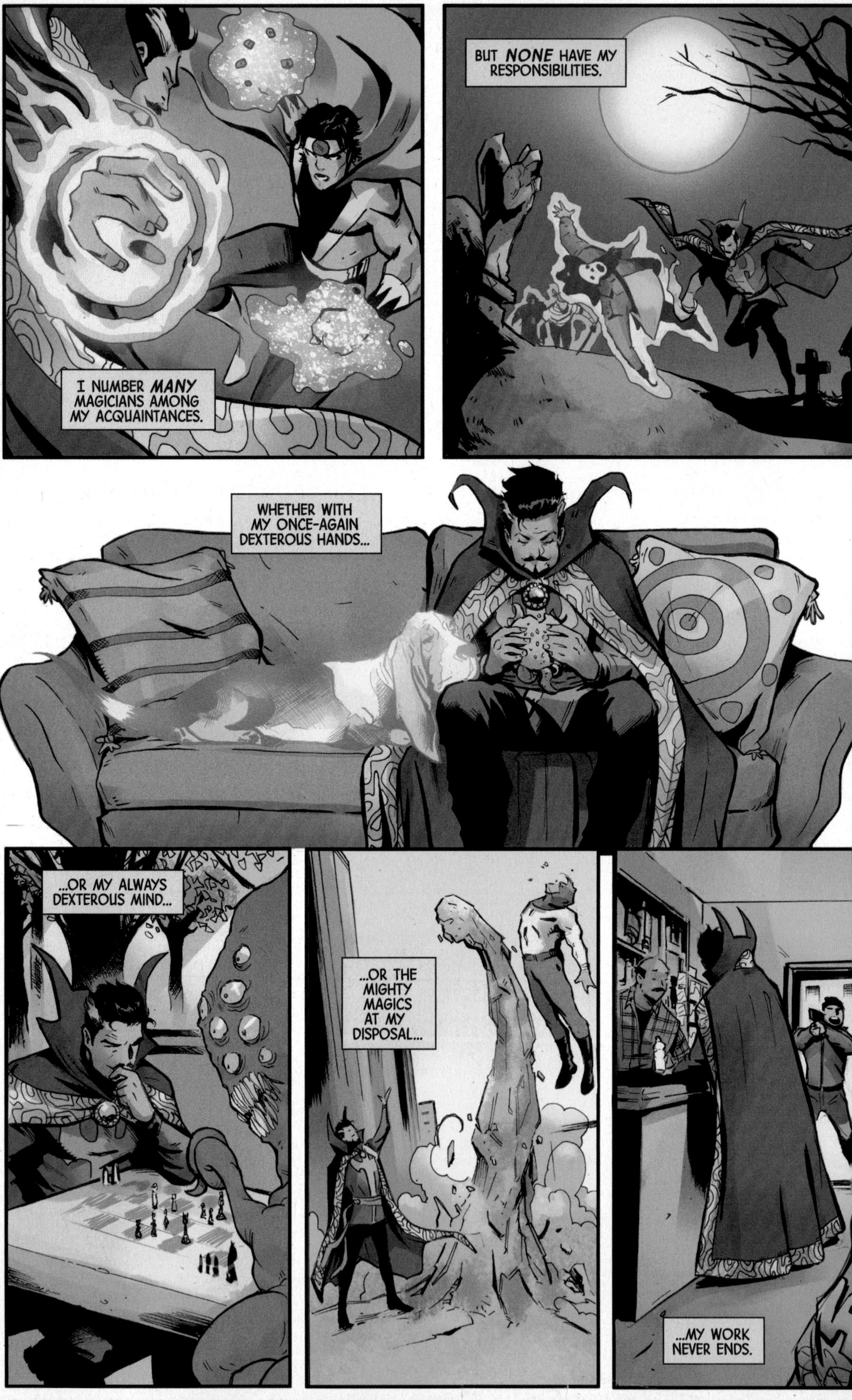
I NUMBER MANY MAGICIANS AMONG MY ACQUAINTANCES.
BUT NONE HAVE MY RESPONSIBILITIES.
WHETHER WITH MY ONCE-AGAIN DEXTEROUS HANDS...
...OR MY ALWAYS DEXTEROUS MIND...
...OR THE MIGHTY MAGICS AT MY DISPOSAL...
...MY WORK NEVER ENDS.

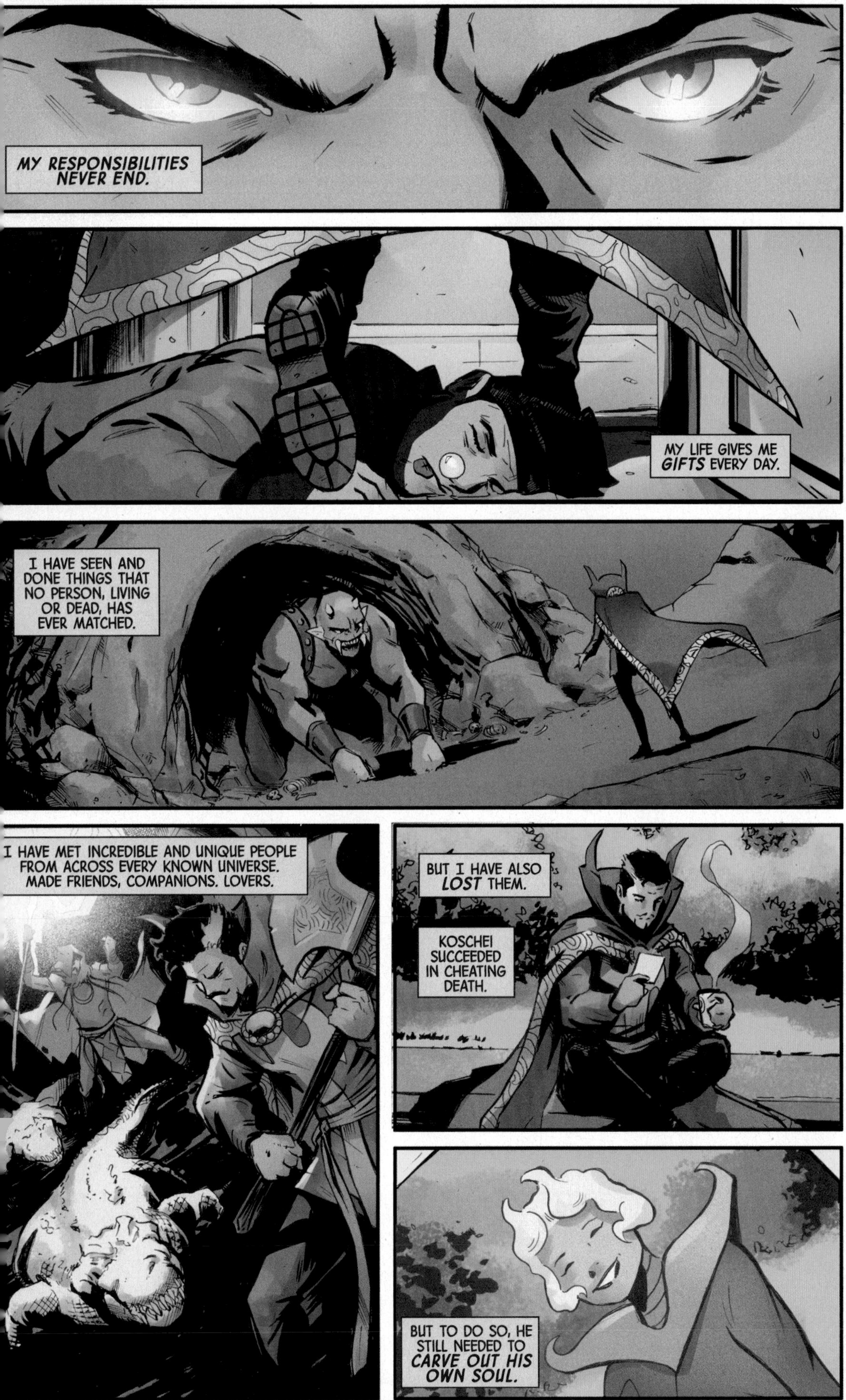
MY RESPONSIBILITIES NEVER END.
MY LIFE GIVES ME GIFTS EVERY DAY.
I HAVE SEEN AND DONE THINGS THAT NO PERSON, LIVING OR DEAD, HAS EVER MATCHED.
I HAVE MET INCREDIBLE AND UNIQUE PEOPLE FROM ACROSS EVERY KNOWN UNIVERSE. MADE FRIENDS, COMPANIONS. LOVERS.
BUT I HAVE ALSO LOST THEM.
KOSCHEI SUCCEEDED IN CHEATING DEATH.
BUT TO DO SO, HE STILL NEEDED TO CARVE OUT HIS OWN SOUL.

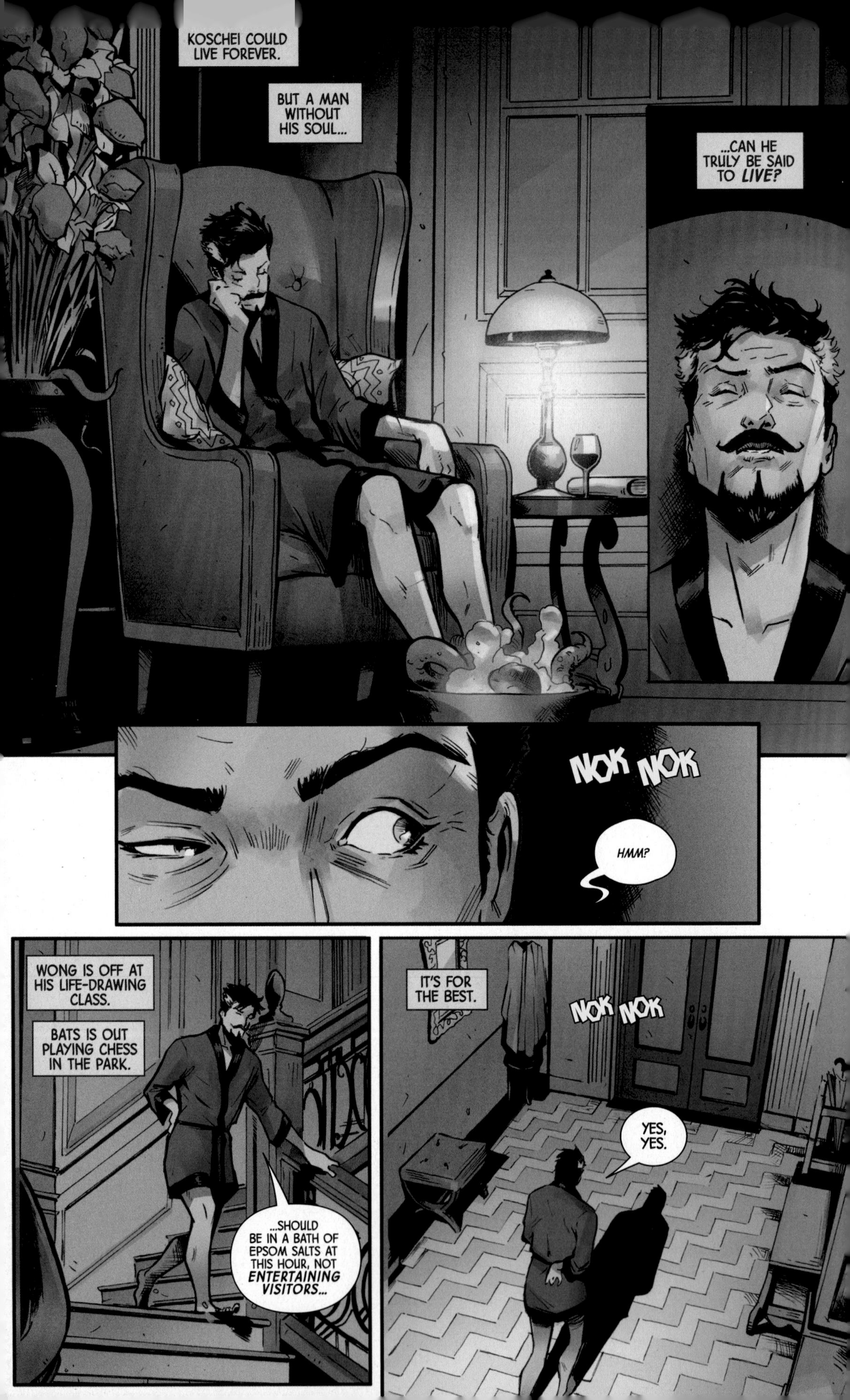
KOSCHEI COULD LIVE FOREVER.
BUT A MAN WITHOUT HIS SOUL...
...CAN HE TRULY BE SAID TO *LIVE?*
NOK NOK
HMM?
WONG IS OFF AT HIS LIFE-DRAWING CLASS.
BATS IS OUT PLAYING CHESS IN THE PARK.
...SHOULD BE IN A BATH OF EPSOM SALTS AT THIS HOUR, NOT *ENTERTAINING VISITORS...*
IT'S FOR THE BEST.
NOK NOK
YES, YES.

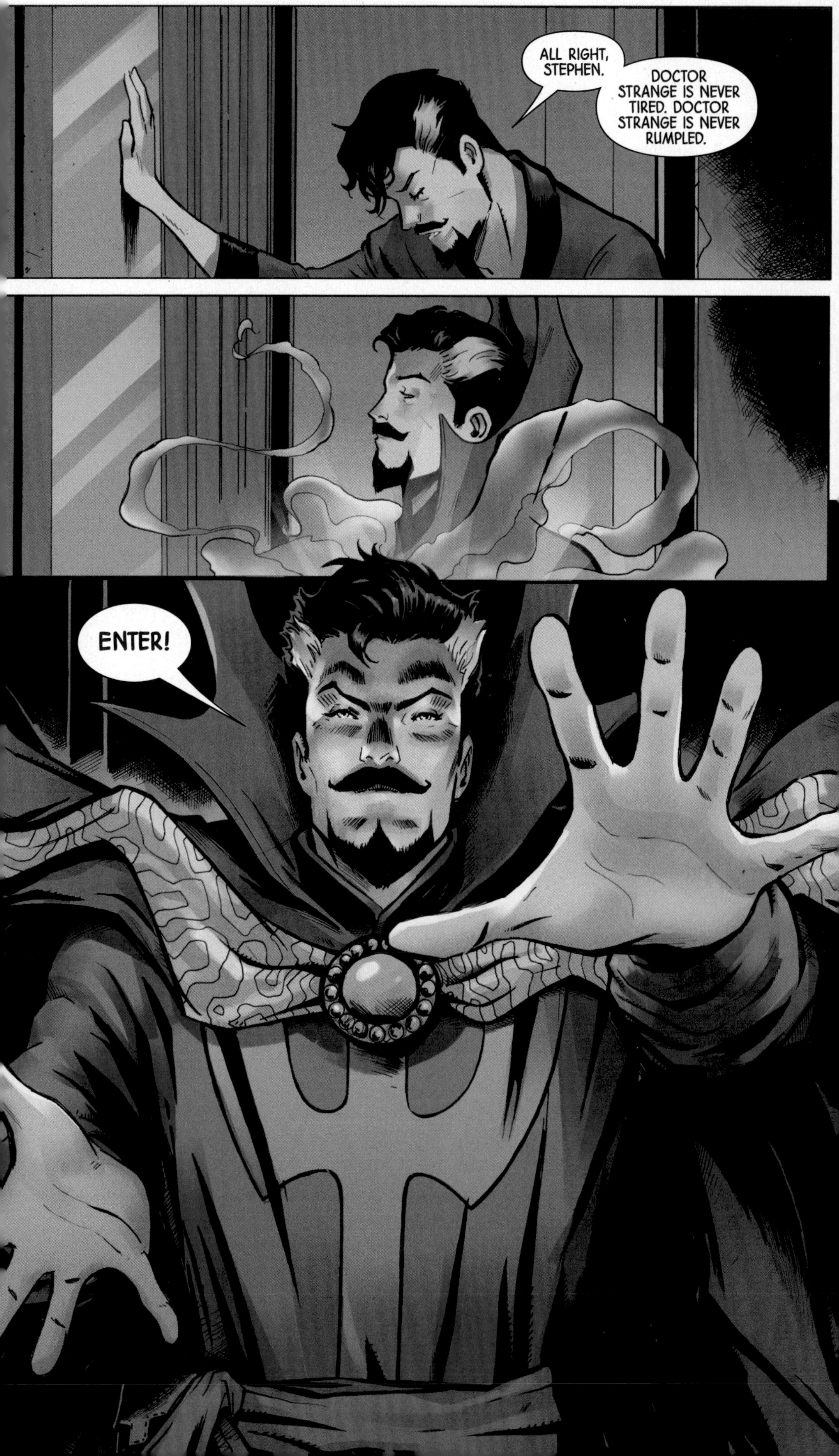
ALL RIGHT, STEPHEN.
DOCTOR STRANGE IS NEVER TIRED. DOCTOR STRANGE IS NEVER RUMPLED.
ENTER!

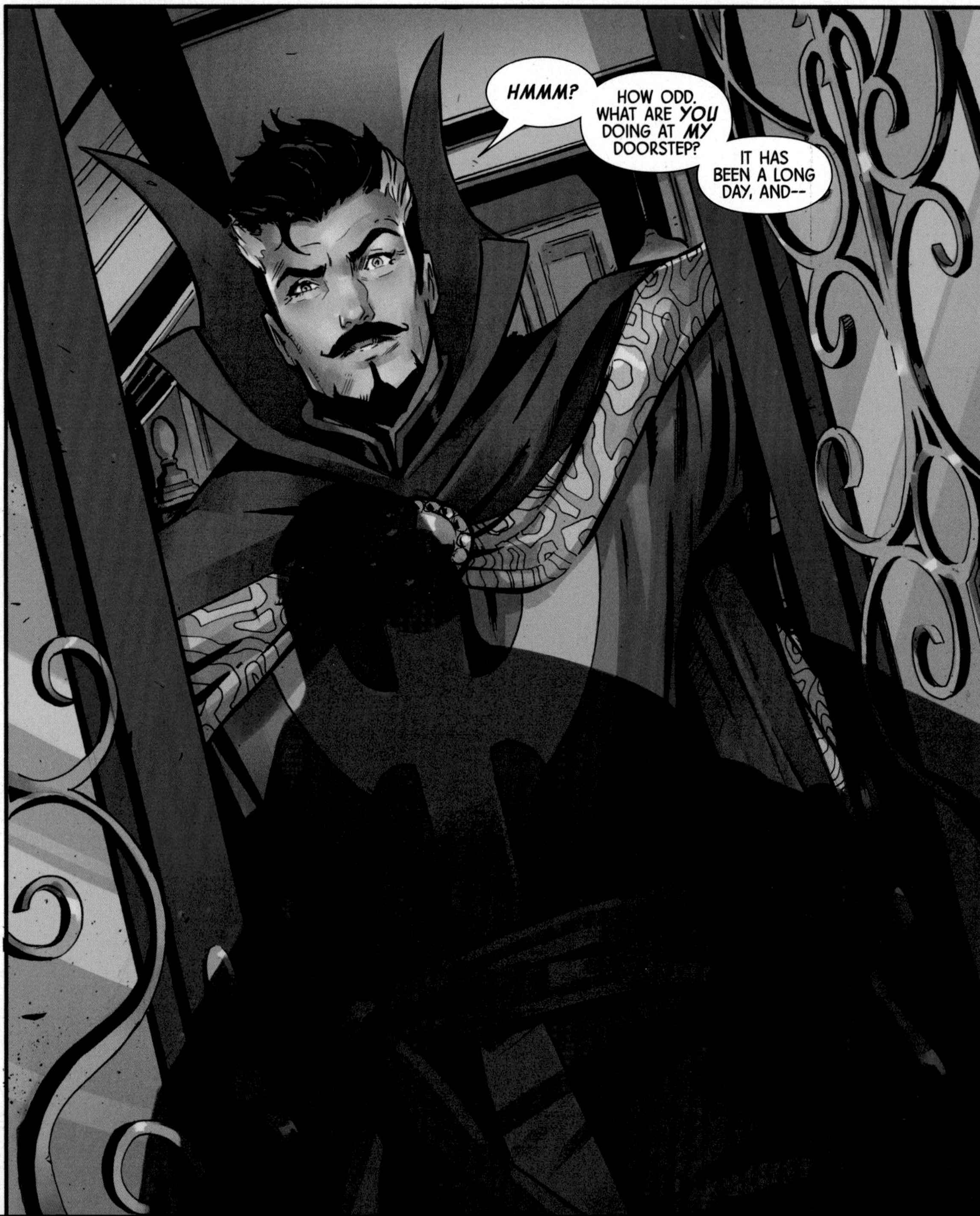
HMMM?
HOW ODD. WHAT ARE YOU DOING AT MY DOORSTEP?
IT HAS BEEN A LONG DAY, AND--

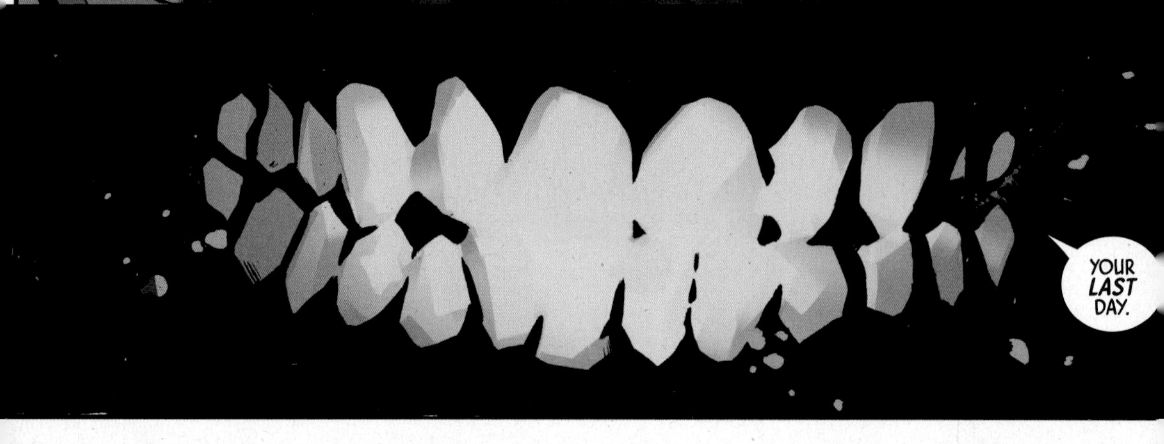
YOUR LAST DAY.

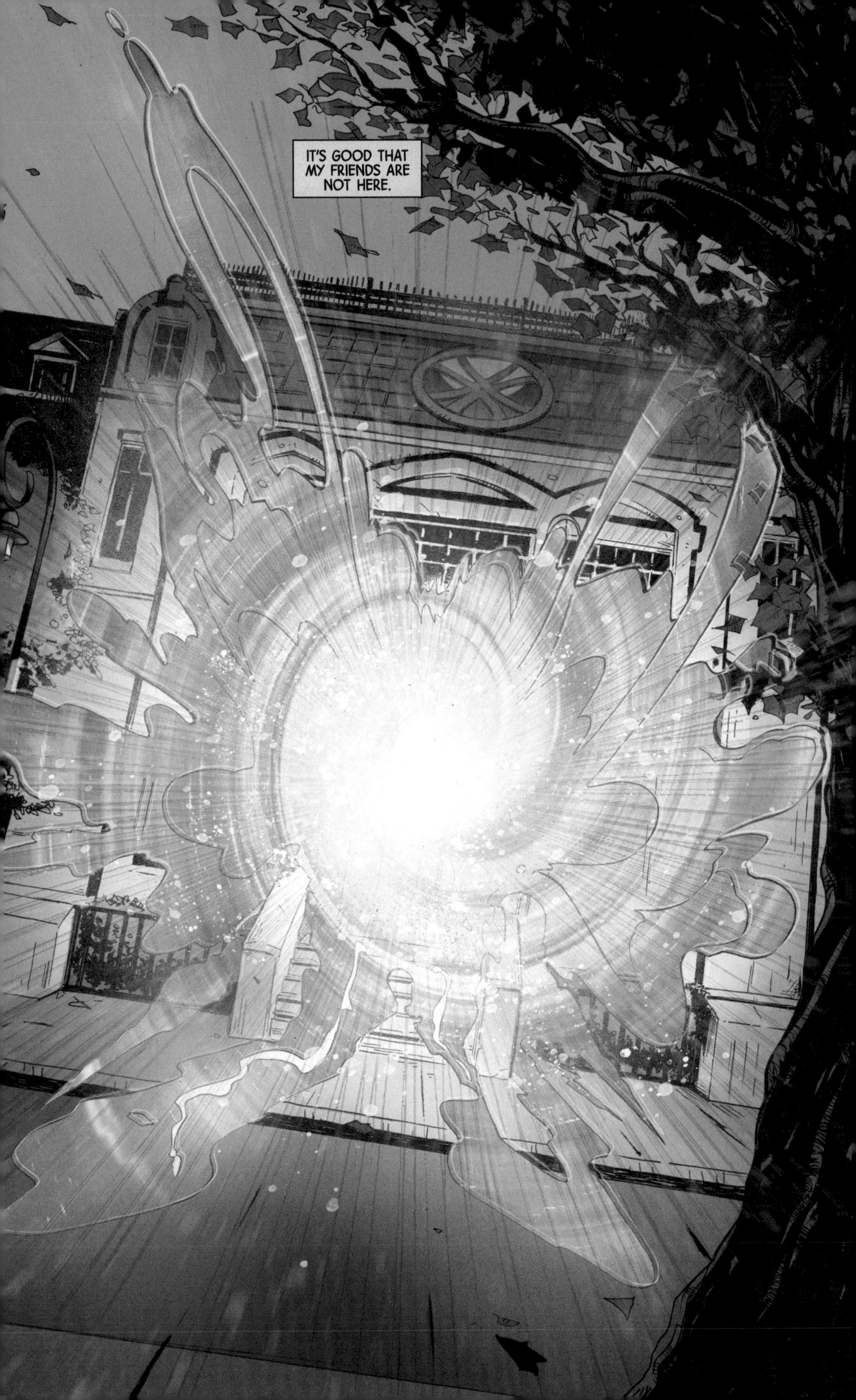
IT'S GOOD THAT MY FRIENDS ARE NOT HERE.

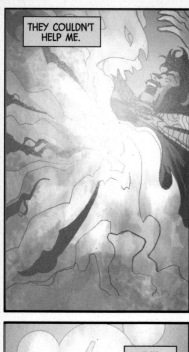

THEY COULDN'T HELP ME.

THIS IS BEYOND THEM.

I *WANT* THEM HERE WITH ME THOUGH.

THIS POWER ARRAYED AGAINST ME--

--THIS *OVERWHELMING, INCONCEIVABLE POWER*--

--IS *FAMILIAR* TO ME.

TERRIBLY SO.

THIS POWER SHOULD NOT *EXIST.*

I WANT MY FRIENDS HERE, EVEN THOUGH I AM GLAD THEY AREN'T.

IT'S SELFISH.

GO ON, THEN.

BUT BE WARNED--THIS WILL NOT END THE WAY YOU WISH.

I JUST DON'T WANT TO DIE ALONE.

CHAPTER TWO

The Lonely Death of Doctor Stephen Strange

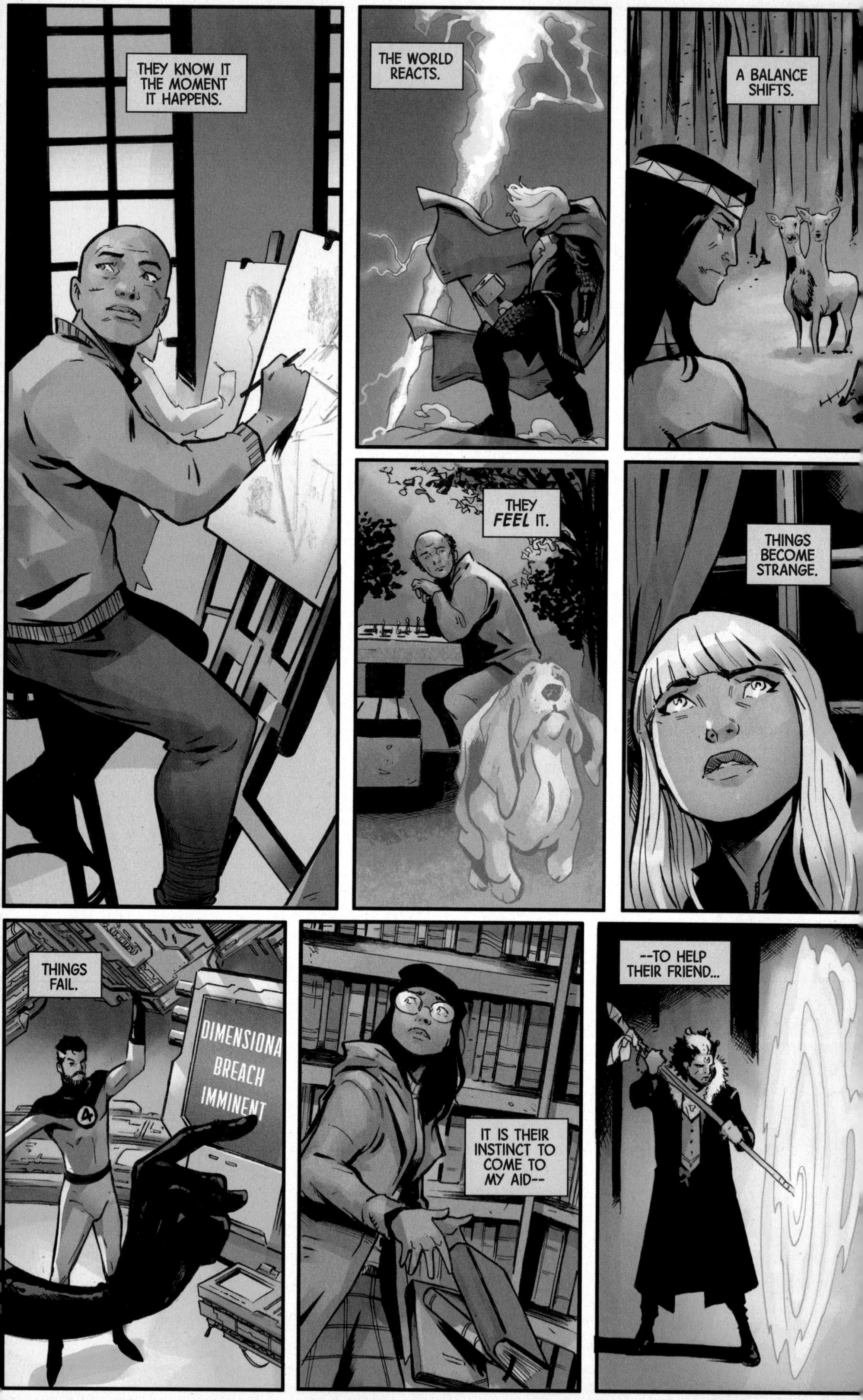
THEY KNOW IT THE MOMENT IT HAPPENS.
THE WORLD REACTS.
A BALANCE SHIFTS.
THEY *FEEL* IT.
THINGS BECOME STRANGE.
THINGS FAIL.
DIMENSIONA BREACH IMMINENT
IT IS THEIR INSTINCT TO COME TO MY AID--
--TO HELP THEIR FRIEND...

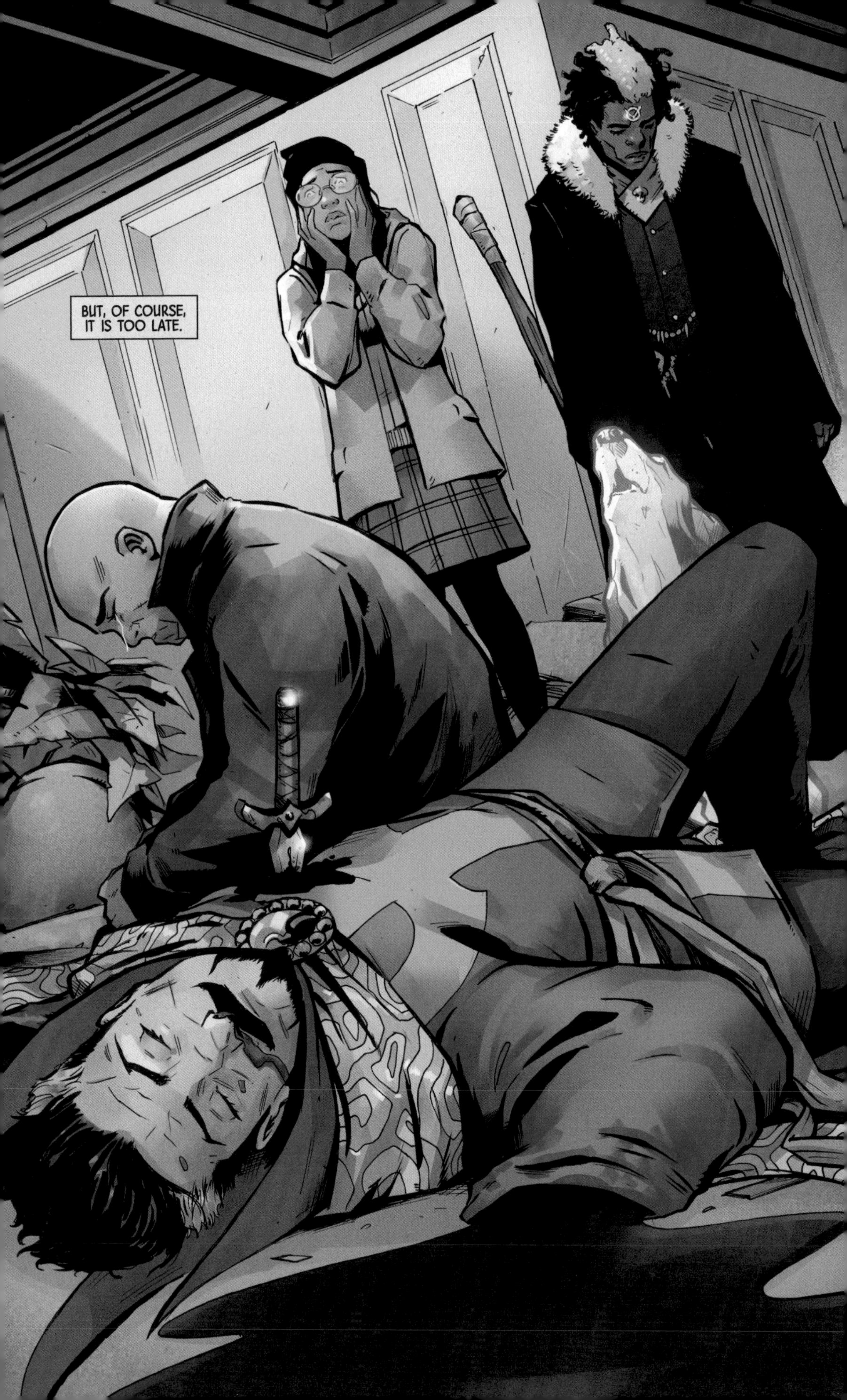
BUT, OF COURSE, IT IS TOO LATE.

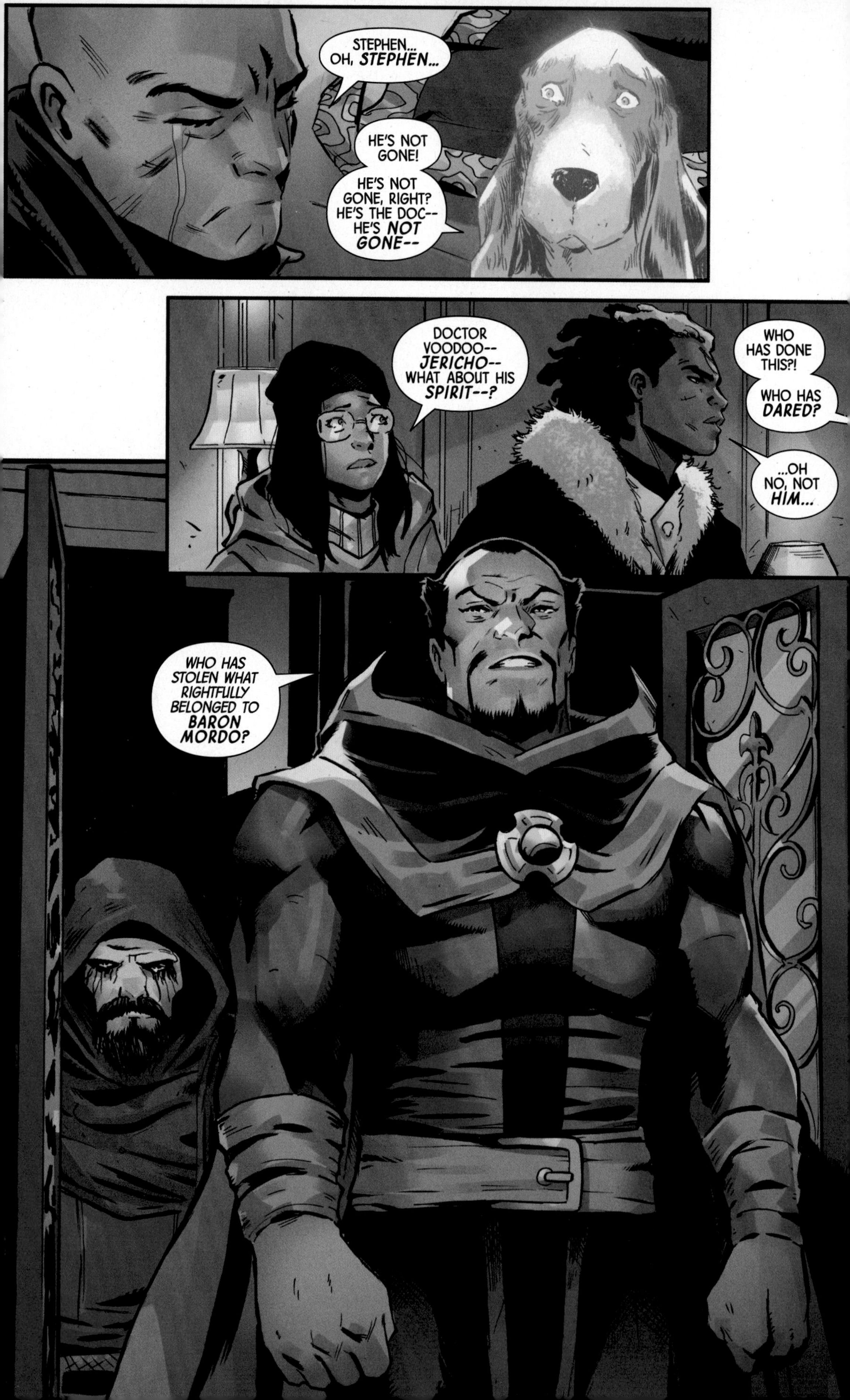
STEPHEN... OH, STEPHEN...
HE'S NOT GONE!
HE'S NOT GONE, RIGHT? HE'S THE DOC-- HE'S NOT GONE--
DOCTOR VOODOO-- JERICHO-- WHAT ABOUT HIS SPIRIT--?
WHO HAS DONE THIS?!
WHO HAS DARED?
...OH NO, NOT HIM...
WHO HAS STOLEN WHAT RIGHTFULLY BELONGED TO BARON MORDO?

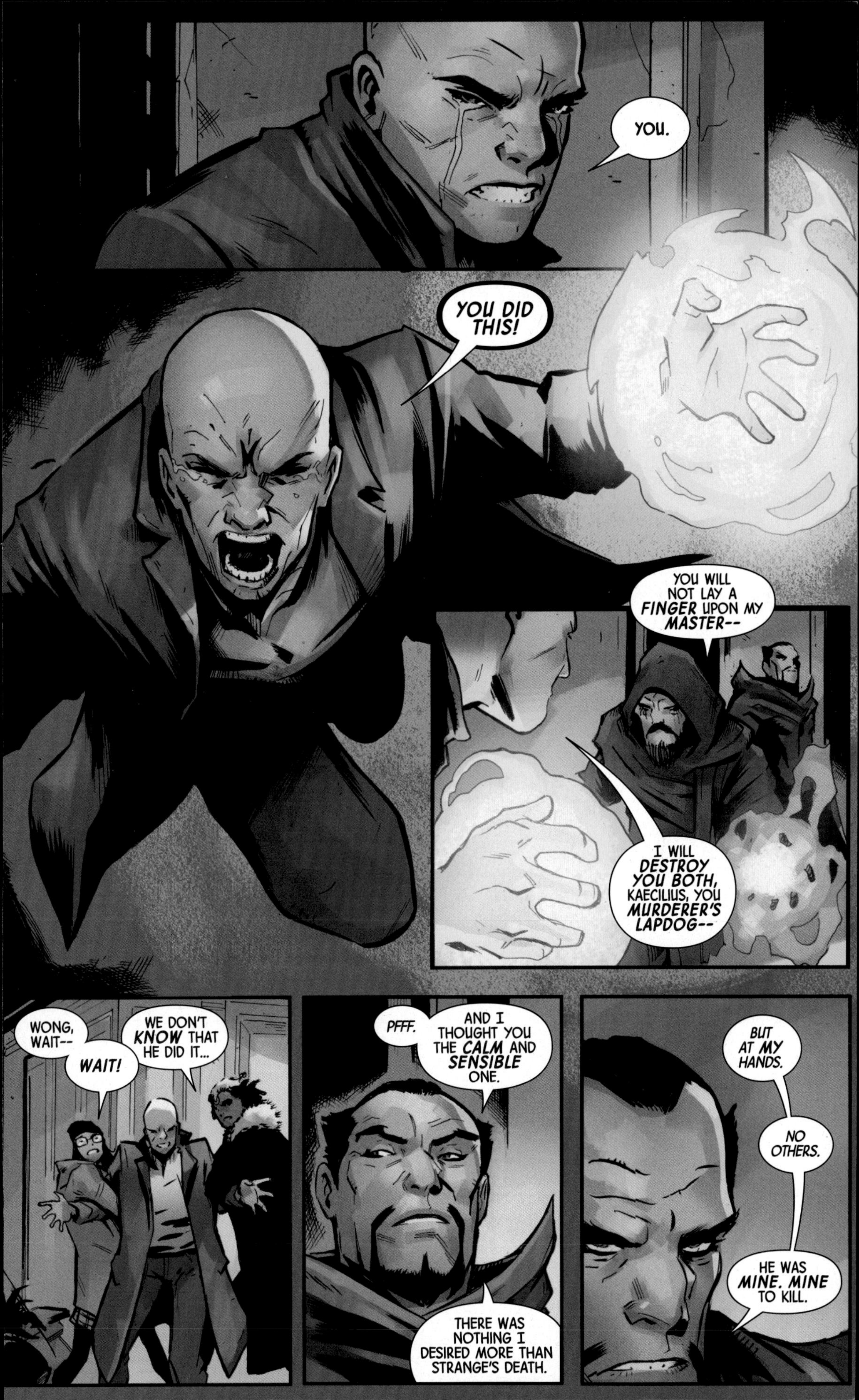
YOU.
YOU DID THIS!
YOU WILL NOT LAY A FINGER UPON MY MASTER--
I WILL DESTROY YOU BOTH, KAECILIUS, YOU MURDERER'S LAPDOG--
WONG, WAIT--
WAIT!
WE DON'T KNOW THAT HE DID IT...
PFFF.
AND I THOUGHT YOU THE CALM AND SENSIBLE ONE.
THERE WAS NOTHING I DESIRED MORE THAN STRANGE'S DEATH.
BUT AT MY HANDS.
NO OTHERS.
HE WAS MINE. MINE TO KILL.

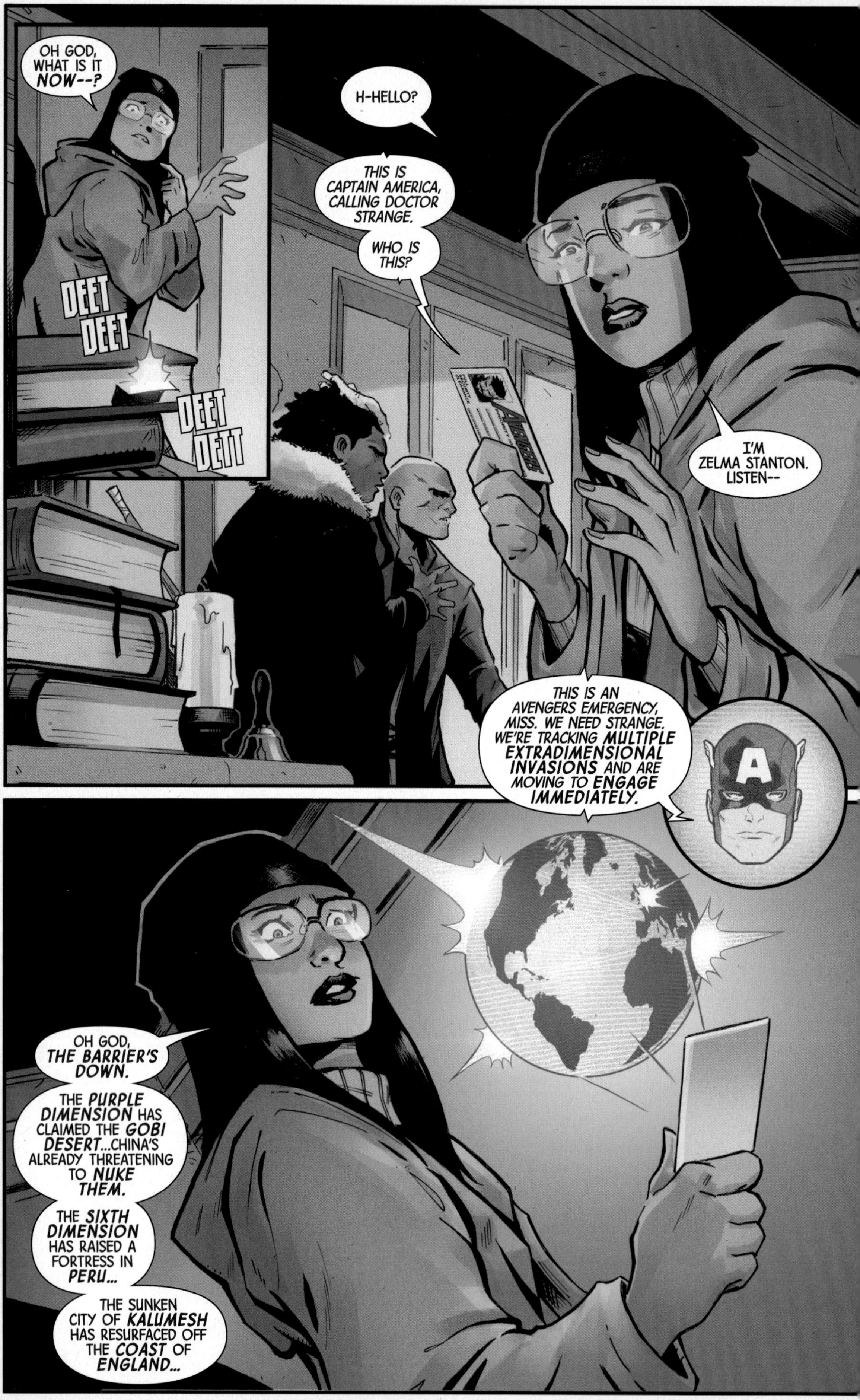

OH GOD, WHAT IS IT NOW--?
DEET
DEET
DEET
DETT
H-HELLO?
THIS IS CAPTAIN AMERICA, CALLING DOCTOR STRANGE.
WHO IS THIS?
I'M ZELMA STANTON. LISTEN--
THIS IS AN AVENGERS EMERGENCY, MISS. WE NEED STRANGE. WE'RE TRACKING MULTIPLE EXTRADIMENSIONAL INVASIONS AND ARE MOVING TO ENGAGE IMMEDIATELY.
OH GOD, THE BARRIER'S DOWN.
THE PURPLE DIMENSION HAS CLAIMED THE GOBI DESERT...CHINA'S ALREADY THREATENING TO NUKE THEM.
THE SIXTH DIMENSION HAS RAISED A FORTRESS IN PERU...
THE SUNKEN CITY OF KALUMESH HAS RESURFACED OFF THE COAST OF ENGLAND...

KOSCHEI THE DEATHLESS.

A MAN WHO SEVERED HIS SOUL AND HID IT...

...SO THAT HE MIGHT LIVE FOREVER.

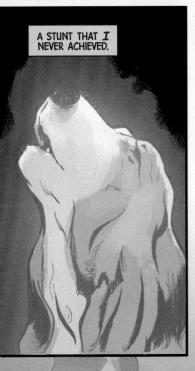

A STUNT THAT *I* NEVER ACHIEVED.

BUT *ONCE*...

...WHEN I WAS *MUCH YOUNGER*...

...IN CASE I MIGHT BE *KILLED* IN THE *FUTURE*...

ZOUNDS.

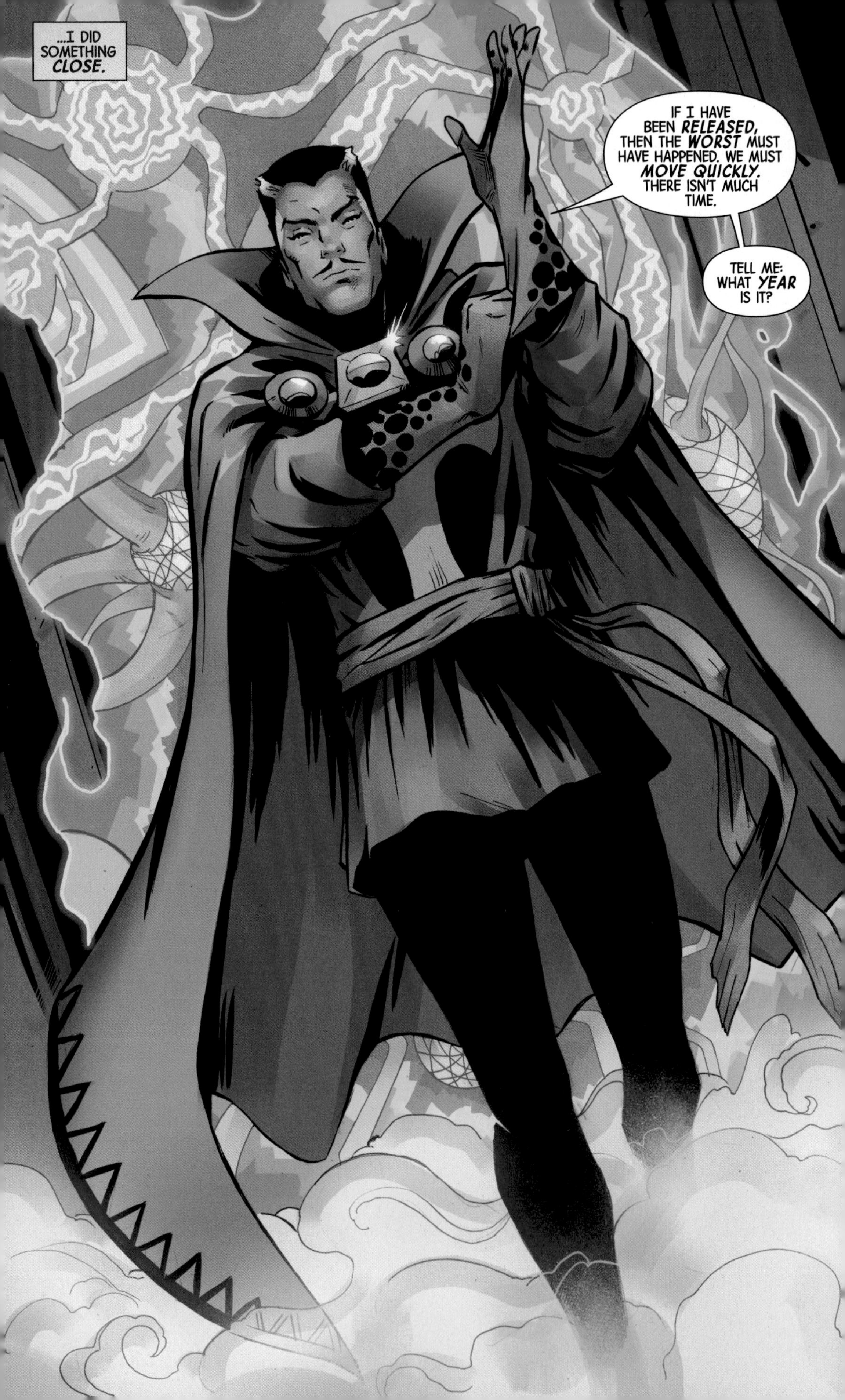
...I DID SOMETHING CLOSE.
IF I HAVE BEEN RELEASED, THEN THE WORST MUST HAVE HAPPENED. WE MUST MOVE QUICKLY. THERE ISN'T MUCH TIME.
TELL ME: WHAT YEAR IS IT?

CHAPTER THREE

The Dance of the Warlords

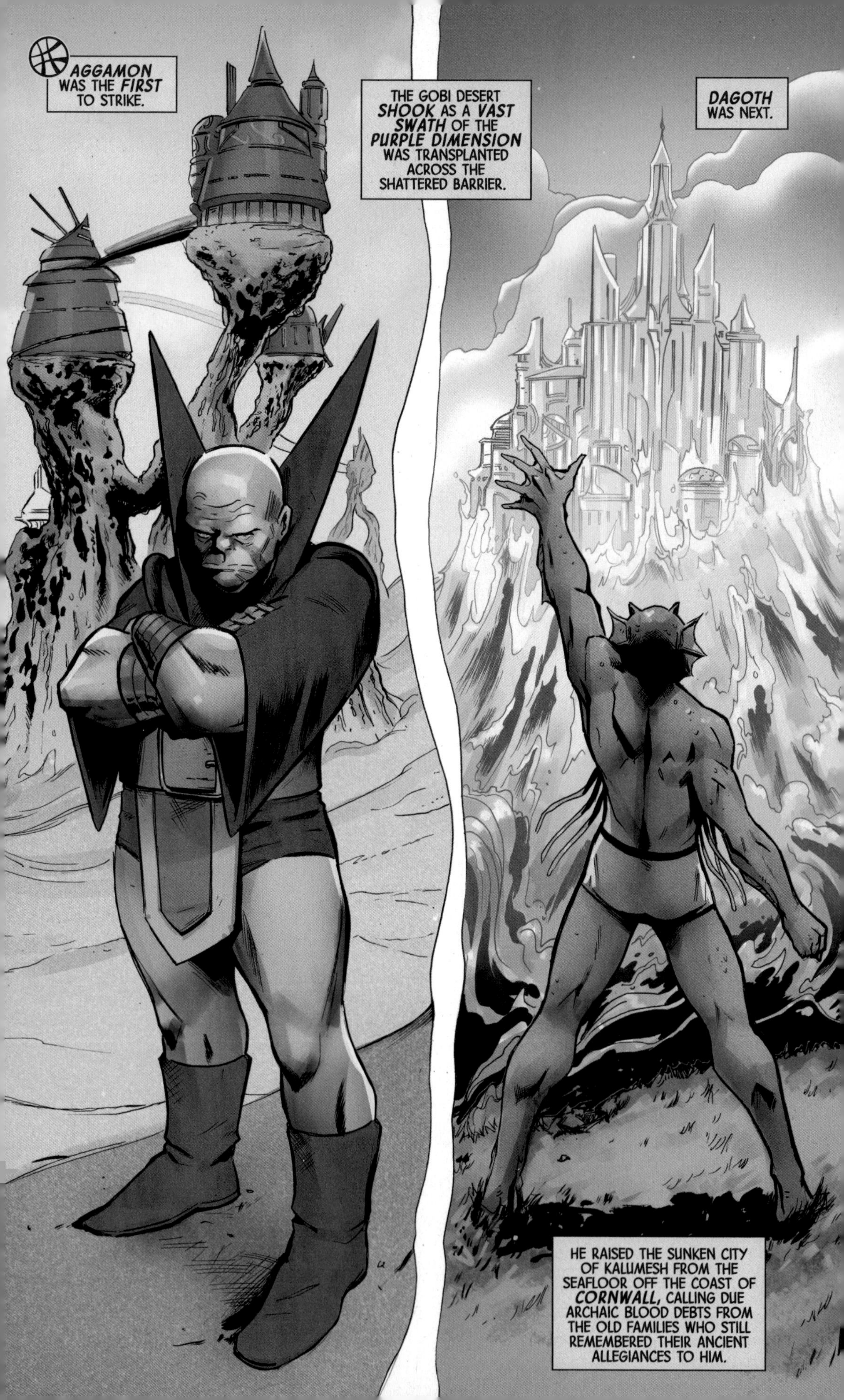
AGGAMON WAS THE FIRST TO STRIKE.
THE GOBI DESERT SHOOK AS A VAST SWATH OF THE PURPLE DIMENSION WAS TRANSPLANTED ACROSS THE SHATTERED BARRIER.
DAGOTH WAS NEXT.
HE RAISED THE SUNKEN CITY OF KALUMESH FROM THE SEAFLOOR OFF THE COAST OF CORNWALL, CALLING DUE ARCHAIC BLOOD DEBTS FROM THE OLD FAMILIES WHO STILL REMEMBERED THEIR ANCIENT ALLEGIANCES TO HIM.

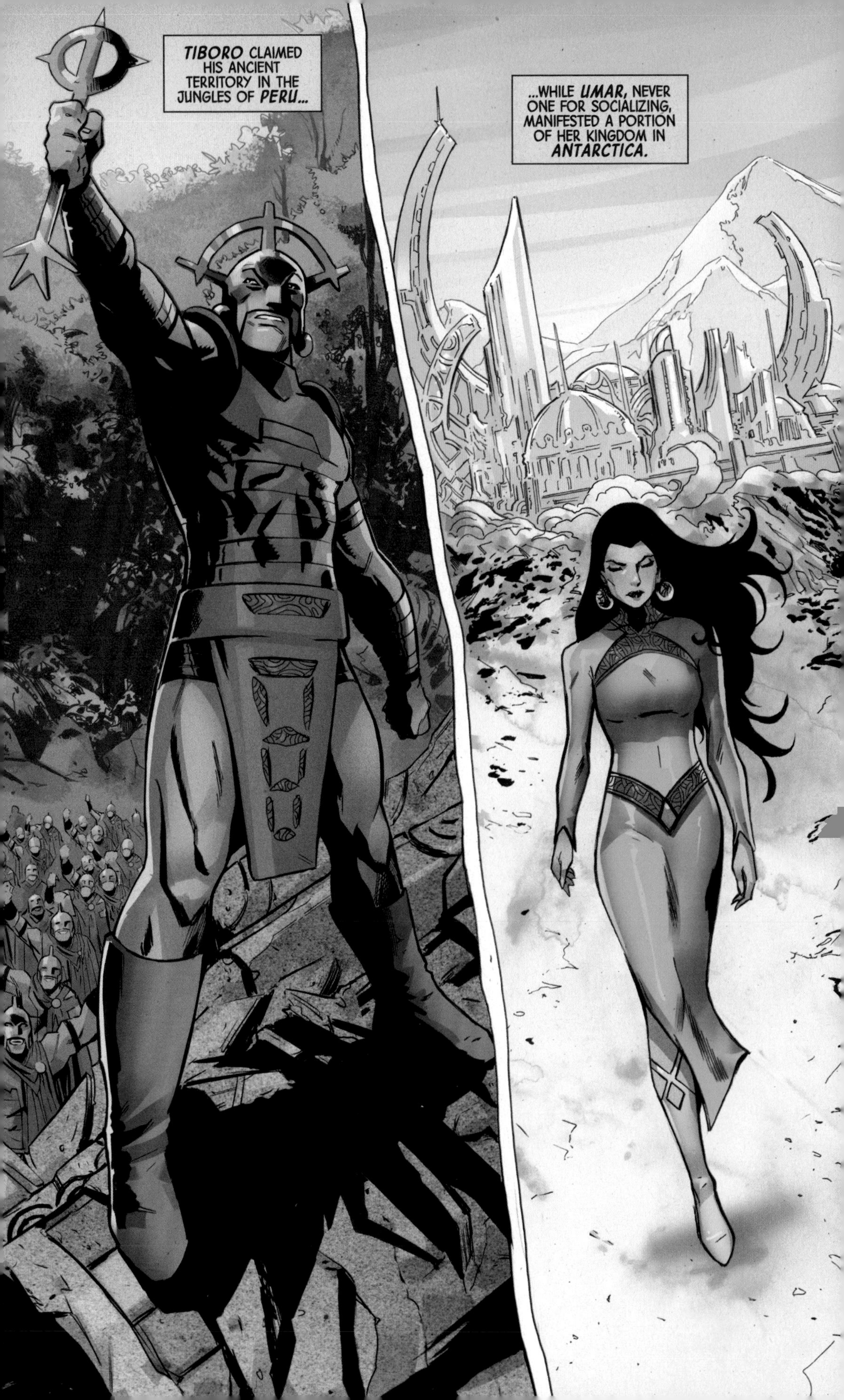
TIBORO CLAIMED HIS ANCIENT TERRITORY IN THE JUNGLES OF PERU...
...WHILE UMAR, NEVER ONE FOR SOCIALIZING, MANIFESTED A PORTION OF HER KINGDOM IN ANTARCTICA.

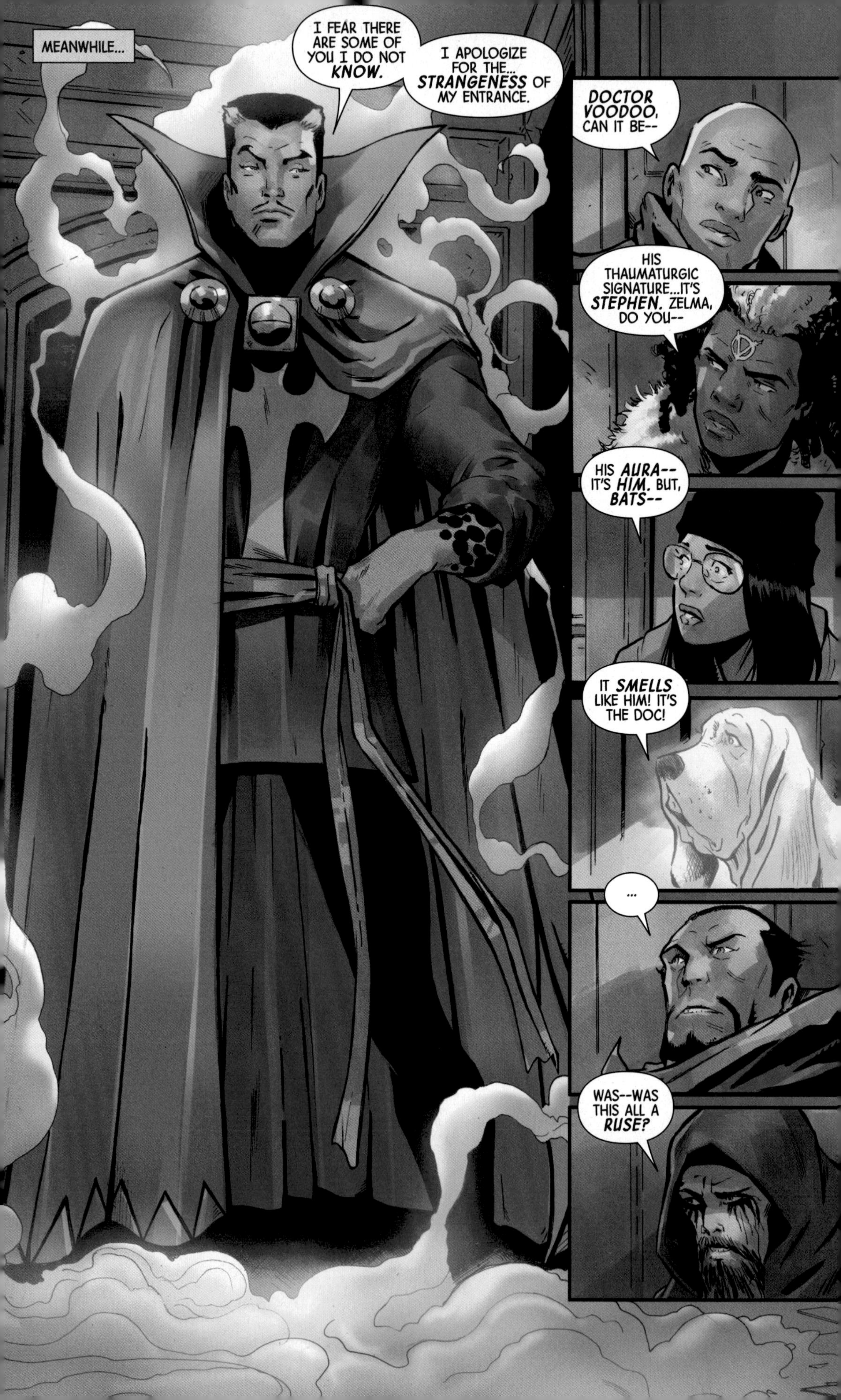
MEANWHILE...
I FEAR THERE ARE SOME OF YOU I DO NOT KNOW.
I APOLOGIZE FOR THE... STRANGENESS OF MY ENTRANCE.
DOCTOR VOODOO, CAN IT BE--
HIS THAUMATURGIC SIGNATURE...IT'S STEPHEN. ZELMA, DO YOU--
HIS AURA-- IT'S HIM. BUT, BATS--
IT SMELLS LIKE HIM! IT'S THE DOC!
...
WAS--WAS THIS ALL A RUSE?

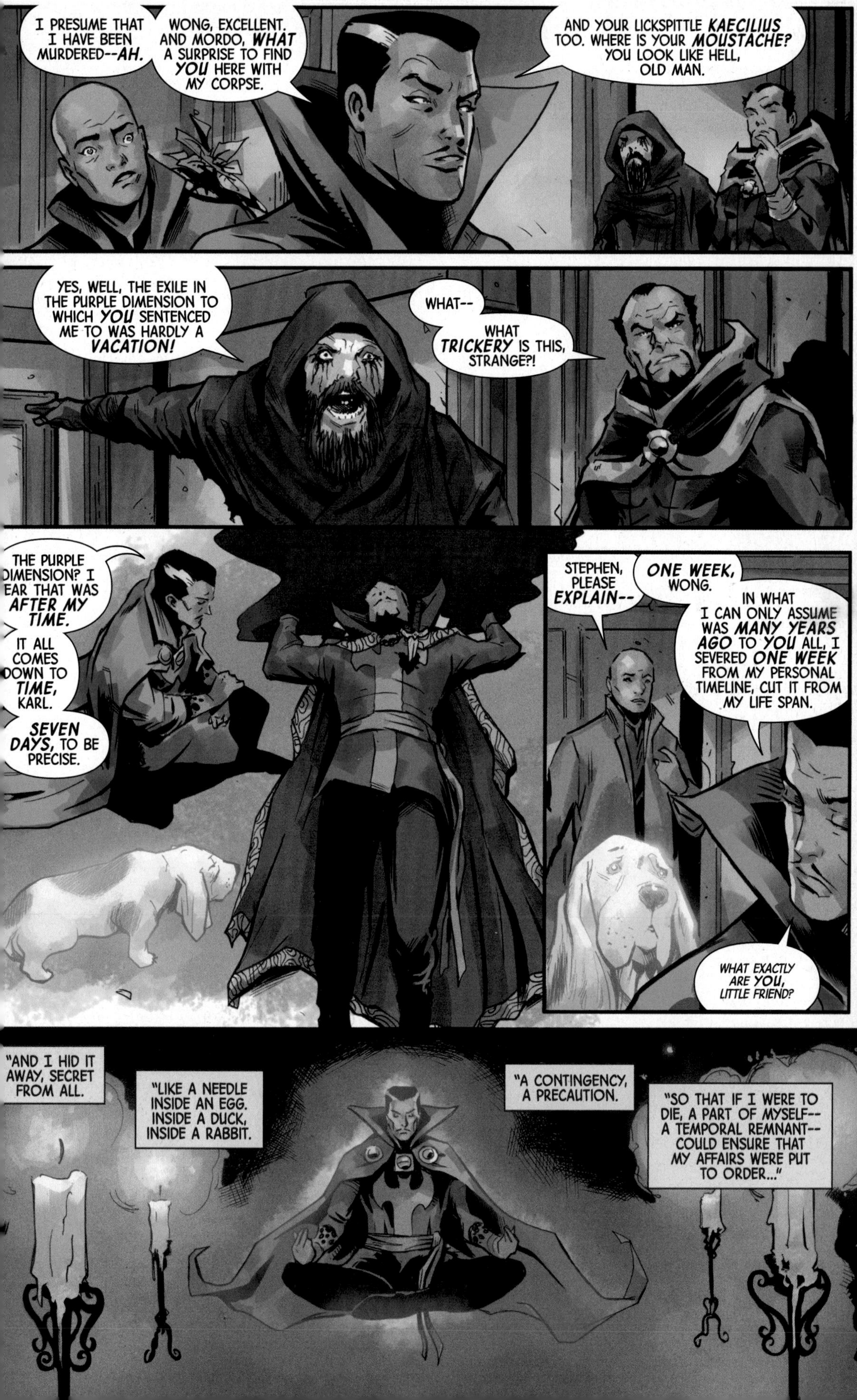
I PRESUME THAT I HAVE BEEN MURDERED--AH.
WONG, EXCELLENT. AND MORDO, WHAT A SURPRISE TO FIND YOU HERE WITH MY CORPSE.
AND YOUR LICKSPITTLE KAECILIUS TOO. WHERE IS YOUR MOUSTACHE? YOU LOOK LIKE HELL, OLD MAN.
YES, WELL, THE EXILE IN THE PURPLE DIMENSION TO WHICH YOU SENTENCED ME TO WAS HARDLY A VACATION!
WHAT--
WHAT TRICKERY IS THIS, STRANGE?!
THE PURPLE DIMENSION? I FEAR THAT WAS AFTER MY TIME.
IT ALL COMES DOWN TO TIME, KARL.
SEVEN DAYS, TO BE PRECISE.
STEPHEN, PLEASE EXPLAIN--
ONE WEEK, WONG.
IN WHAT I CAN ONLY ASSUME WAS MANY YEARS AGO TO YOU ALL, I SEVERED ONE WEEK FROM MY PERSONAL TIMELINE, CUT IT FROM MY LIFE SPAN.
WHAT EXACTLY ARE YOU, LITTLE FRIEND?
"AND I HID IT AWAY, SECRET FROM ALL.
"LIKE A NEEDLE INSIDE AN EGG. INSIDE A DUCK, INSIDE A RABBIT.
"A CONTINGENCY, A PRECAUTION.
"SO THAT IF I WERE TO DIE, A PART OF MYSELF-- A TEMPORAL REMNANT-- COULD ENSURE THAT MY AFFAIRS WERE PUT TO ORDER..."

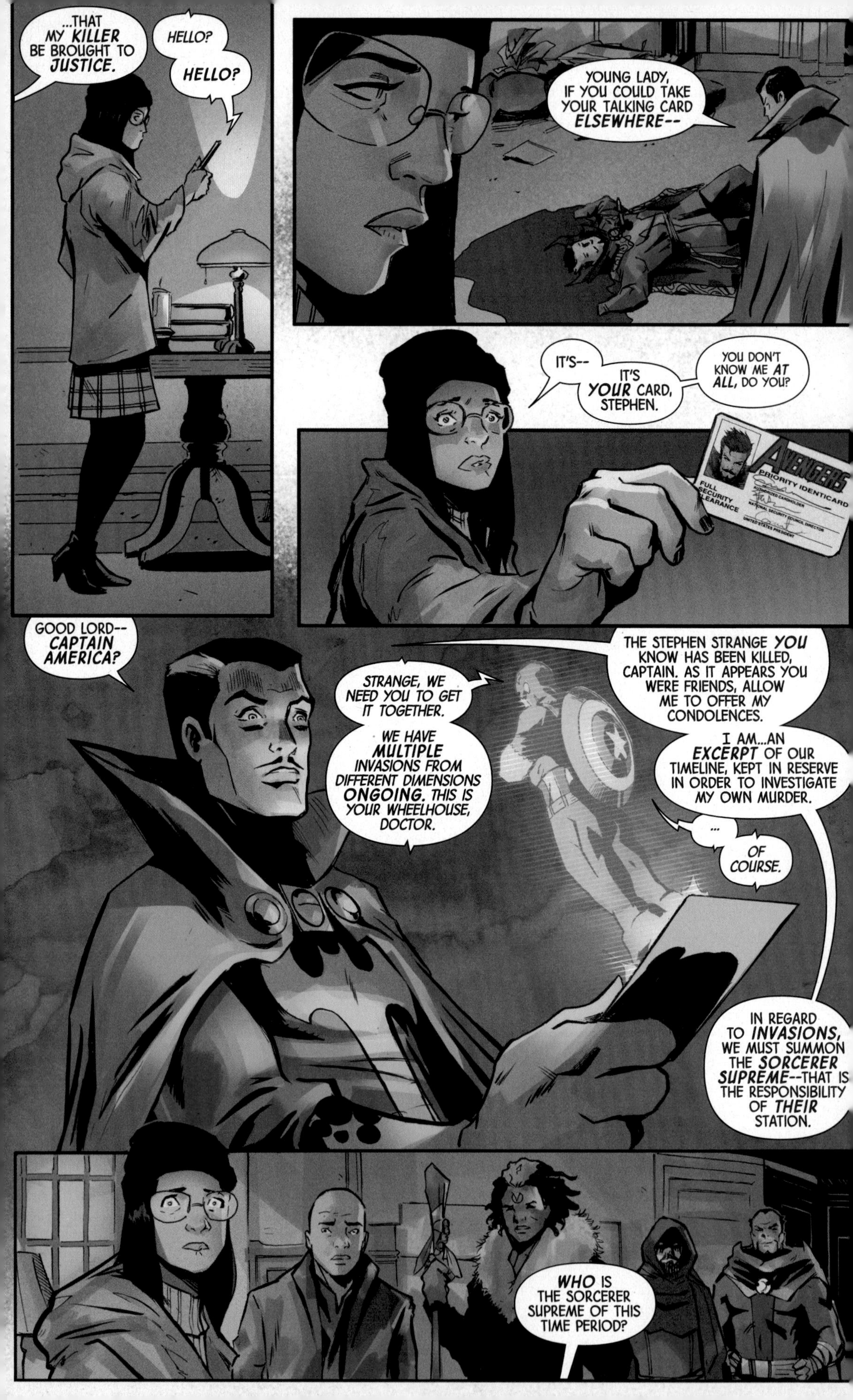

...THAT MY KILLER BE BROUGHT TO JUSTICE.
HELLO?
HELLO?
YOUNG LADY, IF YOU COULD TAKE YOUR TALKING CARD ELSEWHERE--
IT'S--
IT'S YOUR CARD, STEPHEN.
YOU DON'T KNOW ME AT ALL, DO YOU?
AVENGERS
PRIORITY IDENTICARD
GOOD LORD-- CAPTAIN AMERICA?
STRANGE, WE NEED YOU TO GET IT TOGETHER.
WE HAVE MULTIPLE INVASIONS FROM DIFFERENT DIMENSIONS ONGOING. THIS IS YOUR WHEELHOUSE, DOCTOR.
THE STEPHEN STRANGE YOU KNOW HAS BEEN KILLED, CAPTAIN. AS IT APPEARS YOU WERE FRIENDS, ALLOW ME TO OFFER MY CONDOLENCES.
I AM...AN EXCERPT OF OUR TIMELINE, KEPT IN RESERVE IN ORDER TO INVESTIGATE MY OWN MURDER.
...
OF COURSE.
IN REGARD TO INVASIONS, WE MUST SUMMON THE SORCERER SUPREME--THAT IS THE RESPONSIBILITY OF THEIR STATION.
WHO IS THE SORCERER SUPREME OF THIS TIME PERIOD?

CHAPTER FOUR

The Three Mothers

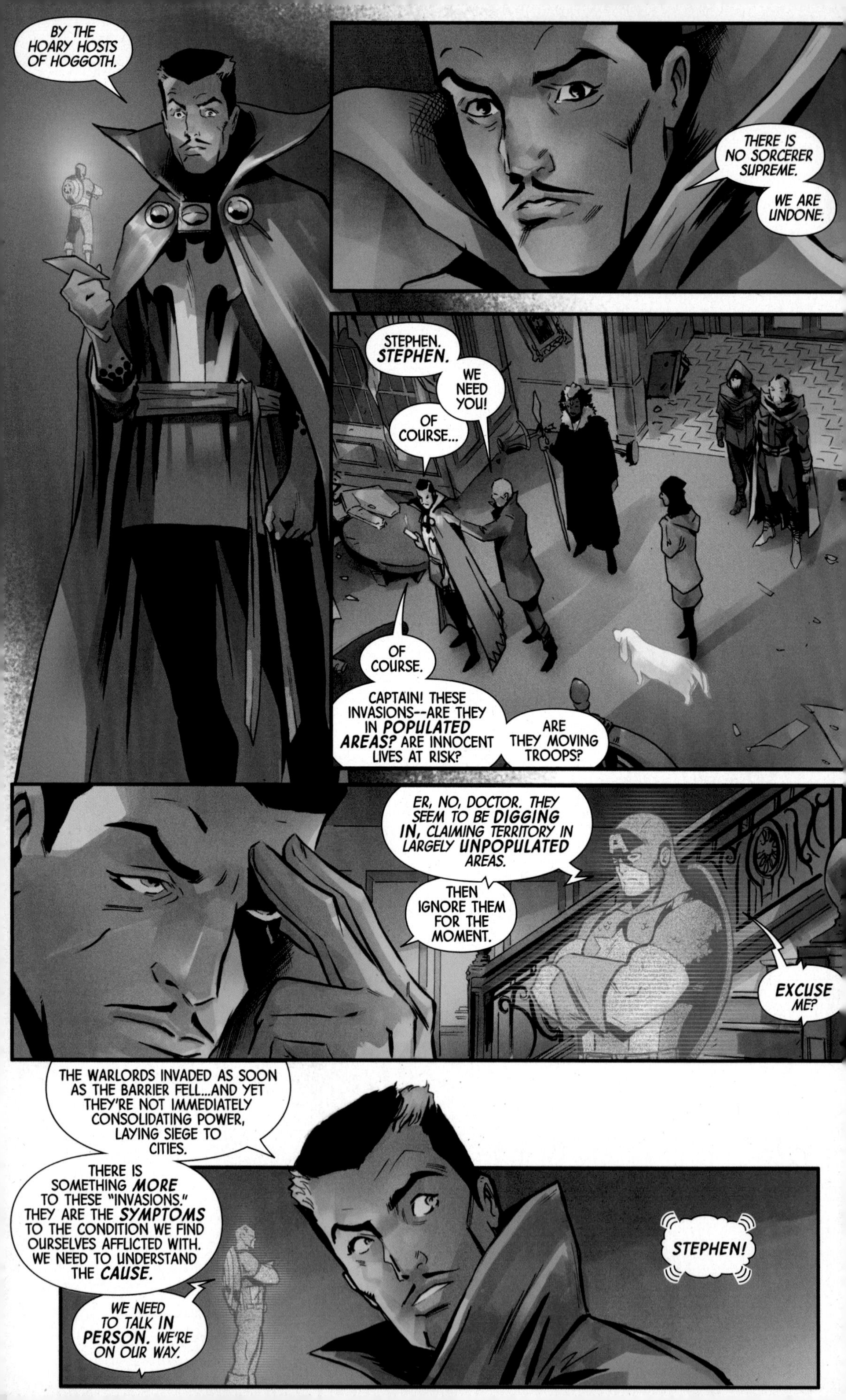
BY THE HOARY HOSTS OF HOGGOTH.
THERE IS NO SORCERER SUPREME.
WE ARE UNDONE.
STEPHEN. STEPHEN.
WE NEED YOU!
OF COURSE...
OF COURSE.
CAPTAIN! THESE INVASIONS--ARE THEY IN POPULATED AREAS? ARE INNOCENT LIVES AT RISK?
ARE THEY MOVING TROOPS?
ER, NO, DOCTOR. THEY SEEM TO BE DIGGING IN, CLAIMING TERRITORY IN LARGELY UNPOPULATED AREAS.
THEN IGNORE THEM FOR THE MOMENT.
EXCUSE ME?
THE WARLORDS INVADED AS SOON AS THE BARRIER FELL...AND YET THEY'RE NOT IMMEDIATELY CONSOLIDATING POWER, LAYING SIEGE TO CITIES.
THERE IS SOMETHING MORE TO THESE "INVASIONS." THEY ARE THE SYMPTOMS TO THE CONDITION WE FIND OURSELVES AFFLICTED WITH. WE NEED TO UNDERSTAND THE CAUSE.
WE NEED TO TALK IN PERSON. WE'RE ON OUR WAY.
STEPHEN!

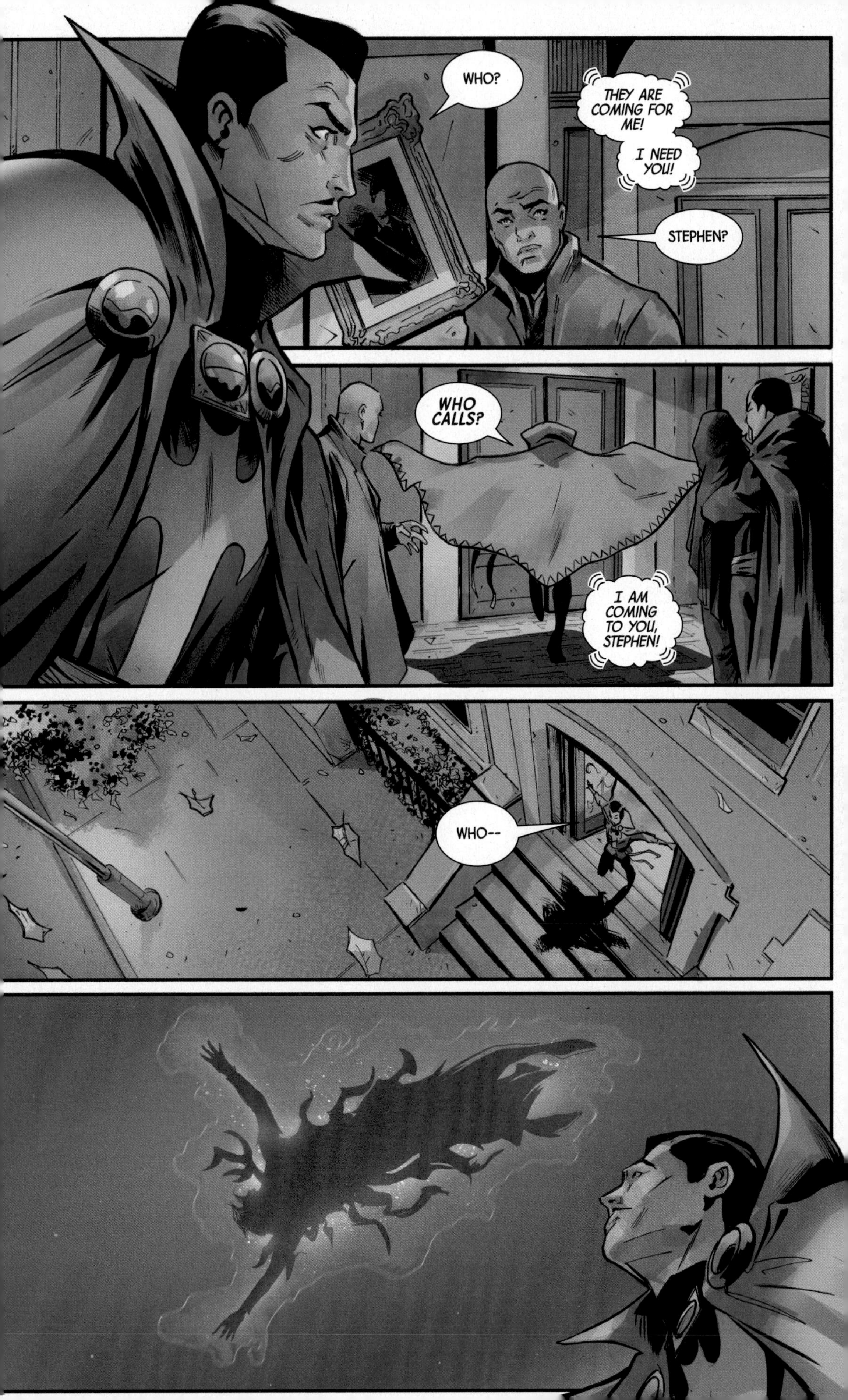
WHO?
THEY ARE COMING FOR ME!
I NEED YOU!
STEPHEN?
WHO CALLS?
I AM COMING TO YOU, STEPHEN!
WHO--

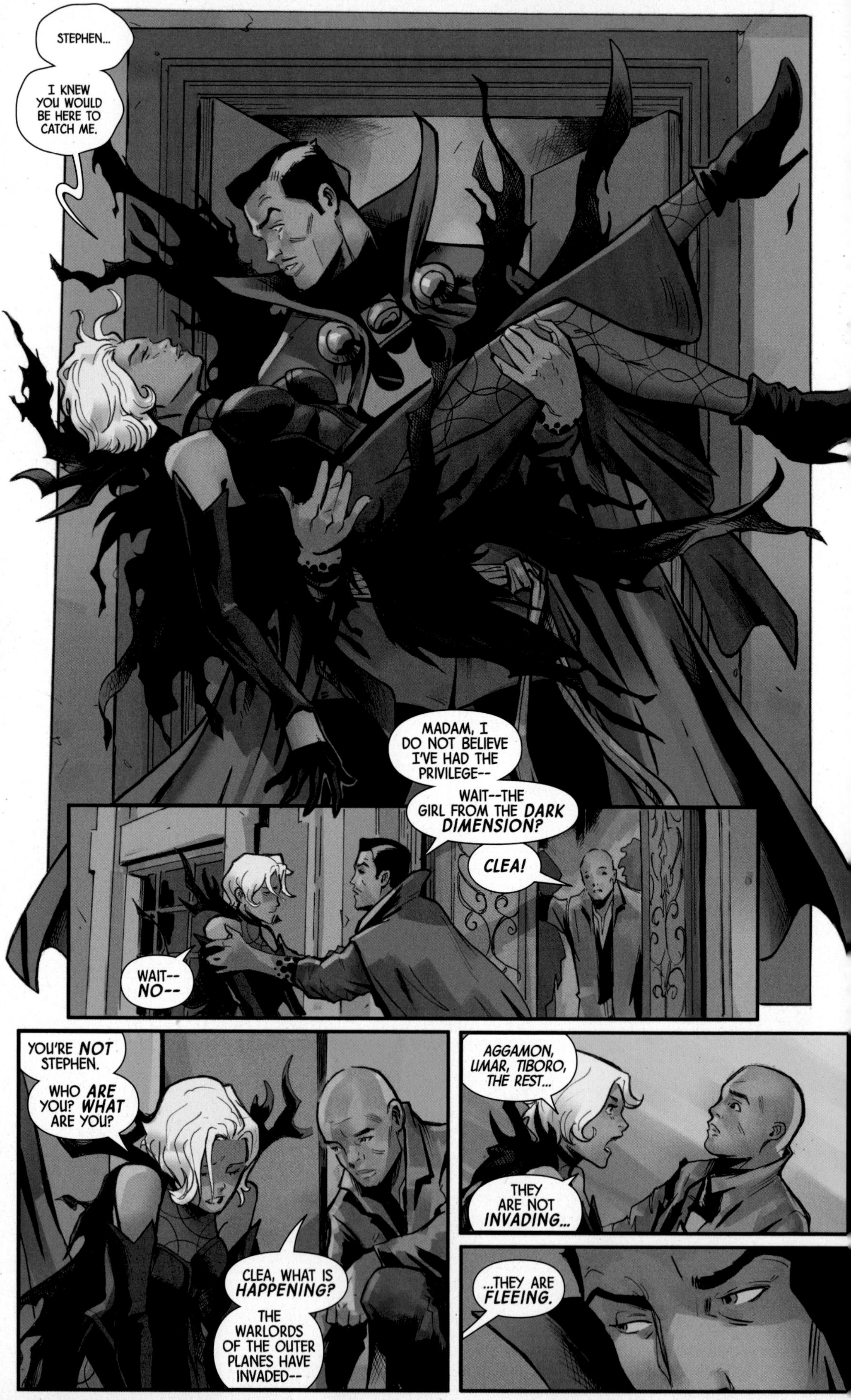
STEPHEN...
I KNEW YOU WOULD BE HERE TO CATCH ME.
MADAM, I DO NOT BELIEVE I'VE HAD THE PRIVILEGE--
WAIT--THE GIRL FROM THE DARK DIMENSION?
CLEA!
WAIT-- NO--
YOU'RE NOT STEPHEN.
WHO ARE YOU? WHAT ARE YOU?
CLEA, WHAT IS HAPPENING?
THE WARLORDS OF THE OUTER PLANES HAVE INVADED--
AGGAMON, UMAR, TIBORO, THE REST...
THEY ARE NOT INVADING...
...THEY ARE FLEEING.

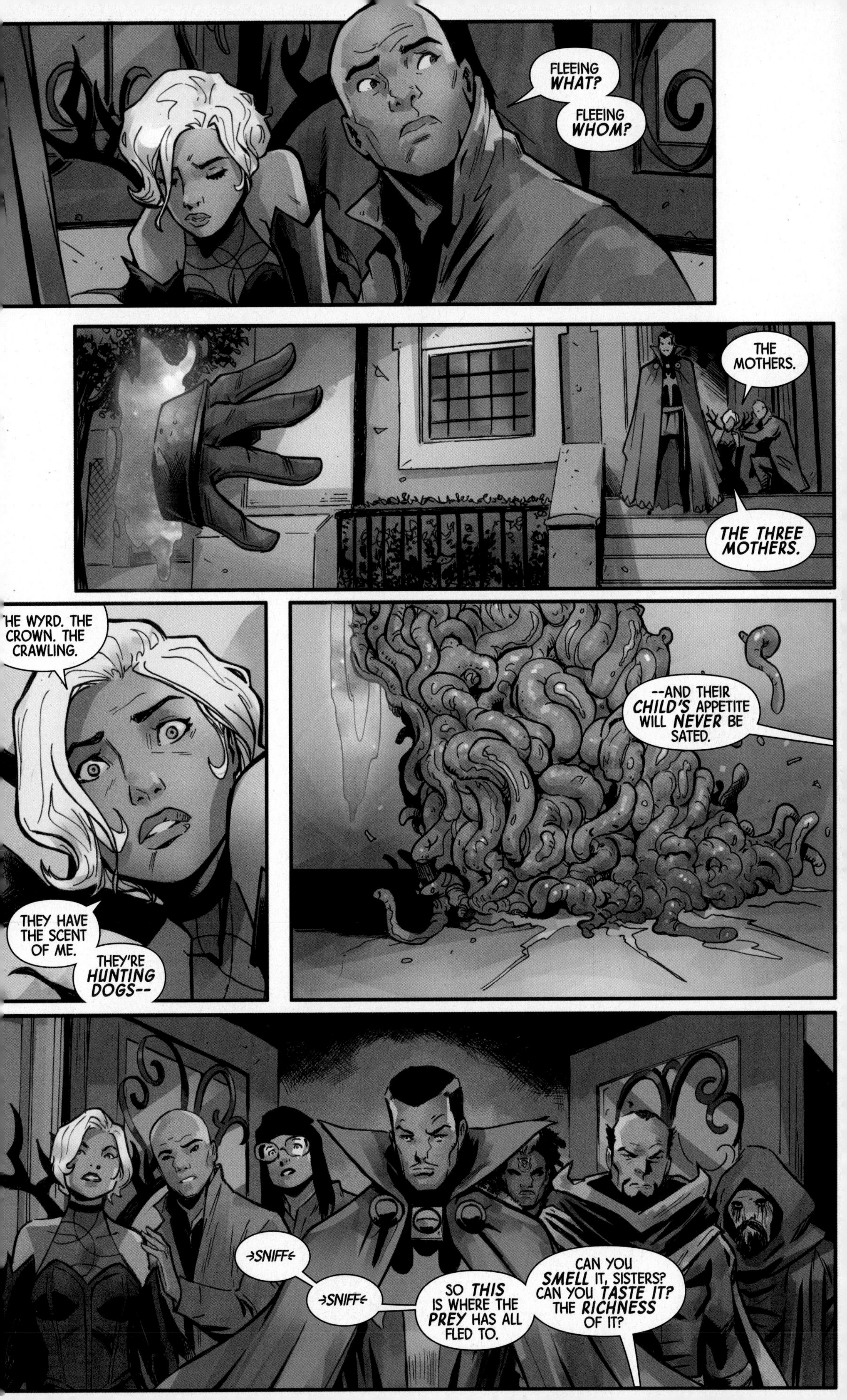
FLEEING WHAT?
FLEEING WHOM?
THE MOTHERS.
THE THREE MOTHERS.
THE WYRD. THE CROWN. THE CRAWLING.
THEY HAVE THE SCENT OF ME.
THEY'RE HUNTING DOGS--
--AND THEIR CHILD'S APPETITE WILL NEVER BE SATED.
SNIFF
SNIFF
SO THIS IS WHERE THE PREY HAS ALL FLED TO.
CAN YOU SMELL IT, SISTERS? CAN YOU TASTE IT? THE RICHNESS OF IT?

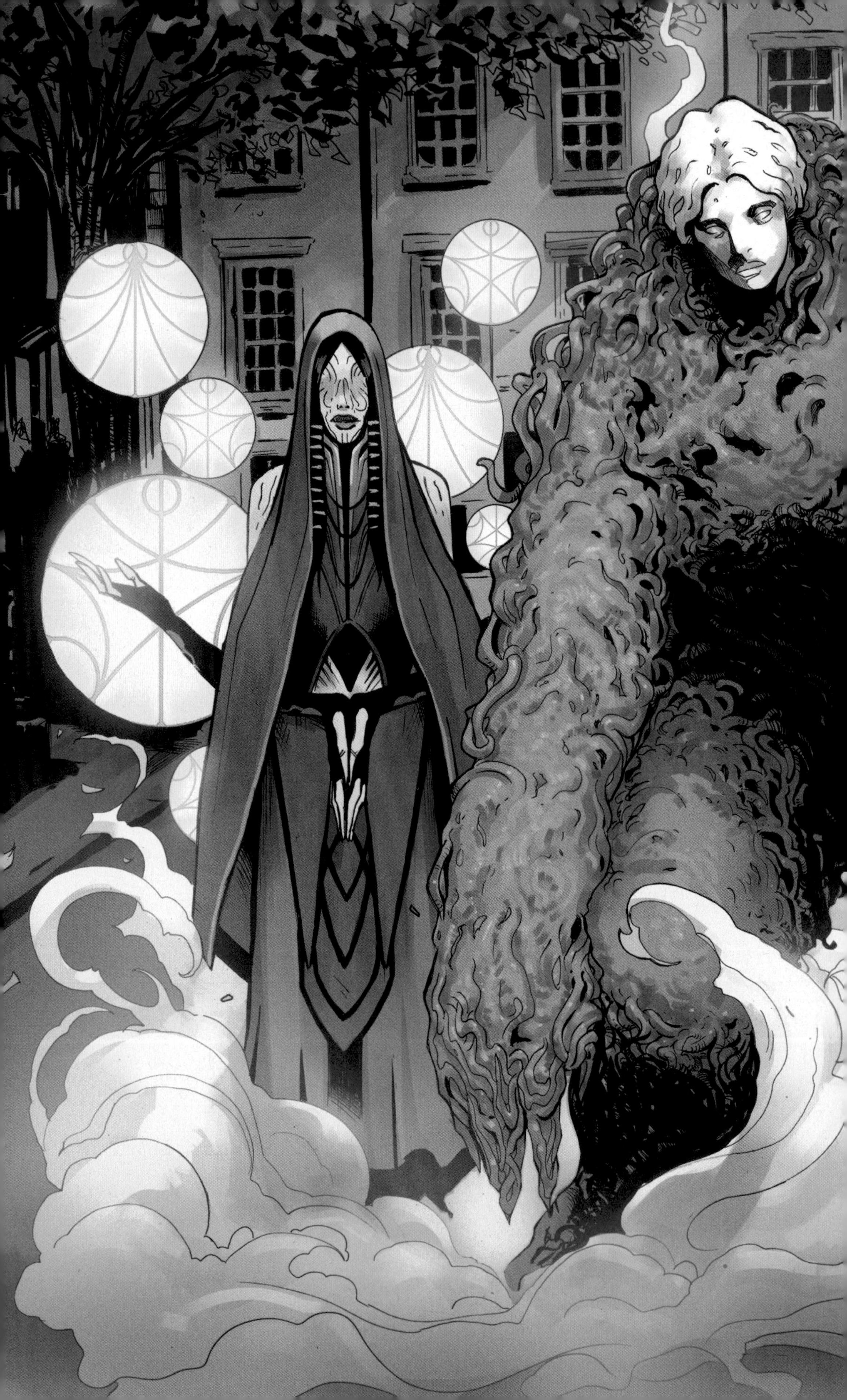

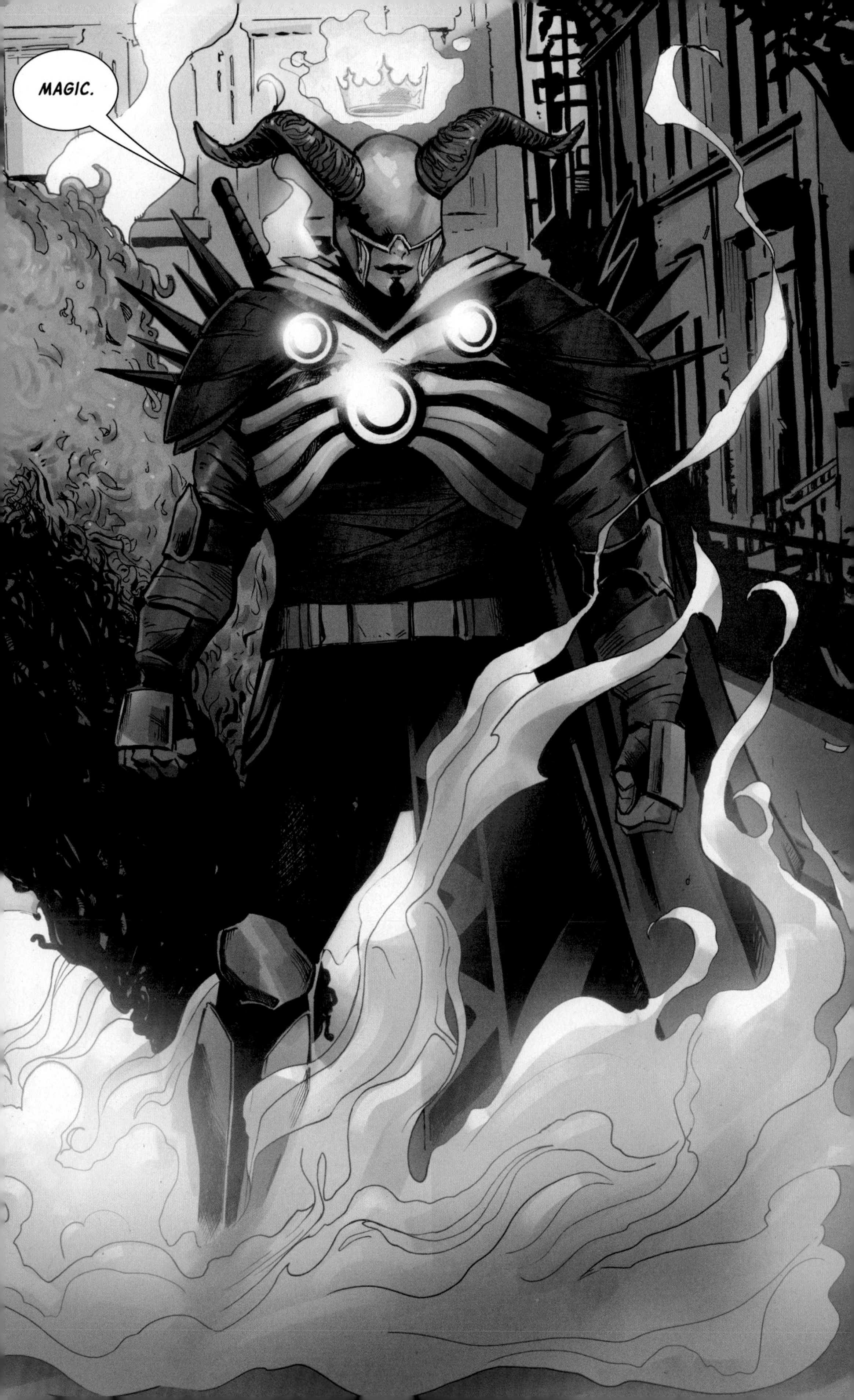
MAGIC.

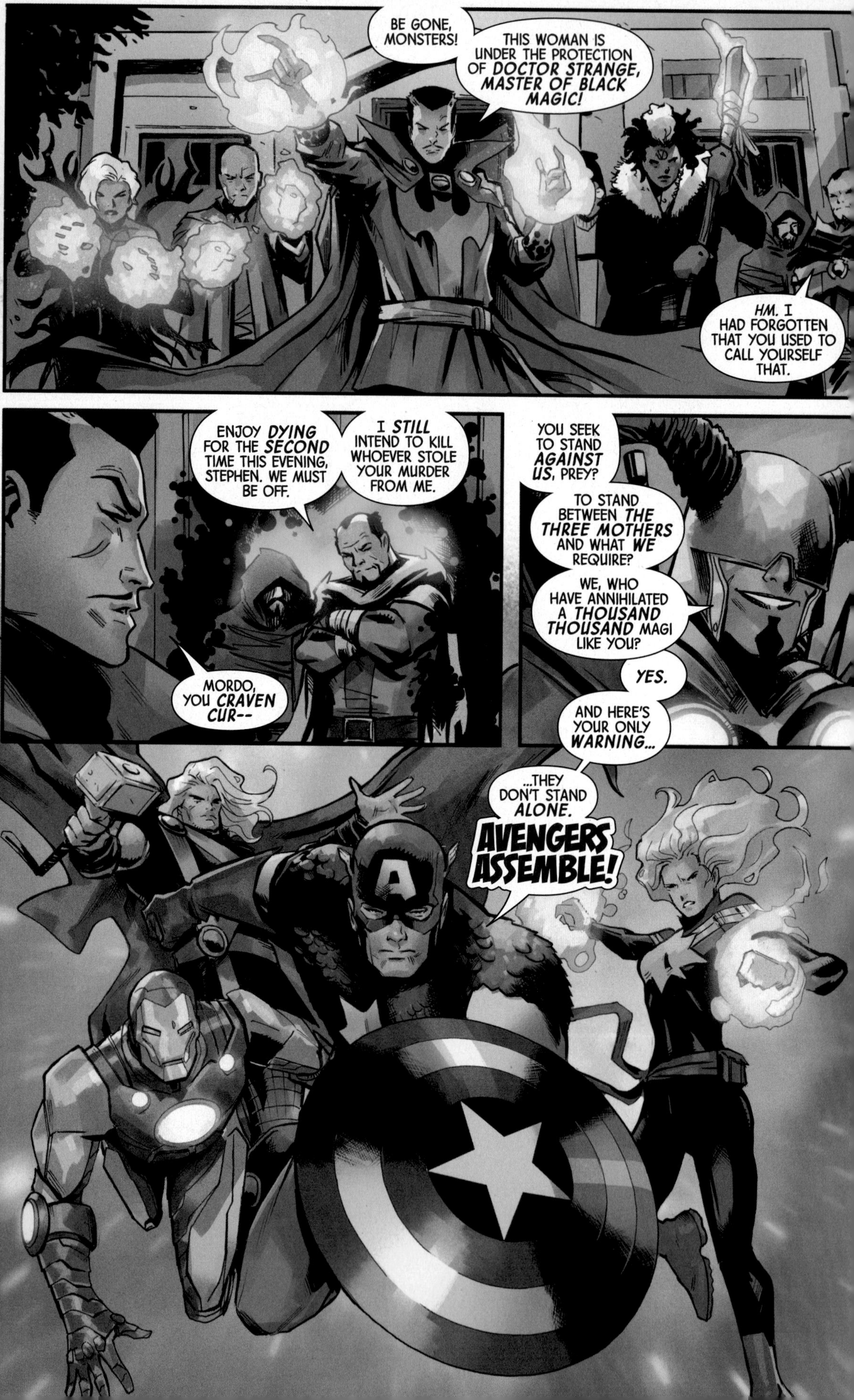
BE GONE, MONSTERS!
THIS WOMAN IS UNDER THE PROTECTION OF DOCTOR STRANGE, MASTER OF BLACK MAGIC!
HM. I HAD FORGOTTEN THAT YOU USED TO CALL YOURSELF THAT.
ENJOY DYING FOR THE SECOND TIME THIS EVENING, STEPHEN. WE MUST BE OFF.
I STILL INTEND TO KILL WHOEVER STOLE YOUR MURDER FROM ME.
MORDO, YOU CRAVEN CUR--
YOU SEEK TO STAND AGAINST US, PREY?
TO STAND BETWEEN THE THREE MOTHERS AND WHAT WE REQUIRE?
WE, WHO HAVE ANNIHILATED A THOUSAND THOUSAND MAGI LIKE YOU?
YES.
AND HERE'S YOUR ONLY WARNING...
...THEY DON'T STAND ALONE.
AVENGERS ASSEMBLE!

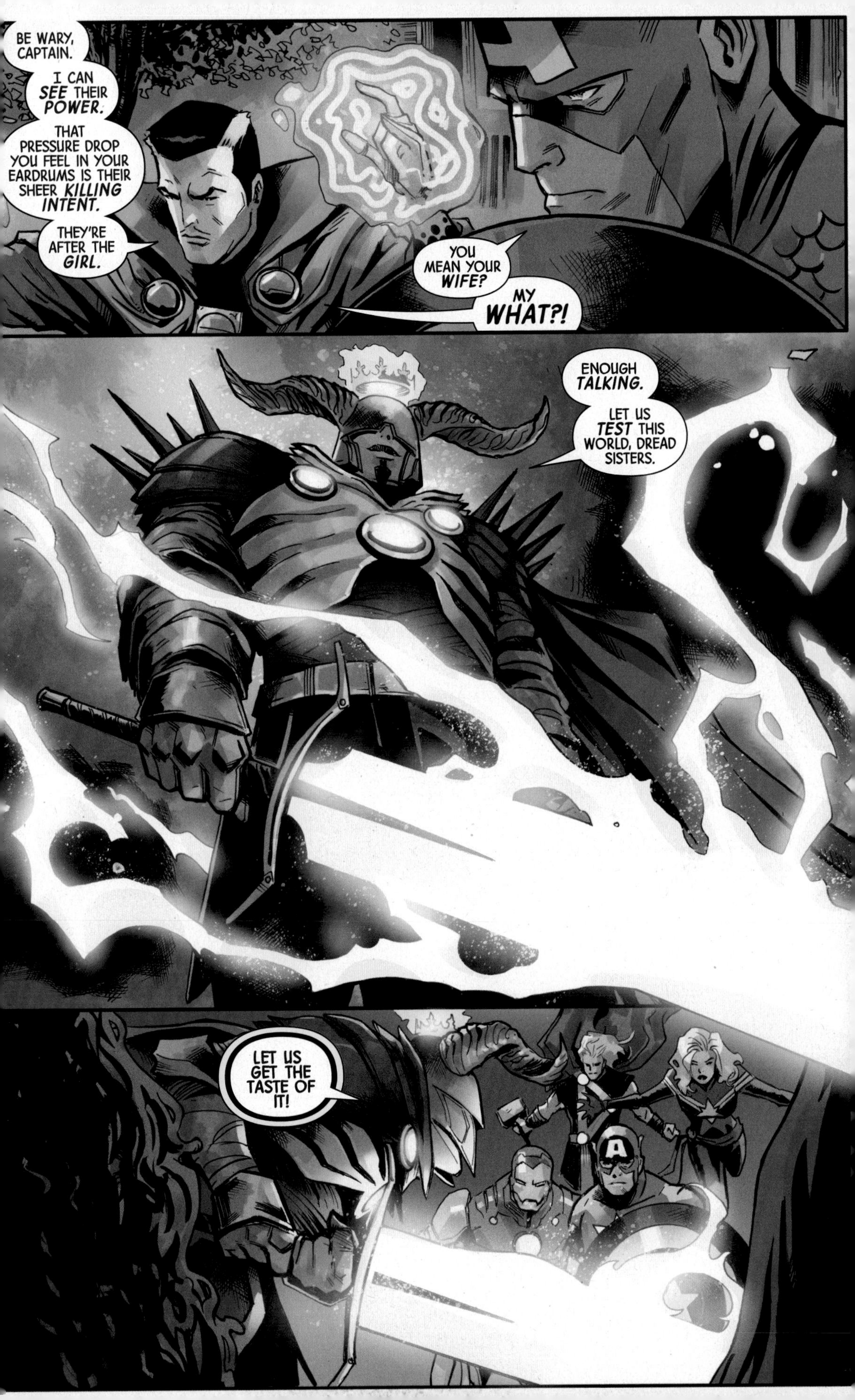
BE WARY, CAPTAIN.
I CAN SEE THEIR POWER.
THAT PRESSURE DROP YOU FEEL IN YOUR EARDRUMS IS THEIR SHEER KILLING INTENT.
THEY'RE AFTER THE GIRL.
YOU MEAN YOUR WIFE?
MY WHAT?!
ENOUGH TALKING.
LET US TEST THIS WORLD, DREAD SISTERS.
LET US GET THE TASTE OF IT!

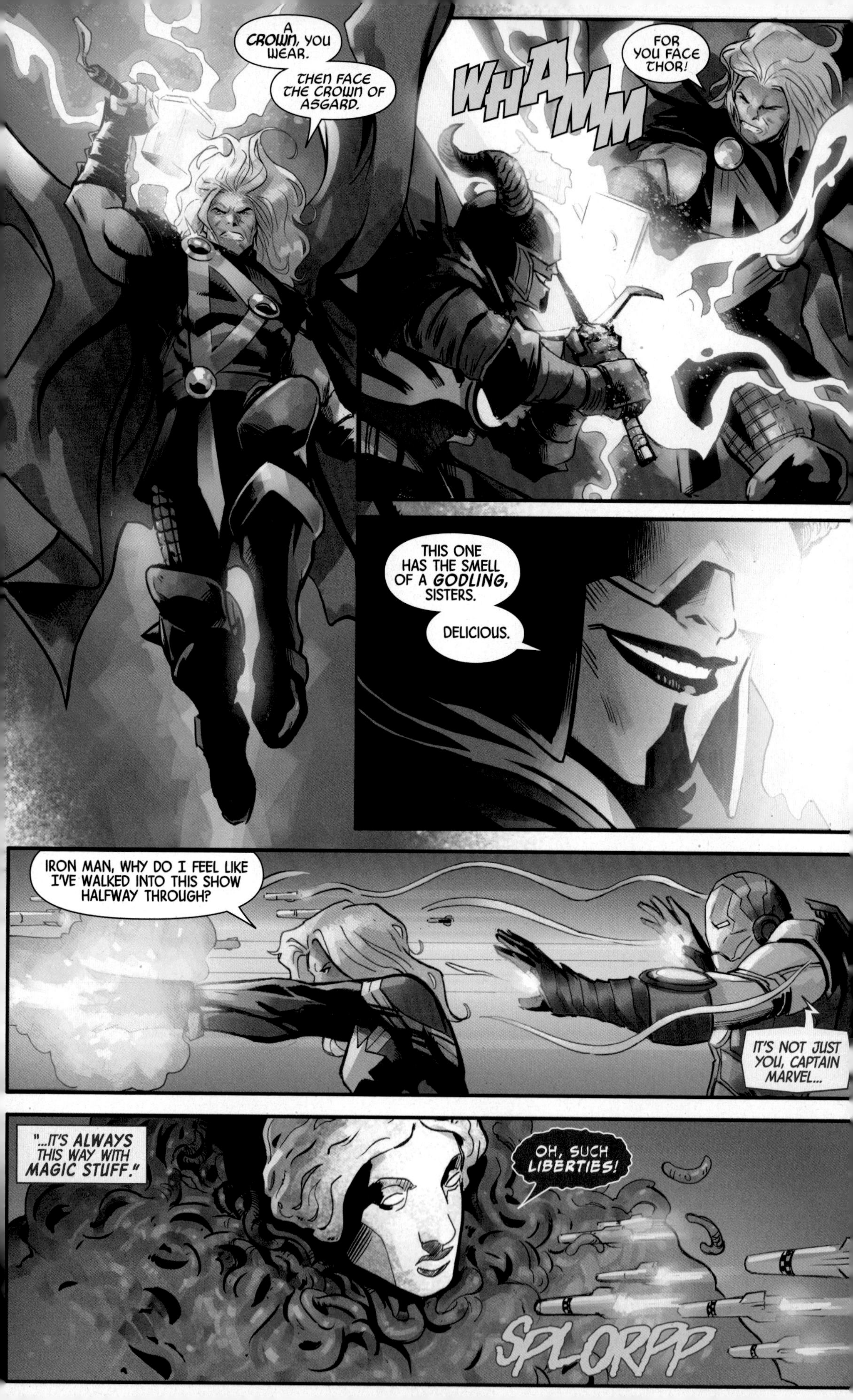

A CROWN, YOU WEAR.
THEN FACE THE CROWN OF ASGARD.
WHAMMM
FOR YOU FACE THOR!
THIS ONE HAS THE SMELL OF A GODLING, SISTERS.
DELICIOUS.
IRON MAN, WHY DO I FEEL LIKE I'VE WALKED INTO THIS SHOW HALFWAY THROUGH?
IT'S NOT JUST YOU, CAPTAIN MARVEL...
"...IT'S ALWAYS THIS WAY WITH MAGIC STUFF."
OH, SUCH LIBERTIES!
SPLORPP

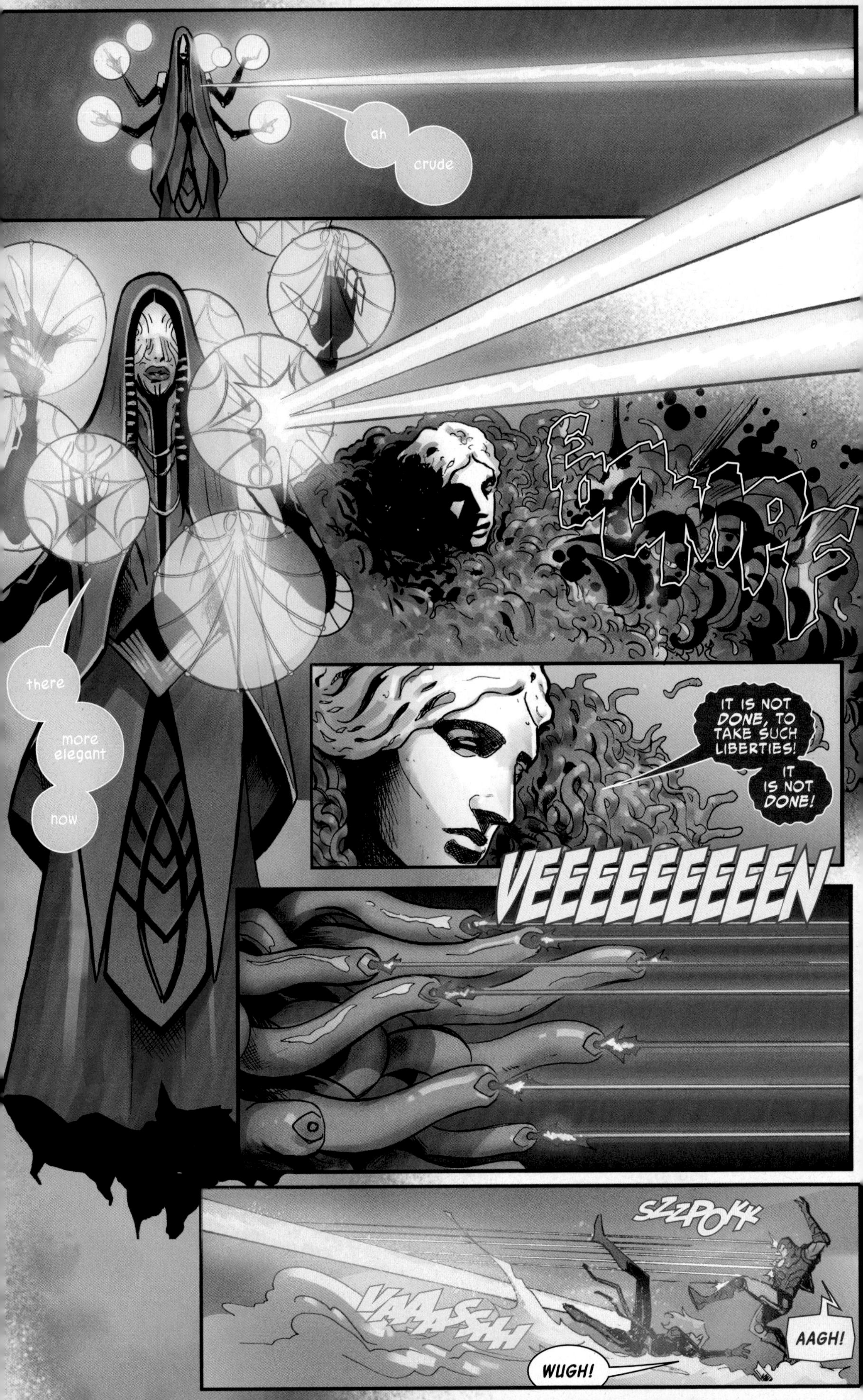
ah
crude
there
more elegant
now
IT IS NOT DONE, TO TAKE SUCH LIBERTIES!
IT IS NOT DONE!
VEEEEEEEEEN
SZZPOKK
VAAASHH
AAGH!
WUGH!

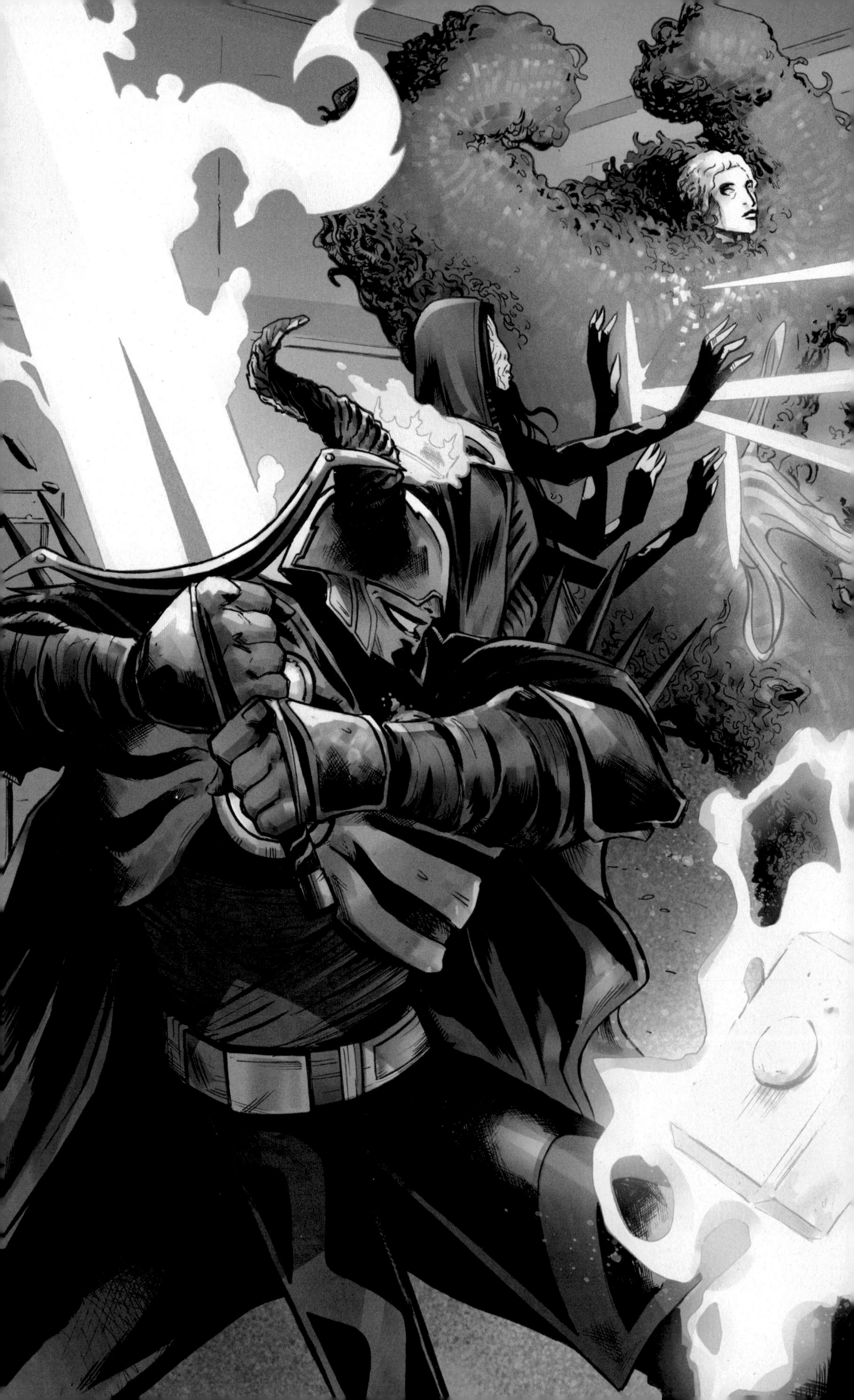

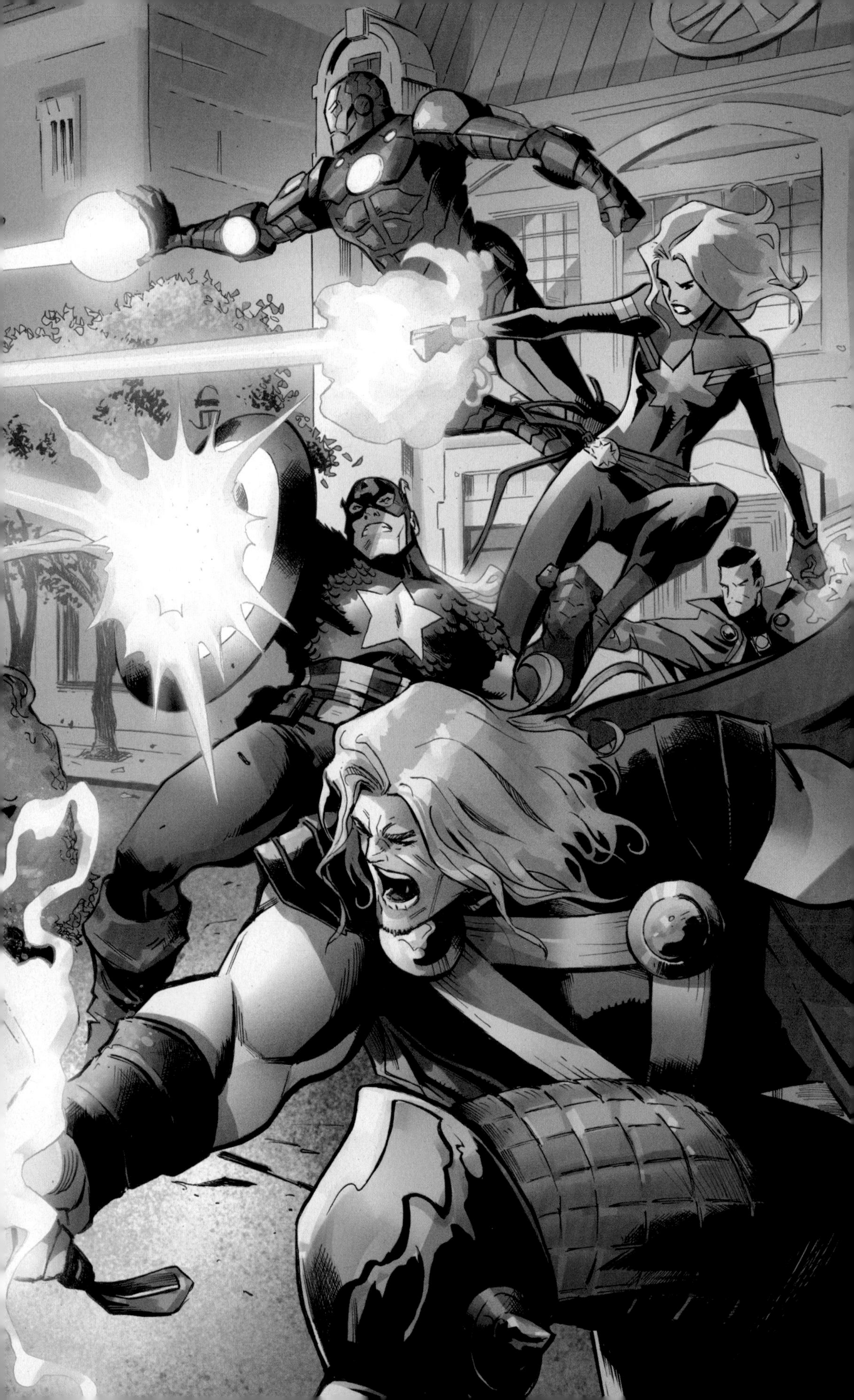

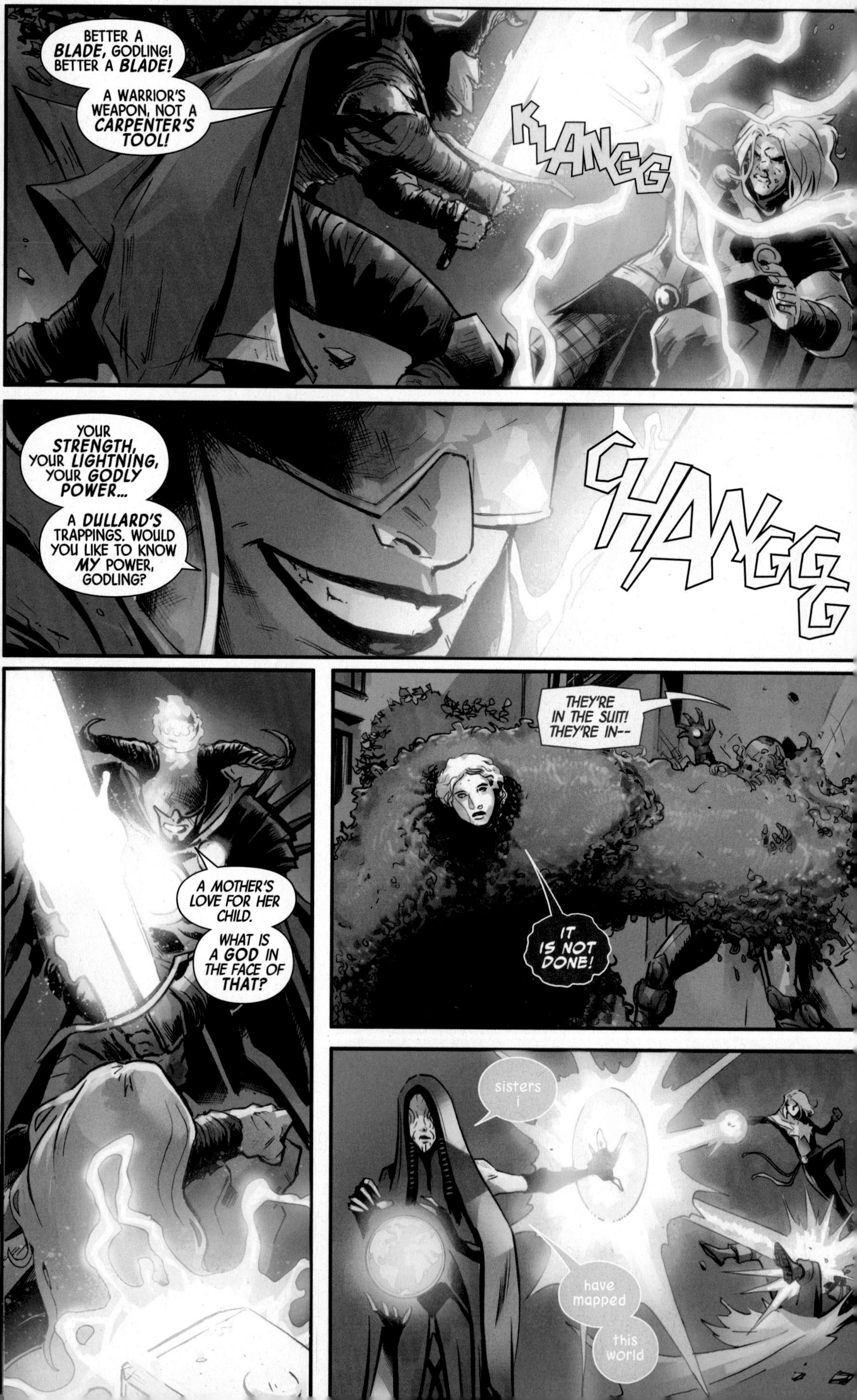
BETTER A BLADE, GODLING! BETTER A BLADE!
A WARRIOR'S WEAPON, NOT A CARPENTER'S TOOL!
KLANGG
YOUR STRENGTH, YOUR LIGHTNING, YOUR GODLY POWER...
A DULLARD'S TRAPPINGS. WOULD YOU LIKE TO KNOW MY POWER, GODLING?
CHANGGG
A MOTHER'S LOVE FOR HER CHILD.
WHAT IS A GOD IN THE FACE OF THAT?
THEY'RE IN THE SUIT! THEY'RE IN--
IT IS NOT DONE!
sisters i
have mapped
this world

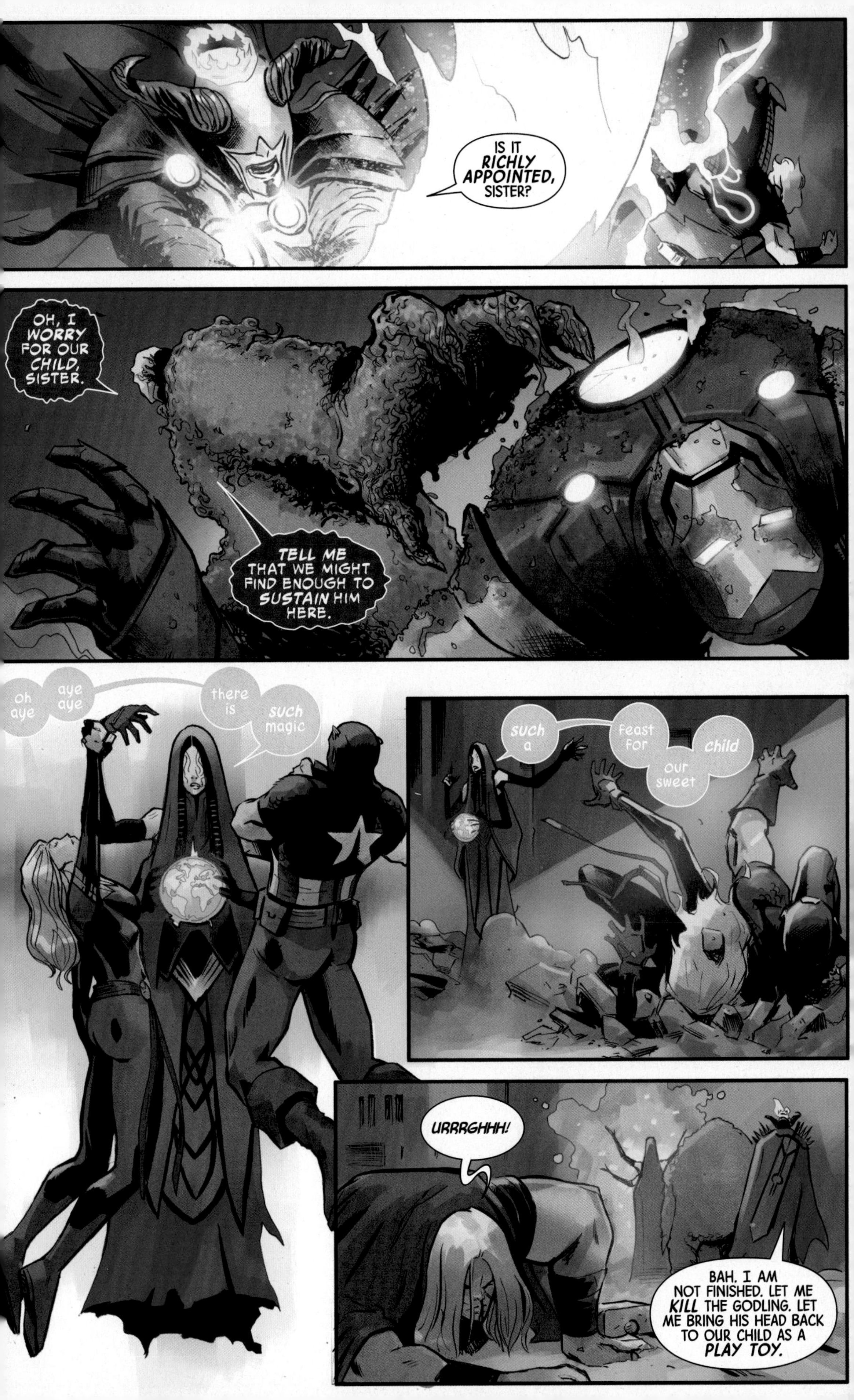
IS IT RICHLY APPOINTED, SISTER?
OH, I WORRY FOR OUR CHILD, SISTER.
TELL ME THAT WE MIGHT FIND ENOUGH TO SUSTAIN HIM HERE.
oh aye
aye aye
there is such magic
such a
feast for
our sweet
child
URRRGHHH!
BAH. I AM NOT FINISHED. LET ME KILL THE GODLING. LET ME BRING HIS HEAD BACK TO OUR CHILD AS A PLAY TOY.

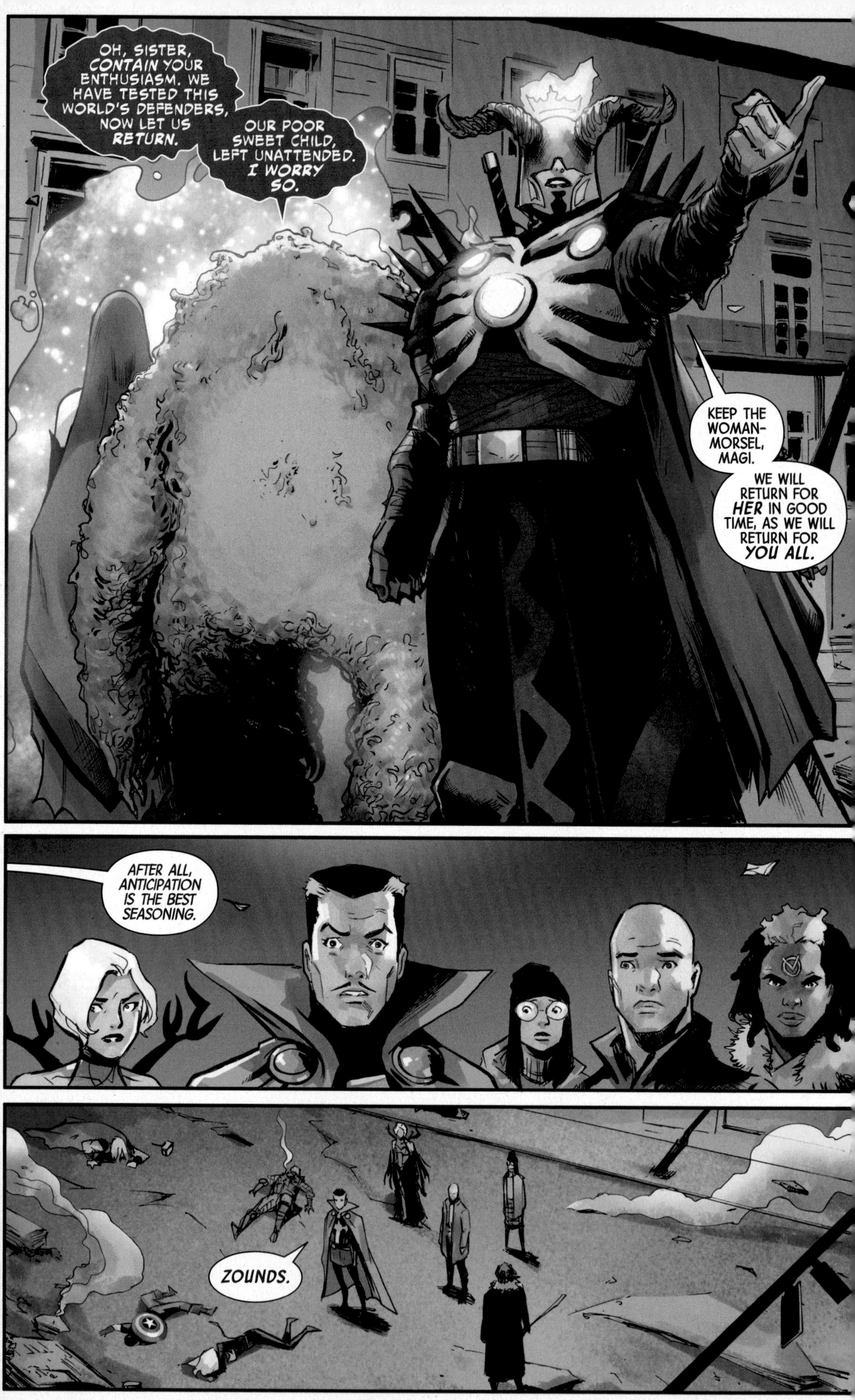
OH, SISTER, CONTAIN YOUR ENTHUSIASM. WE HAVE TESTED THIS WORLD'S DEFENDERS, NOW LET US RETURN.
OUR POOR SWEET CHILD, LEFT UNATTENDED. I WORRY SO.
KEEP THE WOMAN-MORSEL, MAGI.
WE WILL RETURN FOR HER IN GOOD TIME, AS WE WILL RETURN FOR YOU ALL.
AFTER ALL, ANTICIPATION IS THE BEST SEASONING.
ZOUNDS.

CHAPTER FIVE

The
Peregrine
Child

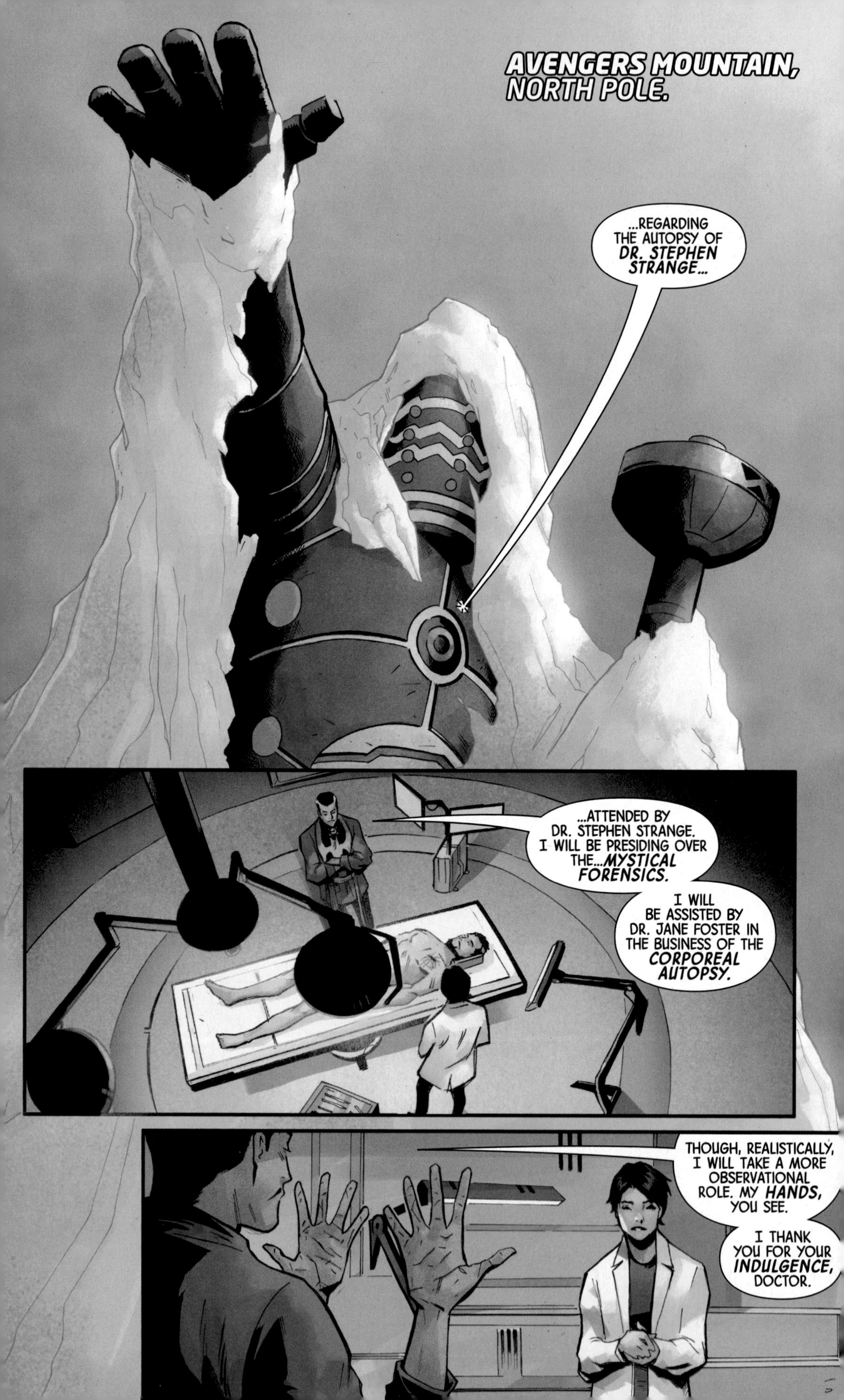
AVENGERS MOUNTAIN, NORTH POLE.
...REGARDING THE AUTOPSY OF DR. STEPHEN STRANGE...
...ATTENDED BY DR. STEPHEN STRANGE. I WILL BE PRESIDING OVER THE...MYSTICAL FORENSICS.
I WILL BE ASSISTED BY DR. JANE FOSTER IN THE BUSINESS OF THE CORPOREAL AUTOPSY.
THOUGH, REALISTICALLY, I WILL TAKE A MORE OBSERVATIONAL ROLE. MY HANDS, YOU SEE.
I THANK YOU FOR YOUR INDULGENCE, DOCTOR.

OF COURSE, DOCTOR.

I MUST CONFESS, THE *CIRCUMSTANCES* OF THIS AUTOPSY... THIS IS A *FIRST.*

IT IS FOR *ME* AS WELL.

I FEAR IF IT WERE NOT FOR MY *RIGOROUS MYSTICAL TRAINING,* I WOULD BE HAVING A *BREAKDOWN* AT THIS VERY MOMENT.

I MEAN, I *SAVED YOUR LIFE* FROM THE *GRIM REAPER* NOT LONG AGO, STRANGE.*

*SEE *VALKYRIE: JANE FOSTER* #4-5! --DS

FROM *DEATH THEMSELF?*

NO, *THE GRIM REAPER,* HE'S--HE'S A COSTUMED IDIOT. A *DEAD* ONE, BUT--

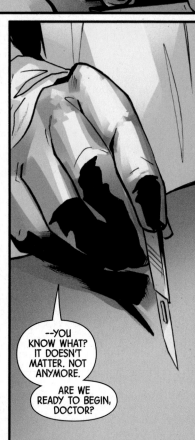

--YOU KNOW WHAT? IT DOESN'T MATTER. NOT ANYMORE.

ARE WE READY TO BEGIN, DOCTOR?

INDEED, DOCTOR.

OPEN ME UP, IF YOU WOULD BE SO KIND.

LET US SEE WHAT *SECRETS* I CONTAIN.

"THE THREE MOTHERS."

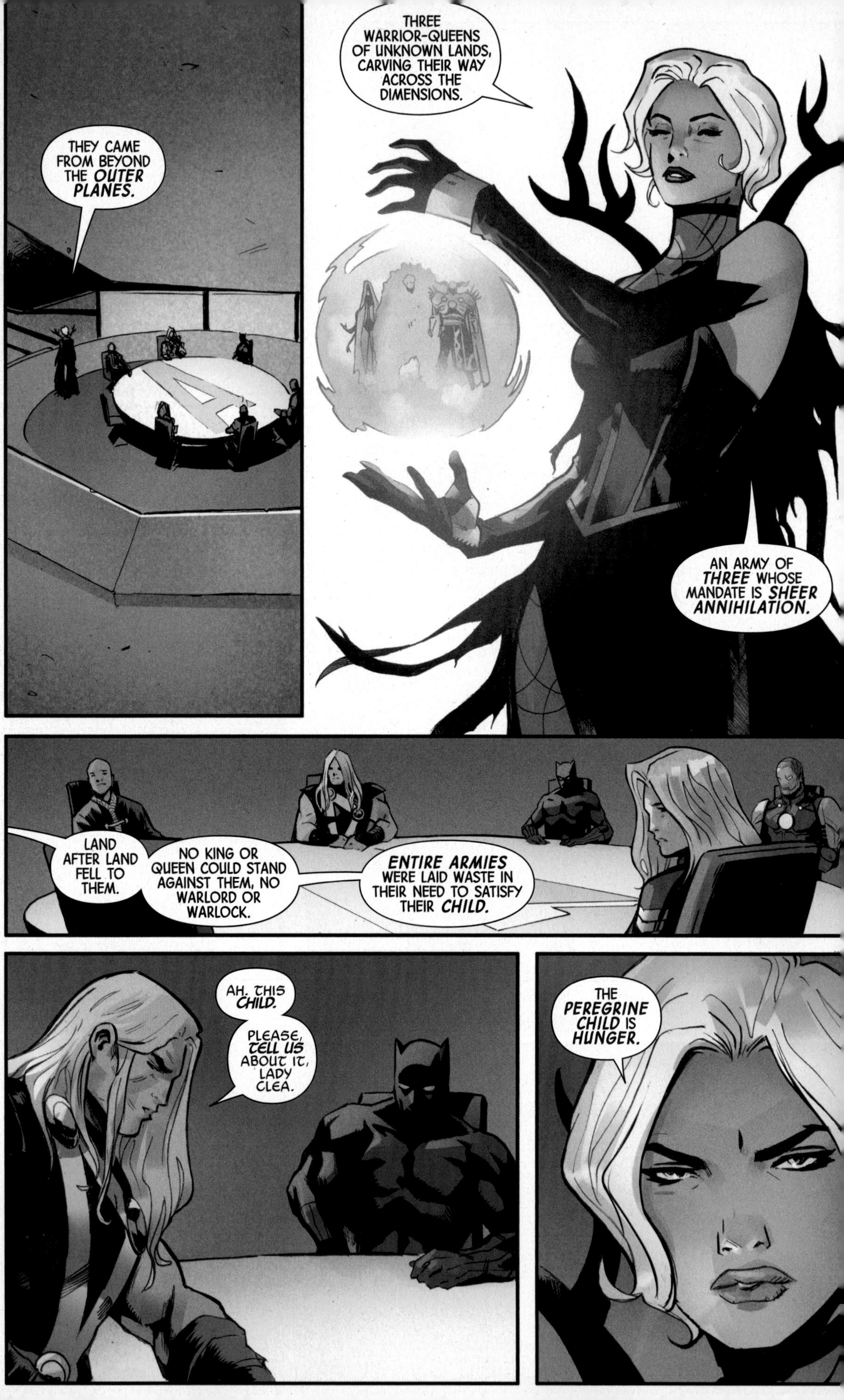
THEY CAME FROM BEYOND THE *OUTER PLANES.*
THREE WARRIOR-QUEENS OF UNKNOWN LANDS, CARVING THEIR WAY ACROSS THE DIMENSIONS.
AN ARMY OF *THREE* WHOSE MANDATE IS *SHEER ANNIHILATION.*
LAND AFTER LAND FELL TO THEM.
NO KING OR QUEEN COULD STAND AGAINST THEM, NO WARLORD OR WARLOCK.
ENTIRE ARMIES WERE LAID WASTE IN THEIR NEED TO SATISFY THEIR *CHILD.*
AH. THIS *CHILD.*
PLEASE, *TELL US* ABOUT IT, LADY CLEA.
THE *PEREGRINE CHILD* IS *HUNGER.*

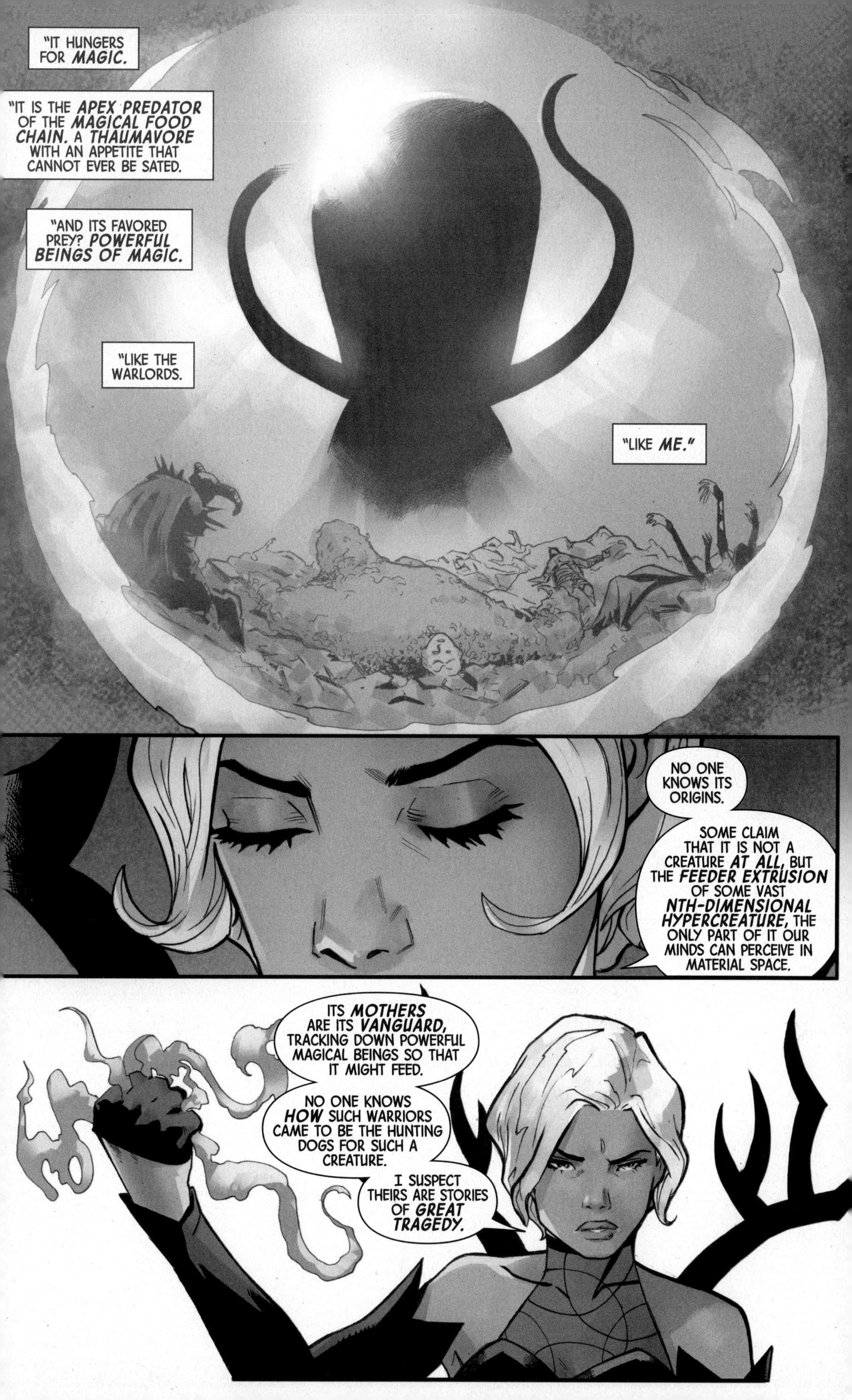
"IT HUNGERS FOR MAGIC.
"IT IS THE APEX PREDATOR OF THE MAGICAL FOOD CHAIN. A THAUMAVORE WITH AN APPETITE THAT CANNOT EVER BE SATED.
"AND ITS FAVORED PREY? POWERFUL BEINGS OF MAGIC.
"LIKE THE WARLORDS.
"LIKE ME."
NO ONE KNOWS ITS ORIGINS.
SOME CLAIM THAT IT IS NOT A CREATURE AT ALL, BUT THE FEEDER EXTRUSION OF SOME VAST NTH-DIMENSIONAL HYPERCREATURE, THE ONLY PART OF IT OUR MINDS CAN PERCEIVE IN MATERIAL SPACE.
ITS MOTHERS ARE ITS VANGUARD, TRACKING DOWN POWERFUL MAGICAL BEINGS SO THAT IT MIGHT FEED.
NO ONE KNOWS HOW SUCH WARRIORS CAME TO BE THE HUNTING DOGS FOR SUCH A CREATURE.
I SUSPECT THEIRS ARE STORIES OF GREAT TRAGEDY.

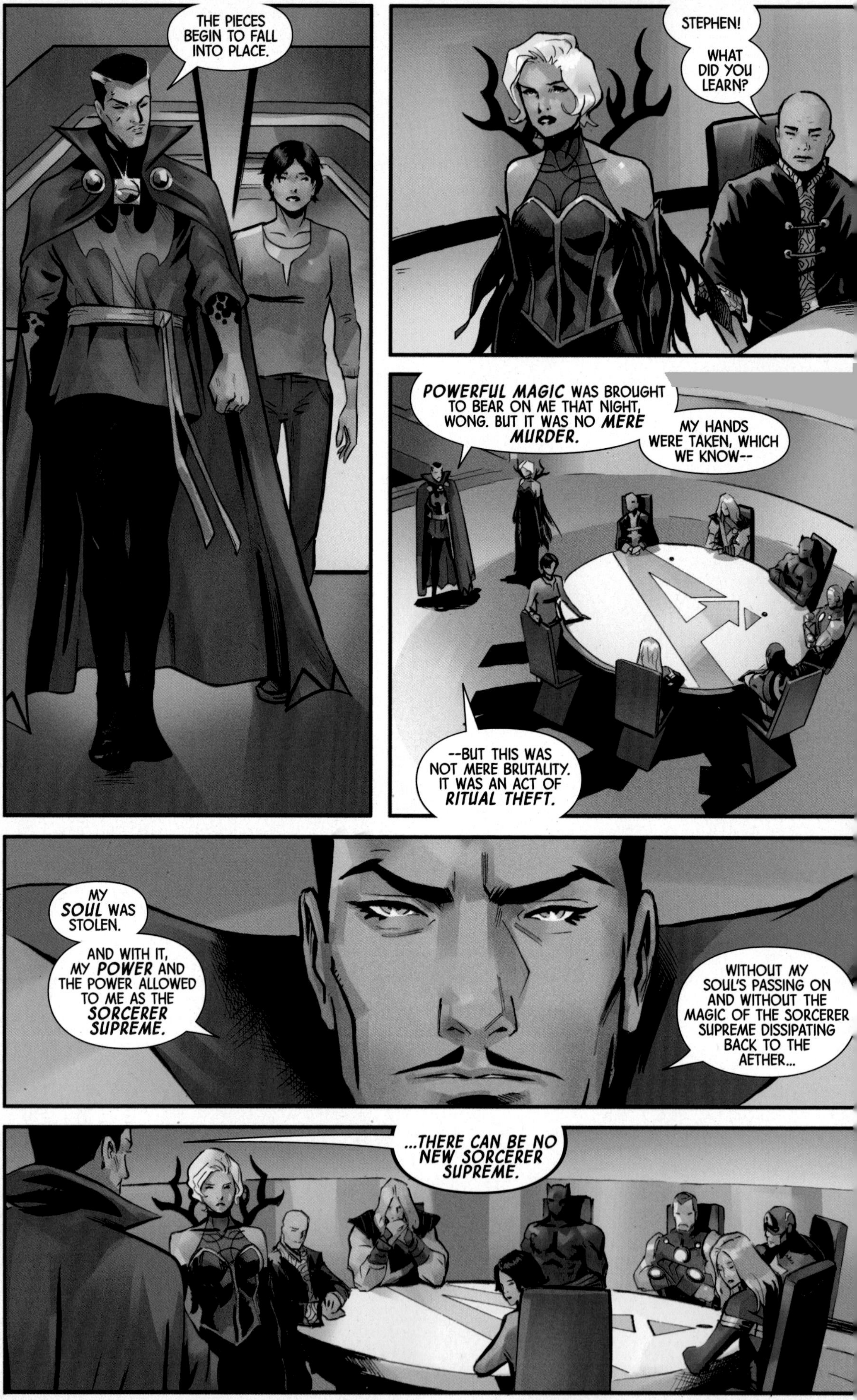
THE PIECES BEGIN TO FALL INTO PLACE.
STEPHEN!
WHAT DID YOU LEARN?
POWERFUL MAGIC WAS BROUGHT TO BEAR ON ME THAT NIGHT, WONG. BUT IT WAS NO MERE MURDER.
MY HANDS WERE TAKEN, WHICH WE KNOW--
--BUT THIS WAS NOT MERE BRUTALITY. IT WAS AN ACT OF RITUAL THEFT.
MY SOUL WAS STOLEN.
AND WITH IT, MY POWER AND THE POWER ALLOWED TO ME AS THE SORCERER SUPREME.
WITHOUT MY SOUL'S PASSING ON AND WITHOUT THE MAGIC OF THE SORCERER SUPREME DISSIPATING BACK TO THE AETHER...
...THERE CAN BE NO NEW SORCERER SUPREME.

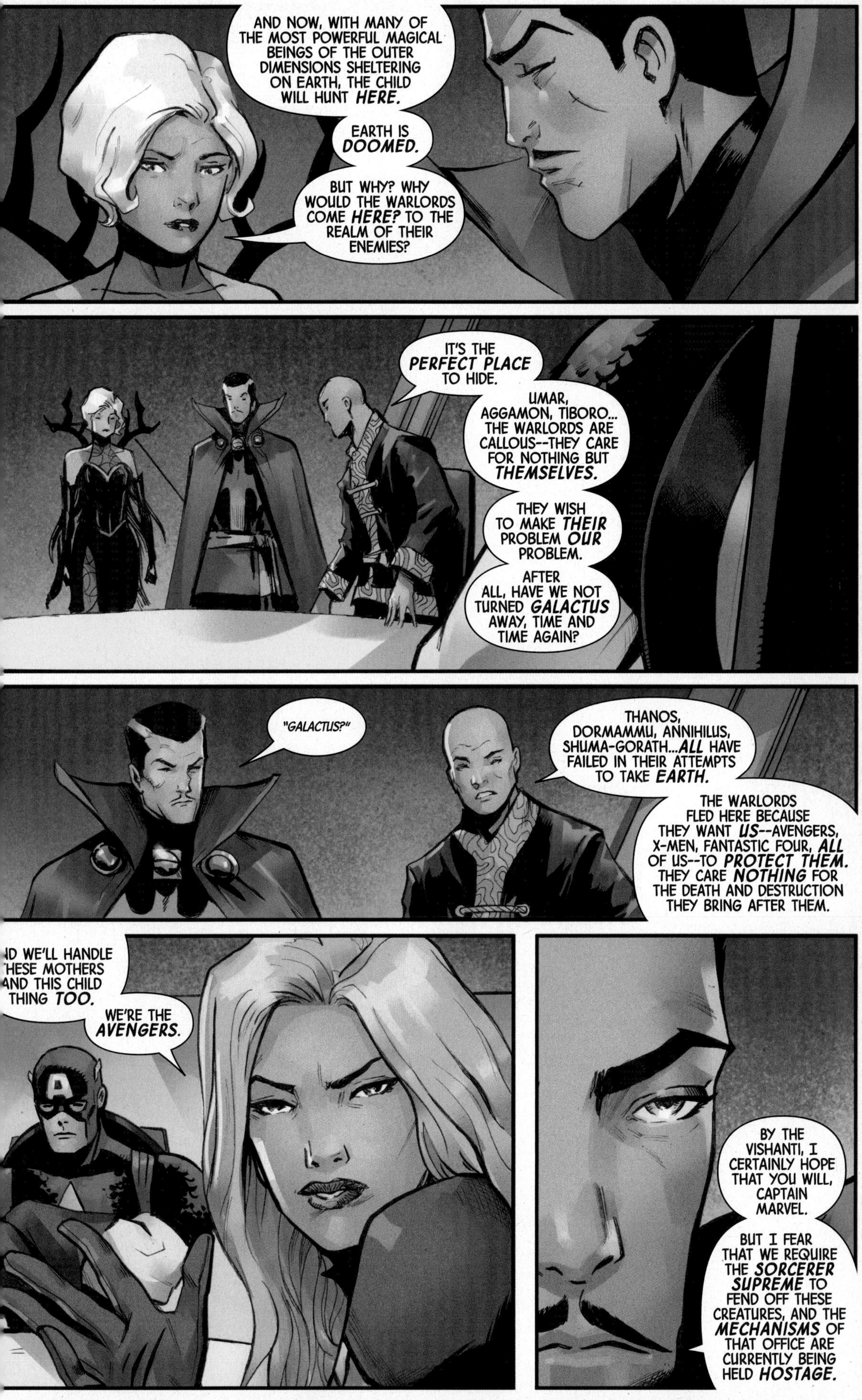
AND NOW, WITH MANY OF THE MOST POWERFUL MAGICAL BEINGS OF THE OUTER DIMENSIONS SHELTERING ON EARTH, THE CHILD WILL HUNT HERE.
EARTH IS DOOMED.
BUT WHY? WHY WOULD THE WARLORDS COME HERE? TO THE REALM OF THEIR ENEMIES?
IT'S THE PERFECT PLACE TO HIDE.
UMAR, AGGAMON, TIBORO... THE WARLORDS ARE CALLOUS--THEY CARE FOR NOTHING BUT THEMSELVES.
THEY WISH TO MAKE THEIR PROBLEM OUR PROBLEM.
AFTER ALL, HAVE WE NOT TURNED GALACTUS AWAY, TIME AND TIME AGAIN?
"GALACTUS?"
THANOS, DORMAMMU, ANNIHILUS, SHUMA-GORATH...ALL HAVE FAILED IN THEIR ATTEMPTS TO TAKE EARTH.
THE WARLORDS FLED HERE BECAUSE THEY WANT US--AVENGERS, X-MEN, FANTASTIC FOUR, ALL OF US--TO PROTECT THEM. THEY CARE NOTHING FOR THE DEATH AND DESTRUCTION THEY BRING AFTER THEM.
ND WE'LL HANDLE THESE MOTHERS AND THIS CHILD THING TOO.
WE'RE THE AVENGERS.
BY THE VISHANTI, I CERTAINLY HOPE THAT YOU WILL, CAPTAIN MARVEL.
BUT I FEAR THAT WE REQUIRE THE SORCERER SUPREME TO FEND OFF THESE CREATURES, AND THE MECHANISMS OF THAT OFFICE ARE CURRENTLY BEING HELD HOSTAGE.

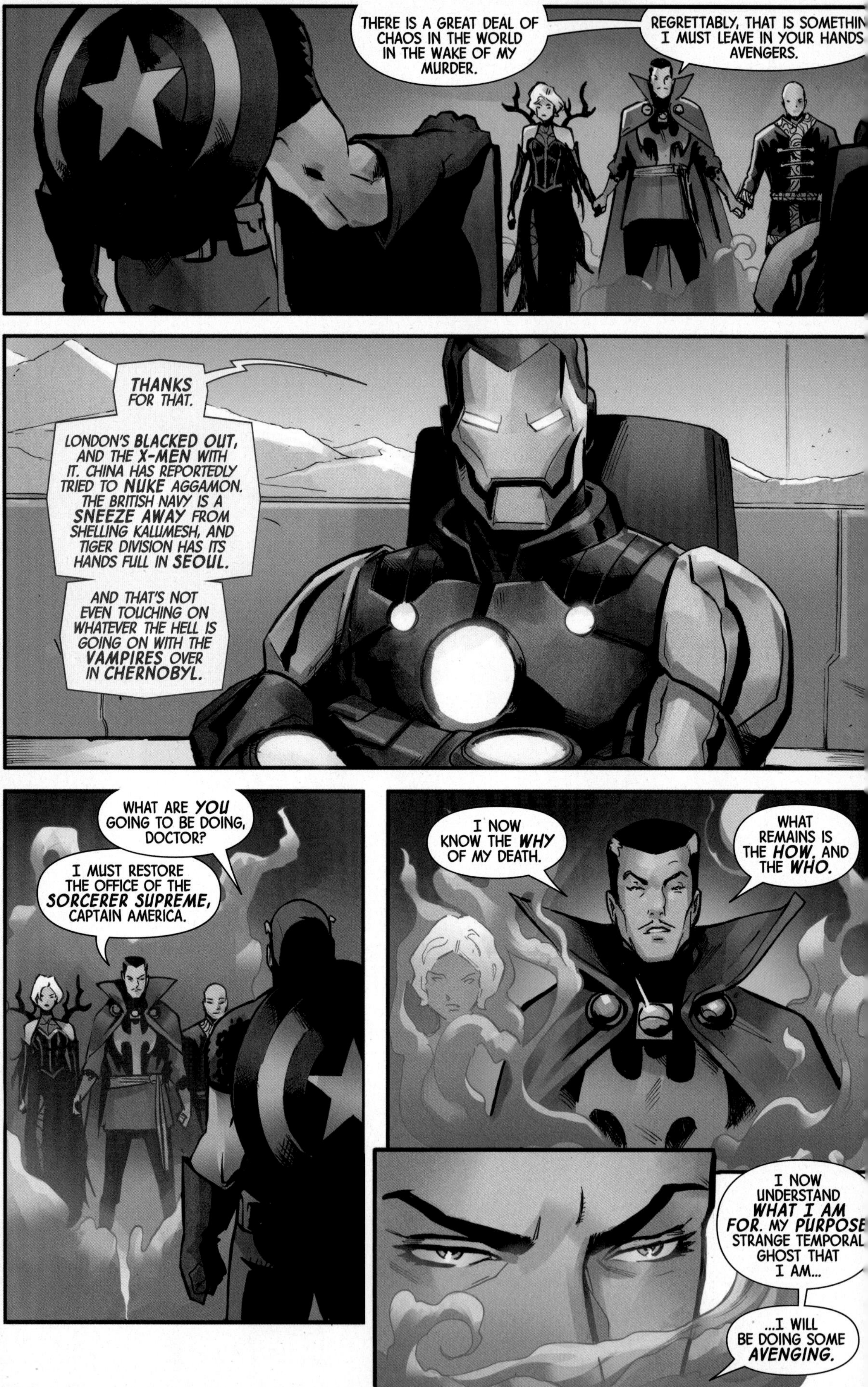

THERE IS A GREAT DEAL OF CHAOS IN THE WORLD IN THE WAKE OF MY MURDER.
REGRETTABLY, THAT IS SOMETHIN I MUST LEAVE IN YOUR HANDS AVENGERS.
THANKS FOR THAT.
LONDON'S BLACKED OUT, AND THE X-MEN WITH IT. CHINA HAS REPORTEDLY TRIED TO NUKE AGGAMON. THE BRITISH NAVY IS A SNEEZE AWAY FROM SHELLING KALUMESH, AND TIGER DIVISION HAS ITS HANDS FULL IN SEOUL.
AND THAT'S NOT EVEN TOUCHING ON WHATEVER THE HELL IS GOING ON WITH THE VAMPIRES OVER IN CHERNOBYL.
WHAT ARE YOU GOING TO BE DOING, DOCTOR?
I MUST RESTORE THE OFFICE OF THE SORCERER SUPREME, CAPTAIN AMERICA.
I NOW KNOW THE WHY OF MY DEATH.
WHAT REMAINS IS THE HOW, AND THE WHO.
I NOW UNDERSTAND WHAT I AM FOR. MY PURPOSE STRANGE TEMPORAL GHOST THAT I AM...
...I WILL BE DOING SOME AVENGING.

CHAPTER SIX

A
Knife
of
Memory

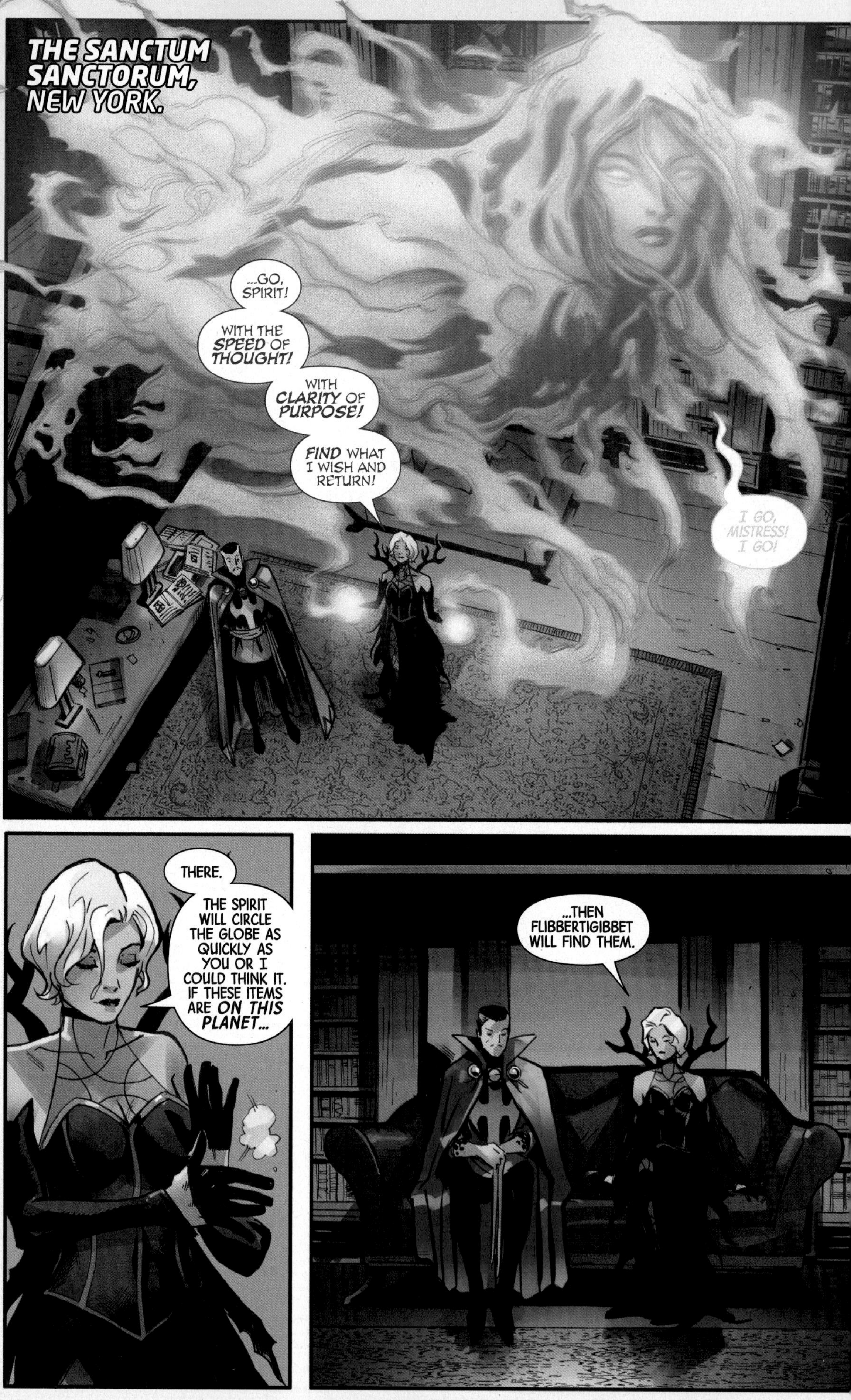
THE SANCTUM SANCTORUM, NEW YORK.
...GO, SPIRIT!
WITH THE SPEED OF THOUGHT!
WITH CLARITY OF PURPOSE!
FIND WHAT I WISH AND RETURN!
I GO, MISTRESS! I GO!
THERE.
THE SPIRIT WILL CIRCLE THE GLOBE AS QUICKLY AS YOU OR I COULD THINK IT. IF THESE ITEMS ARE ON THIS PLANET...
...THEN FLIBBERTIGIBBET WILL FIND THEM.

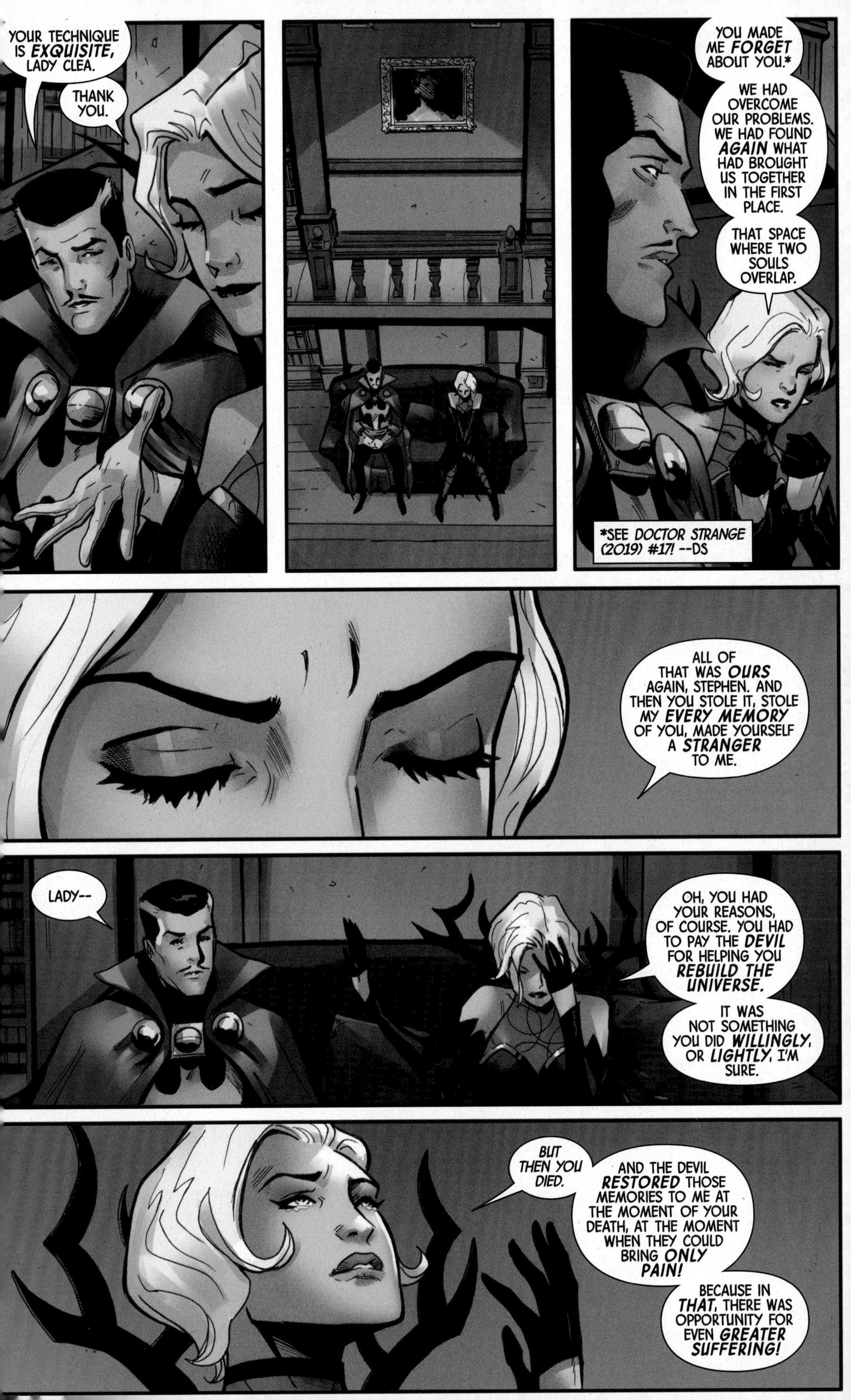
YOUR TECHNIQUE IS EXQUISITE, LADY CLEA.
THANK YOU.
YOU MADE ME FORGET ABOUT YOU.*
WE HAD OVERCOME OUR PROBLEMS. WE HAD FOUND AGAIN WHAT HAD BROUGHT US TOGETHER IN THE FIRST PLACE.
THAT SPACE WHERE TWO SOULS OVERLAP.
*SEE DOCTOR STRANGE (2019) #17! --DS
ALL OF THAT WAS OURS AGAIN, STEPHEN. AND THEN YOU STOLE IT, STOLE MY EVERY MEMORY OF YOU, MADE YOURSELF A STRANGER TO ME.
LADY--
OH, YOU HAD YOUR REASONS, OF COURSE. YOU HAD TO PAY THE DEVIL FOR HELPING YOU REBUILD THE UNIVERSE.
IT WAS NOT SOMETHING YOU DID WILLINGLY, OR LIGHTLY, I'M SURE.
BUT THEN YOU DIED.
AND THE DEVIL RESTORED THOSE MEMORIES TO ME AT THE MOMENT OF YOUR DEATH, AT THE MOMENT WHEN THEY COULD BRING ONLY PAIN!
BECAUSE IN THAT, THERE WAS OPPORTUNITY FOR EVEN GREATER SUFFERING!

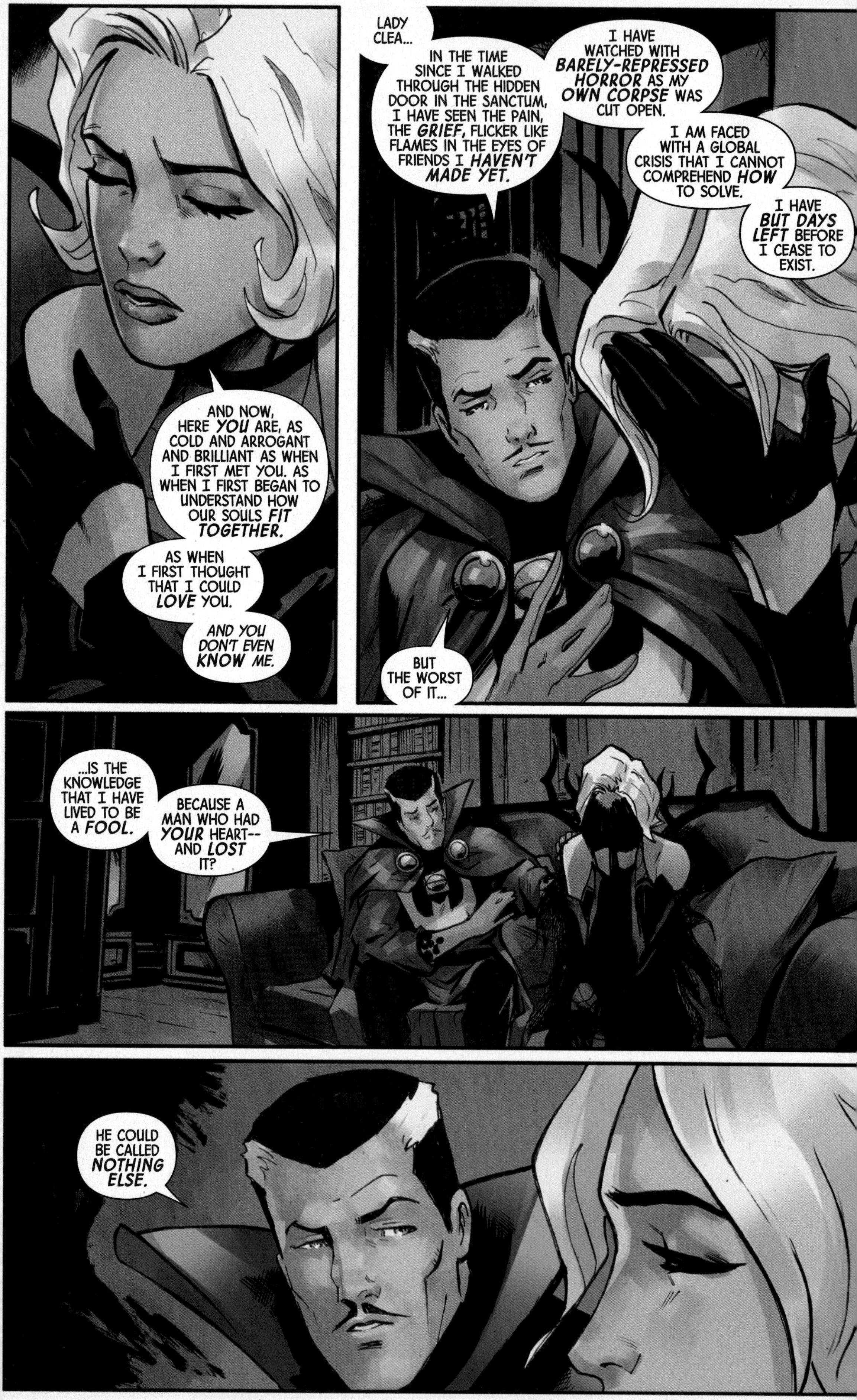
LADY CLEA...
IN THE TIME SINCE I WALKED THROUGH THE HIDDEN DOOR IN THE SANCTUM, I HAVE SEEN THE PAIN, THE GRIEF, FLICKER LIKE FLAMES IN THE EYES OF FRIENDS I HAVEN'T MADE YET.
I HAVE WATCHED WITH BARELY-REPRESSED HORROR AS MY OWN CORPSE WAS CUT OPEN.
I AM FACED WITH A GLOBAL CRISIS THAT I CANNOT COMPREHEND HOW TO SOLVE.
I HAVE BUT DAYS LEFT BEFORE I CEASE TO EXIST.
BUT THE WORST OF IT...
AND NOW, HERE YOU ARE, AS COLD AND ARROGANT AND BRILLIANT AS WHEN I FIRST MET YOU. AS WHEN I FIRST BEGAN TO UNDERSTAND HOW OUR SOULS FIT TOGETHER.
AS WHEN I FIRST THOUGHT THAT I COULD LOVE YOU.
AND YOU DON'T EVEN KNOW ME.
...IS THE KNOWLEDGE THAT I HAVE LIVED TO BE A FOOL.
BECAUSE A MAN WHO HAD YOUR HEART-- AND LOST IT?
HE COULD BE CALLED NOTHING ELSE.

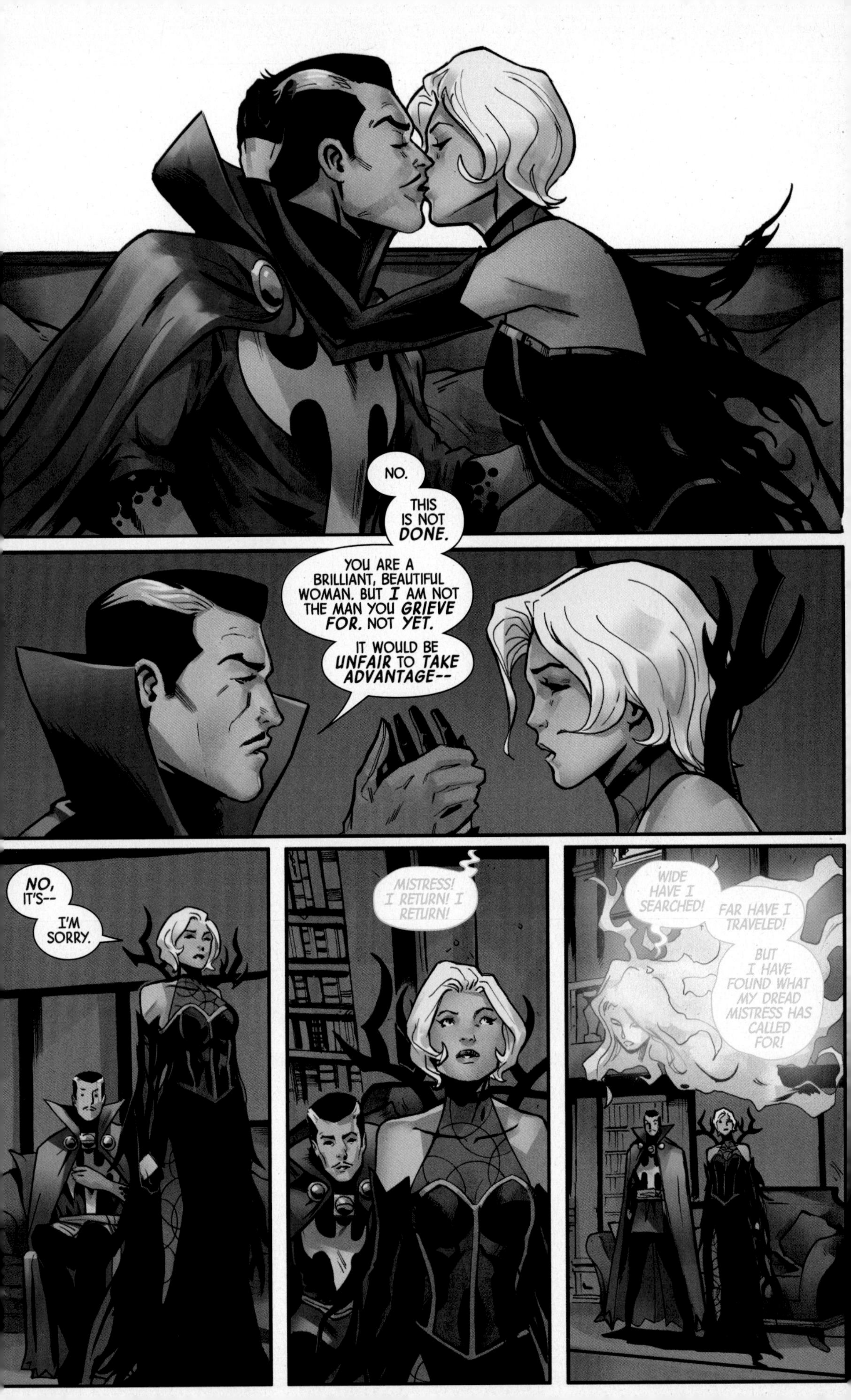

NO.
THIS IS NOT DONE.
YOU ARE A BRILLIANT, BEAUTIFUL WOMAN. BUT I AM NOT THE MAN YOU GRIEVE FOR. NOT YET.
IT WOULD BE UNFAIR TO TAKE ADVANTAGE--
NO, IT'S--
I'M SORRY.
MISTRESS! I RETURN! I RETURN!
WIDE HAVE I SEARCHED!
FAR HAVE I TRAVELED!
BUT I HAVE FOUND WHAT MY DREAD MISTRESS HAS CALLED FOR!

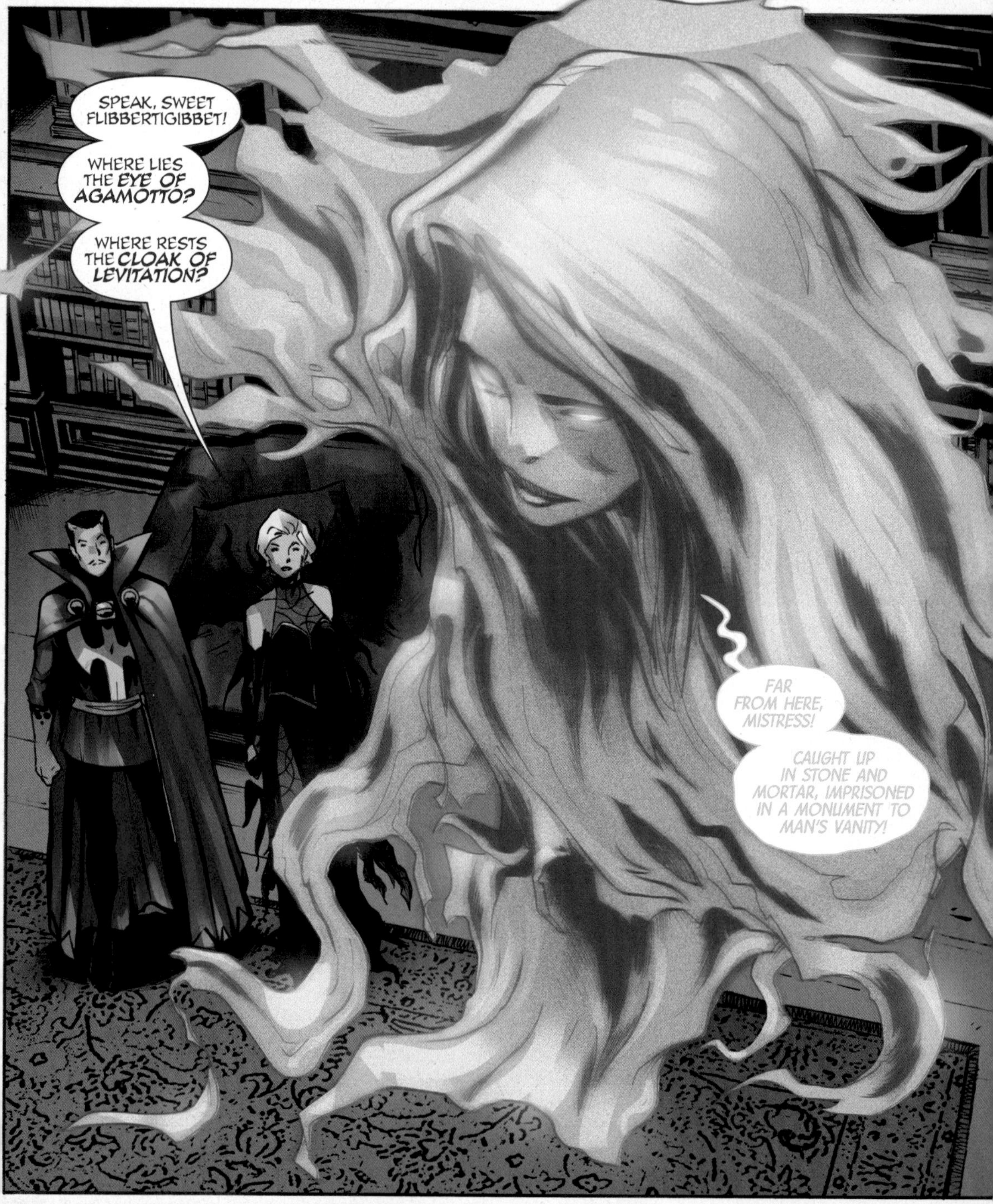
SPEAK, SWEET FLIBBERTIGIBBET!
WHERE LIES THE EYE OF AGAMOTTO?
WHERE RESTS THE CLOAK OF LEVITATION?
FAR FROM HERE, MISTRESS!
CAUGHT UP IN STONE AND MORTAR, IMPRISONED IN A MONUMENT TO MAN'S VANITY!

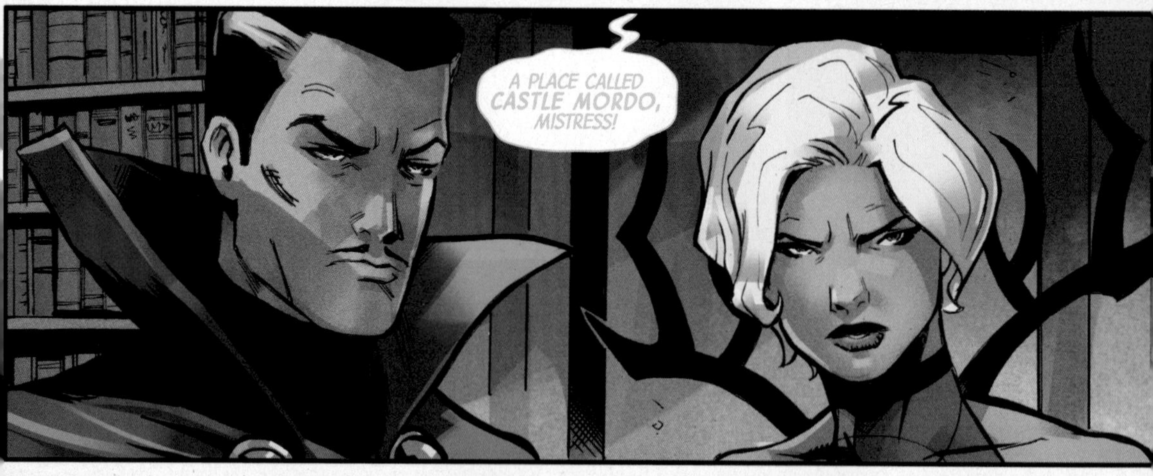
A PLACE CALLED CASTLE MORDO, MISTRESS!

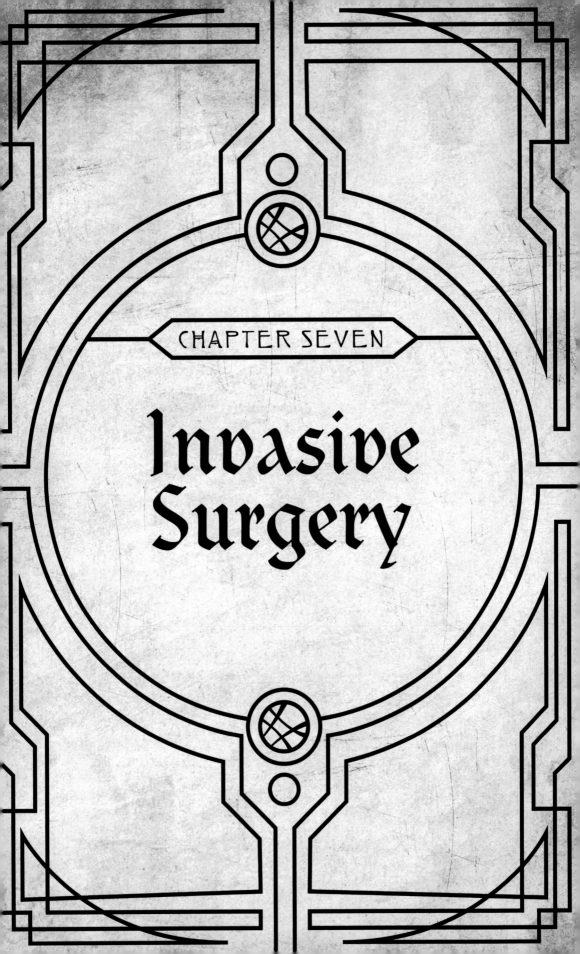

CHAPTER SEVEN

Invasive Surgery

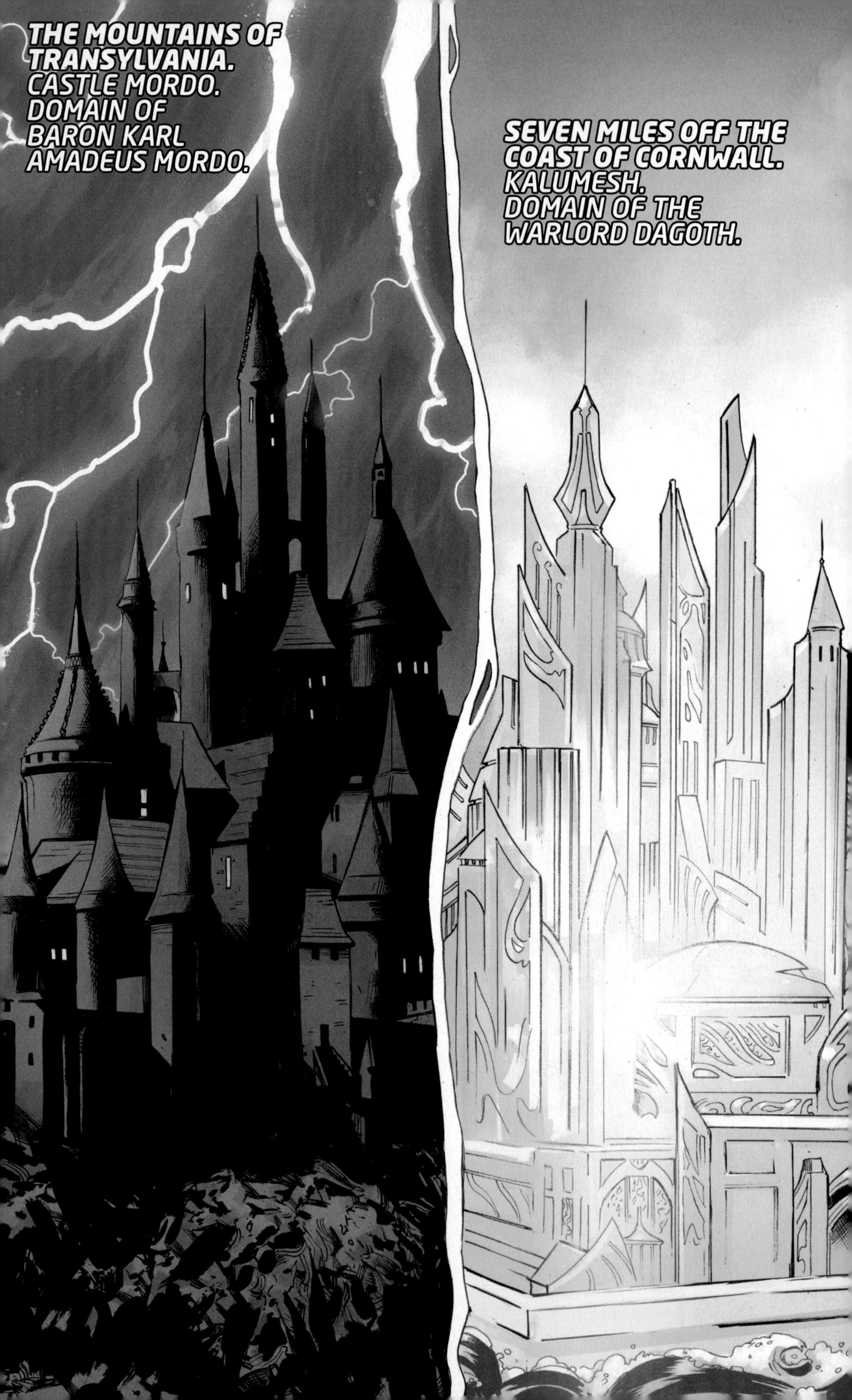
THE MOUNTAINS OF TRANSYLVANIA. CASTLE MORDO. DOMAIN OF BARON KARL AMADEUS MORDO.
SEVEN MILES OFF THE COAST OF CORNWALL. KALUMESH. DOMAIN OF THE WARLORD DAGOTH.

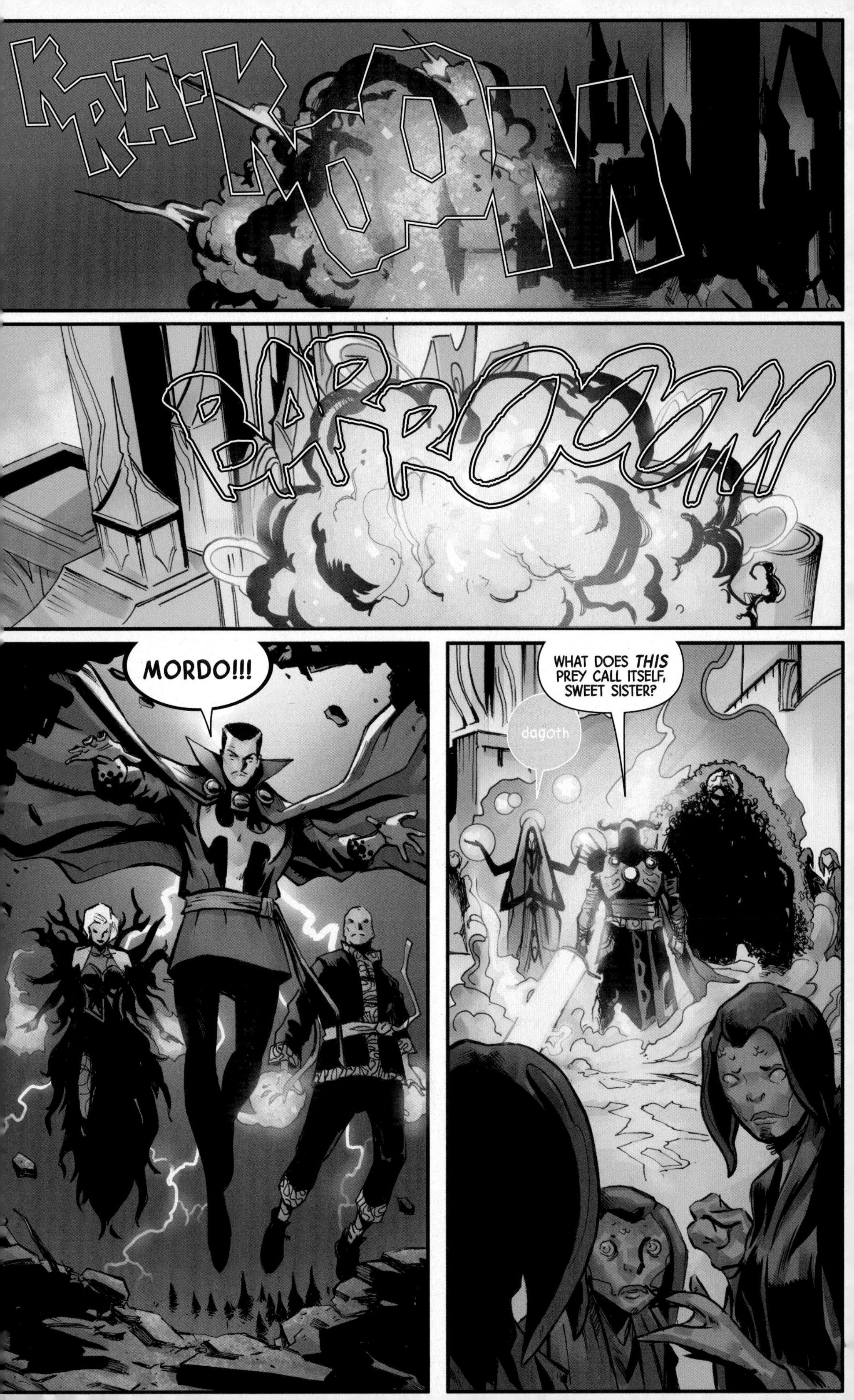
KRA-KOOOM
BARROOOM
MORDO!!!
WHAT DOES *THIS* PREY CALL ITSELF, SWEET SISTER?
dagoth

UP TO YOUR *OLD TRICKS*, KARL?

DID YOU THINK I WOULDN'T *SNIFF YOU OUT?!*

DID YOU *THINK* I WOULD NOT *NOTICE* THAT THE *EYE OF AGAMOTTO* AND THE *CLOAK OF LEVITATION* LEFT BEHIND WERE POOR *COUNTERFEITS?!*

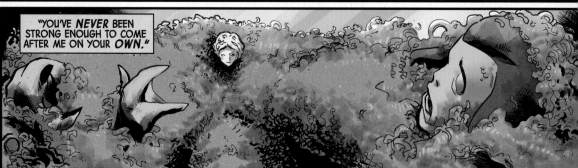

"YOU'VE *NEVER* BEEN STRONG ENOUGH TO COME AFTER ME ON YOUR *OWN.*"

BUT YOU WOULD *BORROW* POWER, WOULDN'T YOU?

"MEWLING TO *DORMAMMU* FOR THE STRENGTH TO FACE ME."

BUT IT WASN'T THE STINK OF *DORMAMMU'S* MAGIC THAT WAS LEFT ON MY BODY.

"NO."

MY *THIRD EYE* PERCEIVED THE MAGICAL SIGNATURES OF *SEVERAL POWERFUL BEINGS.*

AGGAMON, TIBORO, UMAR...

"...AND *DAGOTH.*"

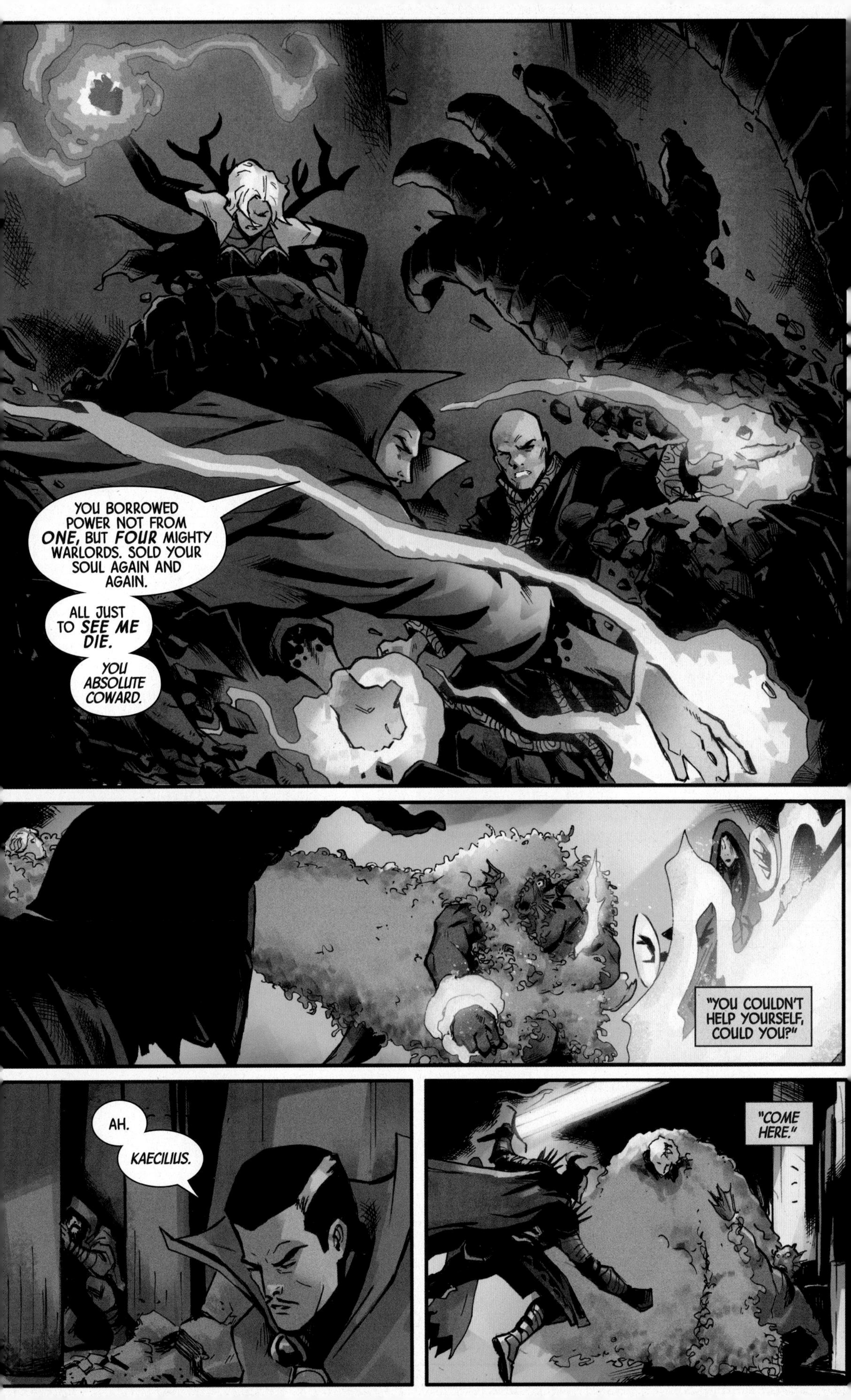

YOU BORROWED POWER NOT FROM ONE, BUT FOUR MIGHTY WARLORDS. SOLD YOUR SOUL AGAIN AND AGAIN.
ALL JUST TO SEE ME DIE.
YOU ABSOLUTE COWARD.
"YOU COULDN'T HELP YOURSELF, COULD YOU?"
AH.
KAECILIUS.
"COME HERE."

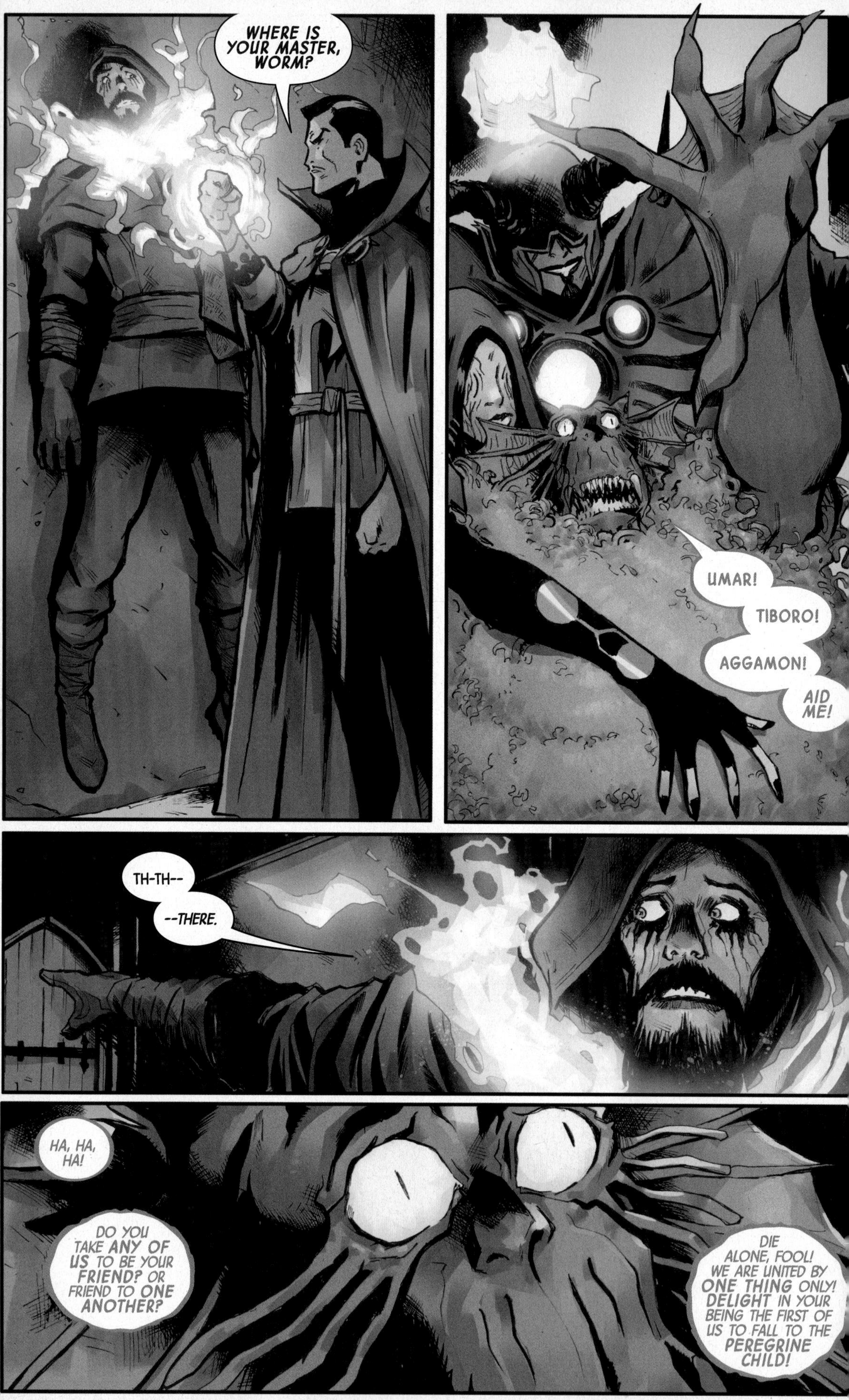
WHERE IS YOUR MASTER, WORM?
UMAR!
TIBORO!
AGGAMON!
AID ME!
TH-TH--
--THERE.
HA, HA, HA!
DO YOU TAKE ANY OF US TO BE YOUR FRIEND? OR FRIEND TO ONE ANOTHER?
DIE ALONE, FOOL! WE ARE UNITED BY ONE THING ONLY! DELIGHT IN YOUR BEING THE FIRST OF US TO FALL TO THE PEREGRINE CHILD!

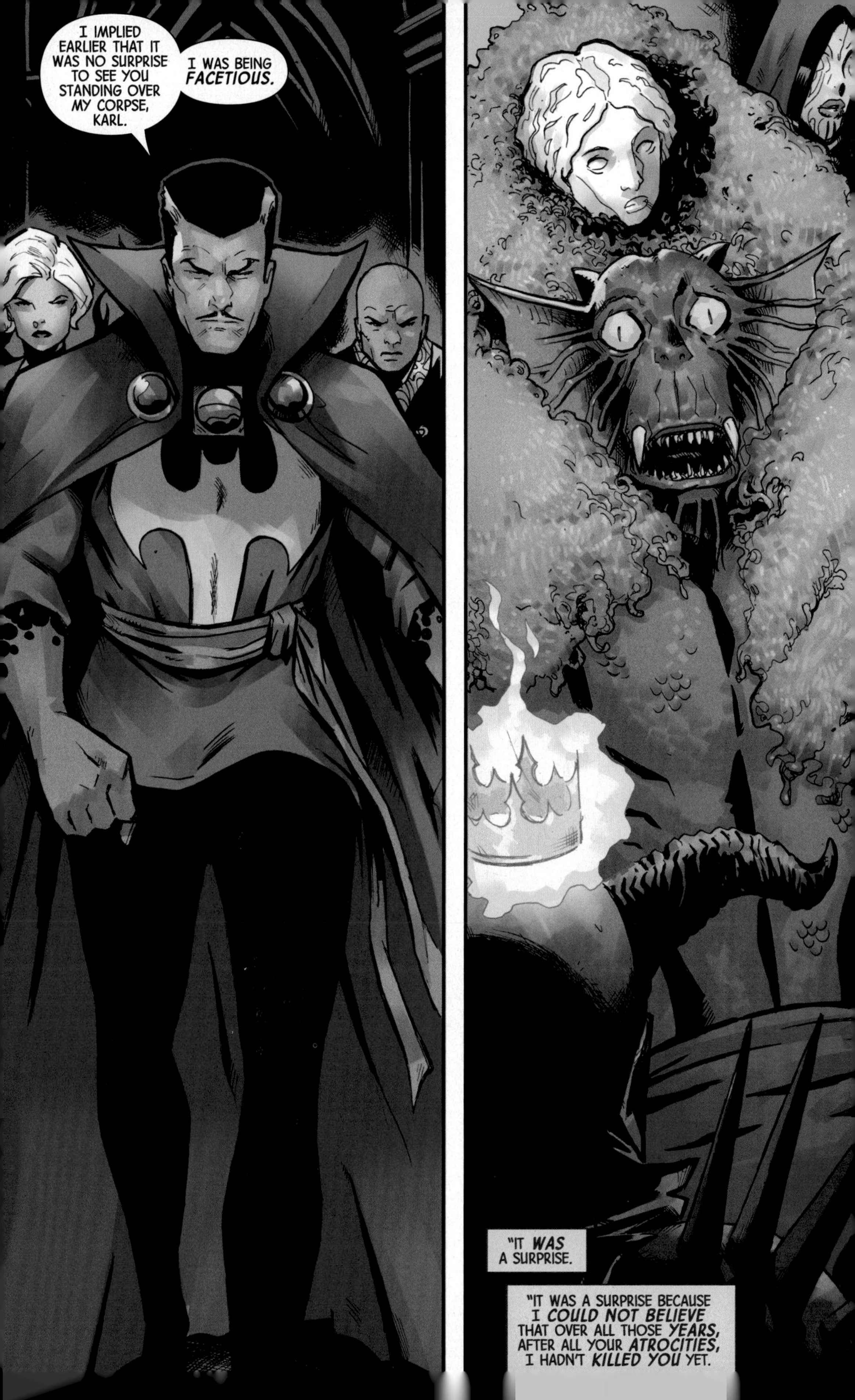
I IMPLIED EARLIER THAT IT WAS NO SURPRISE TO SEE YOU STANDING OVER MY CORPSE, KARL.
I WAS BEING FACETIOUS.
"IT WAS A SURPRISE.
"IT WAS A SURPRISE BECAUSE I COULD NOT BELIEVE THAT OVER ALL THOSE YEARS, AFTER ALL YOUR ATROCITIES, I HADN'T KILLED YOU YET.

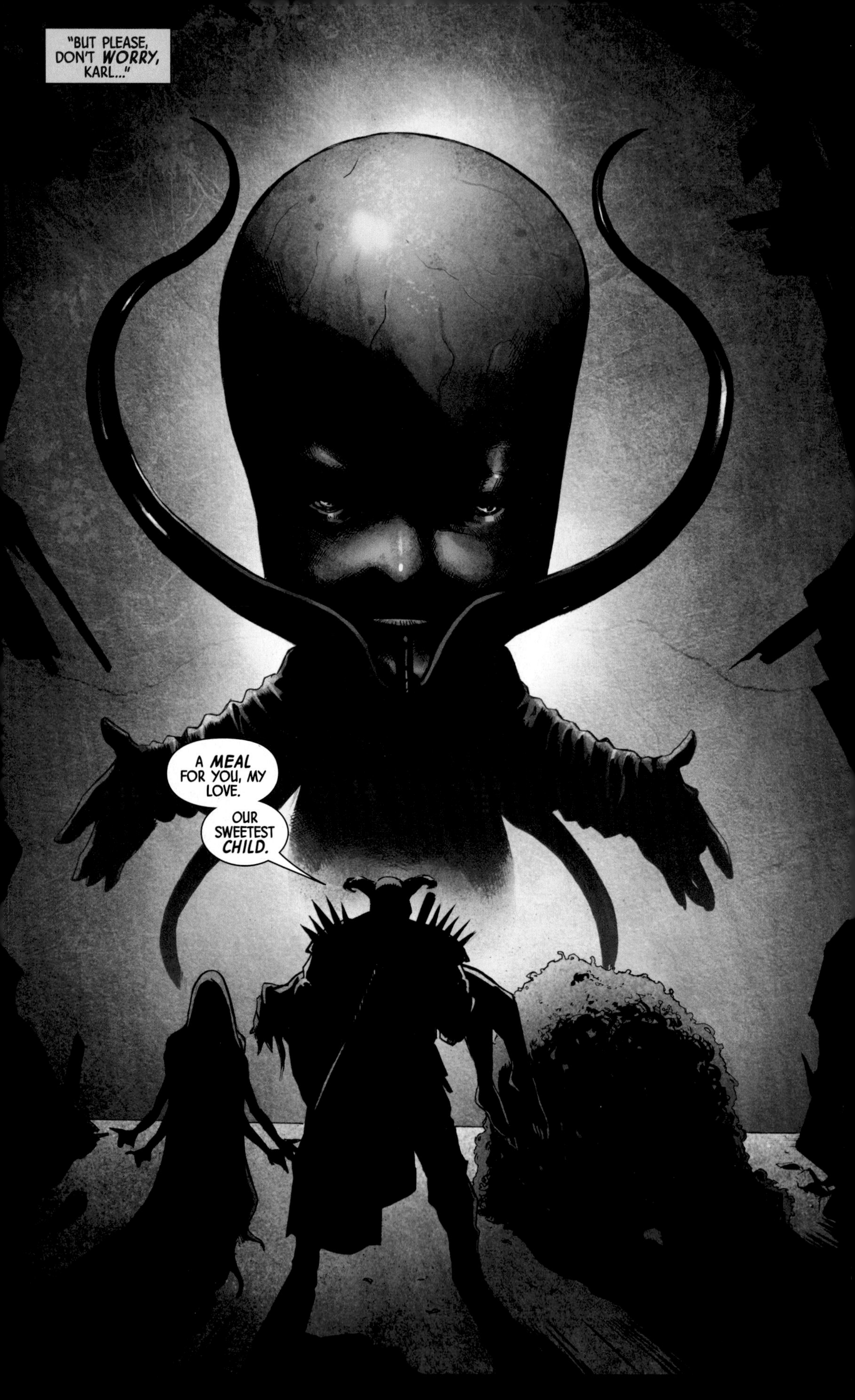
"BUT PLEASE, DON'T WORRY, KARL..."
A MEAL FOR YOU, MY LOVE.
OUR SWEETEST CHILD.

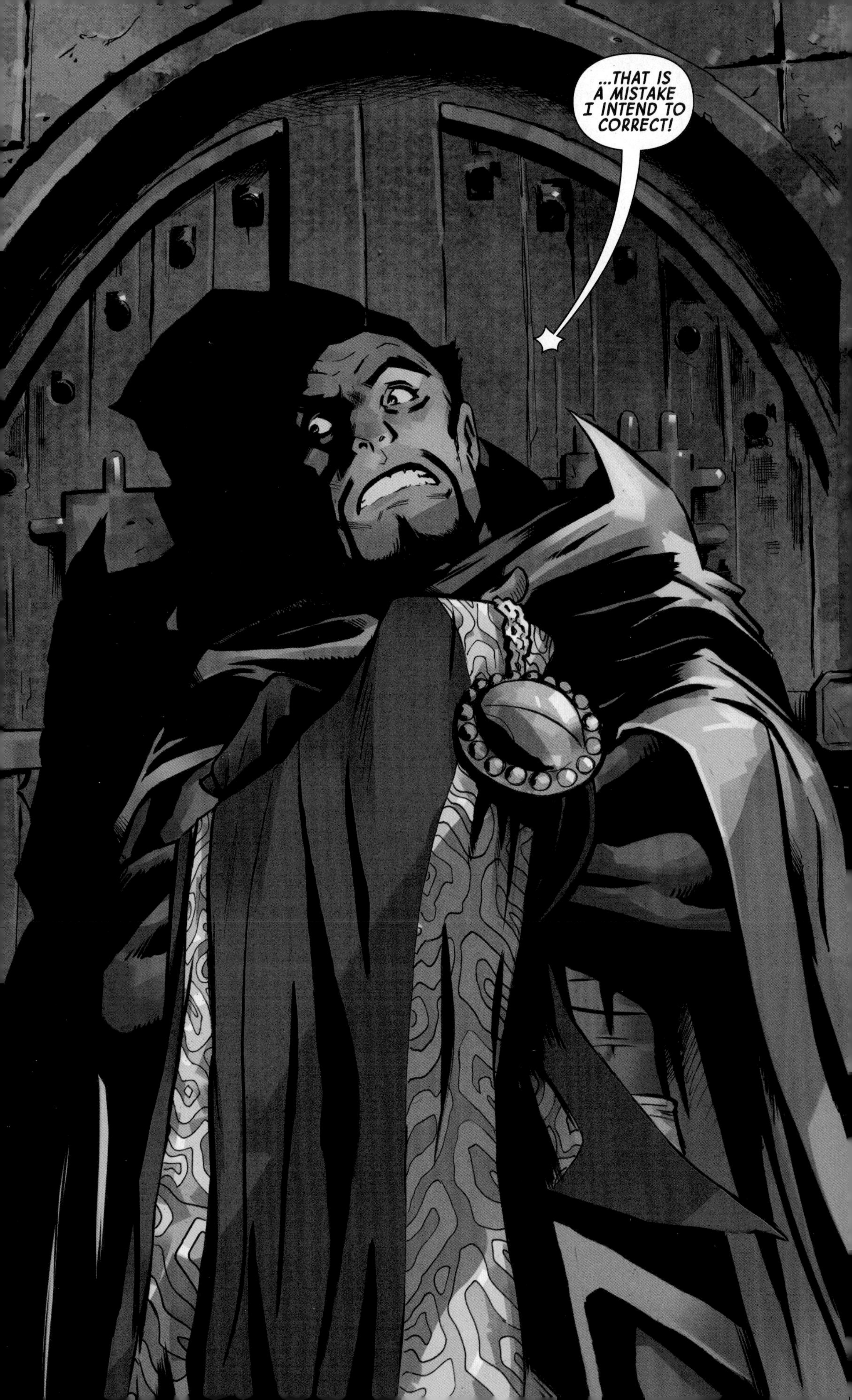
...THAT IS A MISTAKE I INTEND TO CORRECT!

CHAPTER EIGHT

Mordo

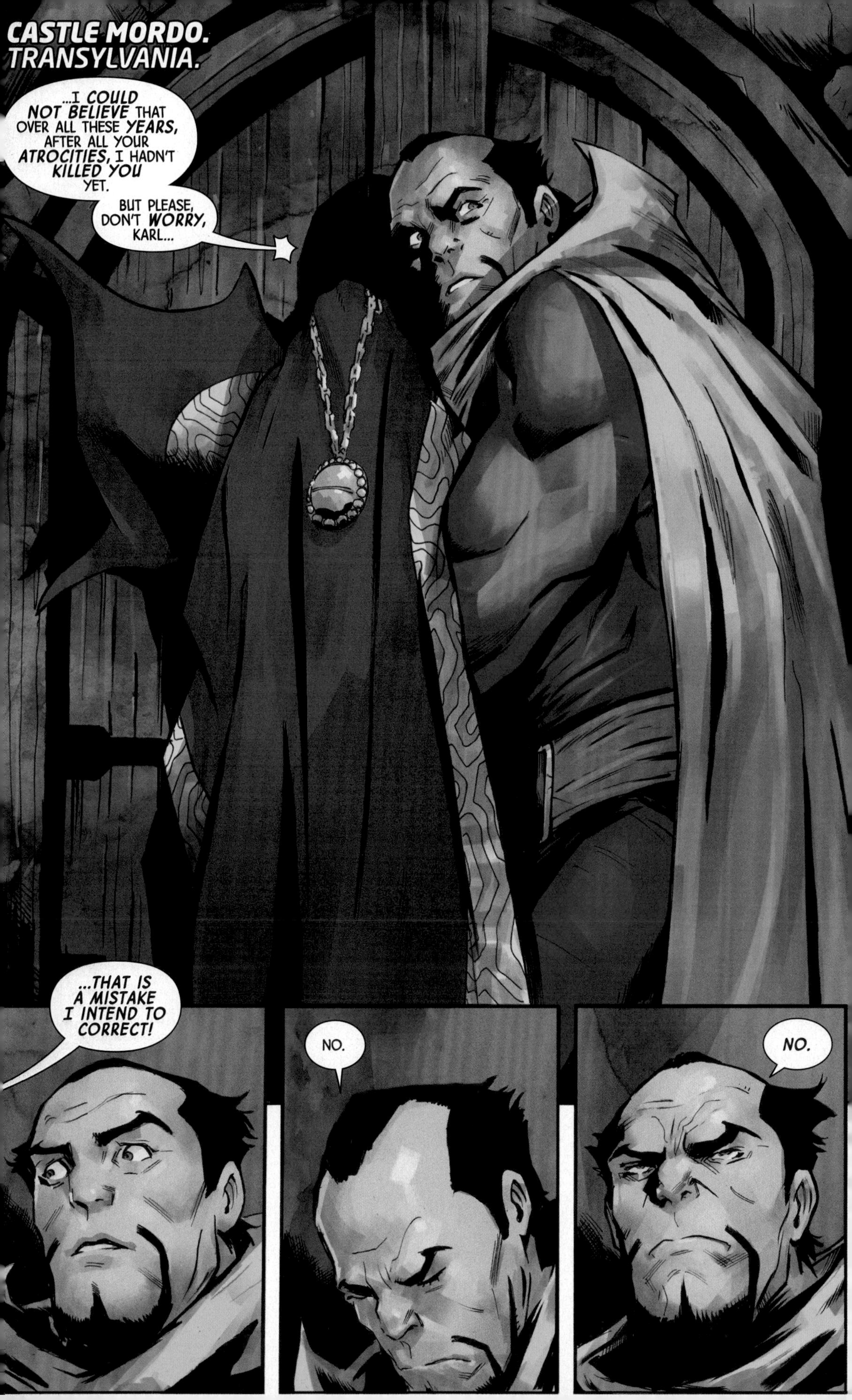
CASTLE MORDO. TRANSYLVANIA.
...I COULD NOT BELIEVE THAT OVER ALL THESE YEARS, AFTER ALL YOUR ATROCITIES, I HADN'T KILLED YOU YET.
BUT PLEASE, DON'T WORRY, KARL...
...THAT IS A MISTAKE I INTEND TO CORRECT!
NO.
NO.

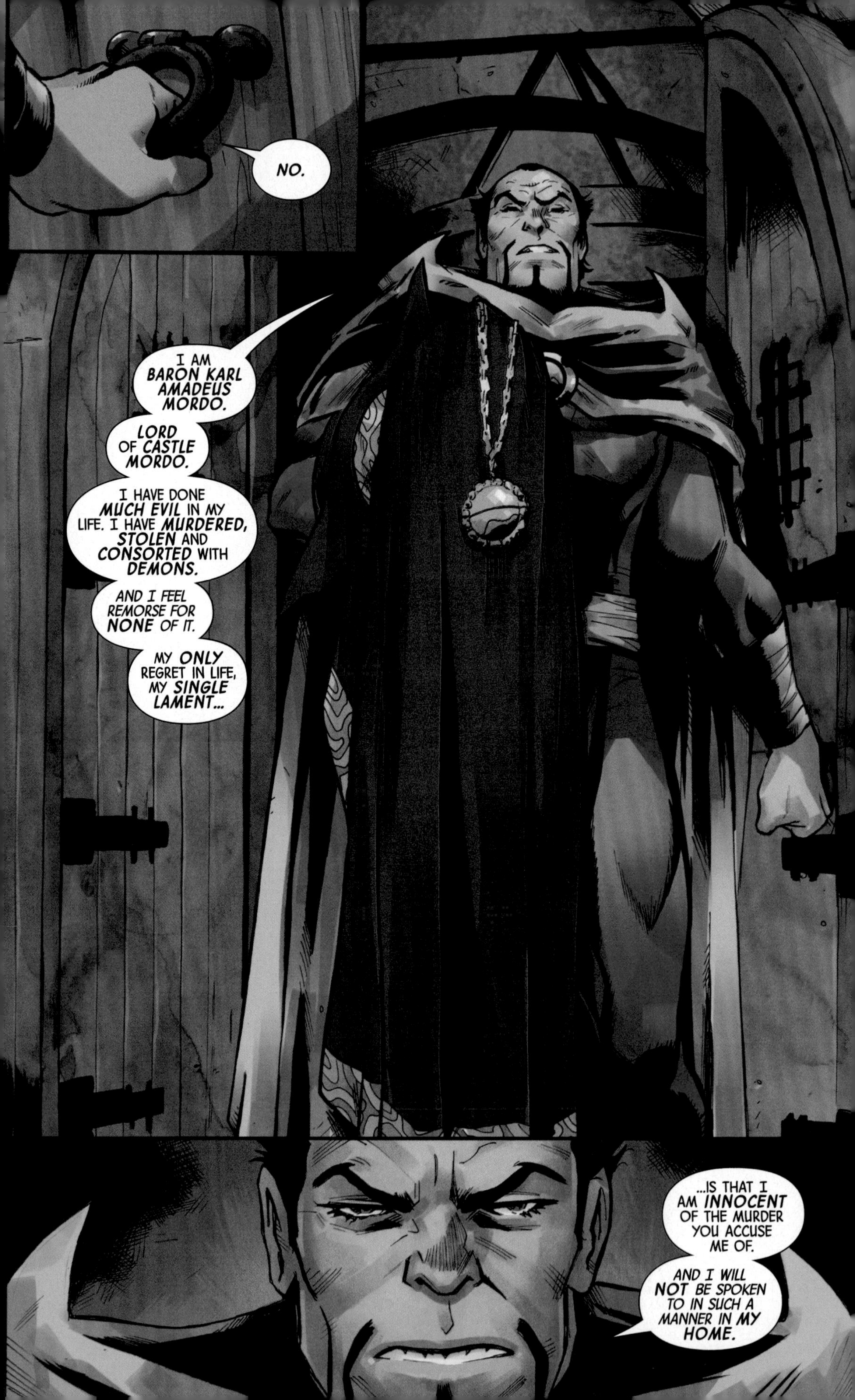
NO.
I AM BARON KARL AMADEUS MORDO.
LORD OF CASTLE MORDO.
I HAVE DONE MUCH EVIL IN MY LIFE. I HAVE MURDERED, STOLEN AND CONSORTED WITH DEMONS.
AND I FEEL REMORSE FOR NONE OF IT.
MY ONLY REGRET IN LIFE, MY SINGLE LAMENT...
...IS THAT I AM INNOCENT OF THE MURDER YOU ACCUSE ME OF.
AND I WILL NOT BE SPOKEN TO IN SUCH A MANNER IN MY HOME.

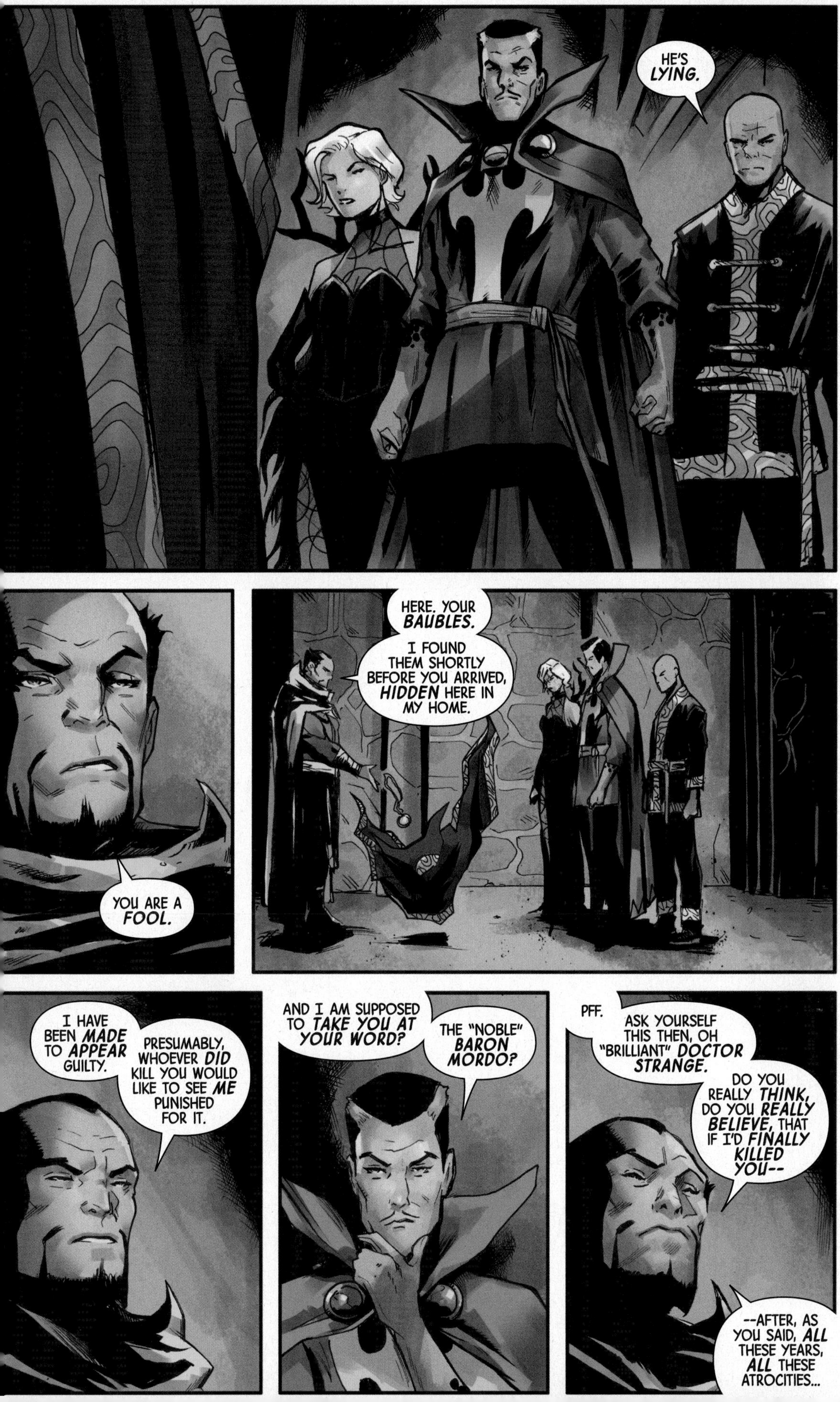
HE'S LYING.
YOU ARE A FOOL.
HERE. YOUR BAUBLES.
I FOUND THEM SHORTLY BEFORE YOU ARRIVED, HIDDEN HERE IN MY HOME.
I HAVE BEEN MADE TO APPEAR GUILTY.
PRESUMABLY, WHOEVER DID KILL YOU WOULD LIKE TO SEE ME PUNISHED FOR IT.
AND I AM SUPPOSED TO TAKE YOU AT YOUR WORD?
THE "NOBLE" BARON MORDO?
PFF.
ASK YOURSELF THIS THEN, OH "BRILLIANT" DOCTOR STRANGE.
DO YOU REALLY THINK, DO YOU REALLY BELIEVE, THAT IF I'D FINALLY KILLED YOU--
--AFTER, AS YOU SAID, ALL THESE YEARS, ALL THESE ATROCITIES...

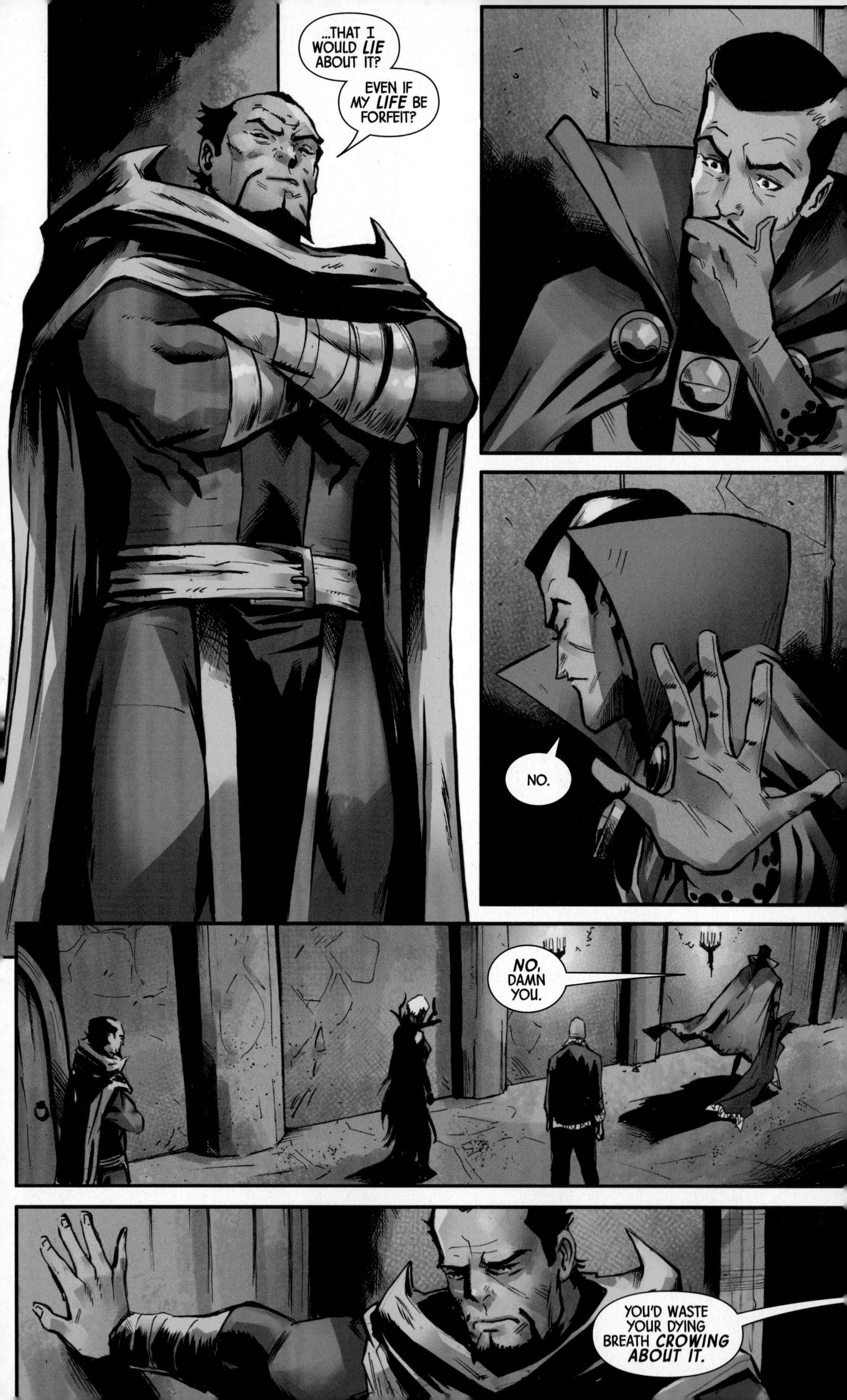
...THAT I WOULD *LIE* ABOUT IT?
EVEN IF MY *LIFE* BE FORFEIT?
NO.
NO, DAMN YOU.
YOU'D WASTE YOUR DYING BREATH *CROWING ABOUT IT.*

CHAPTER NINE

Down
and Out
on
Bleecker
Street

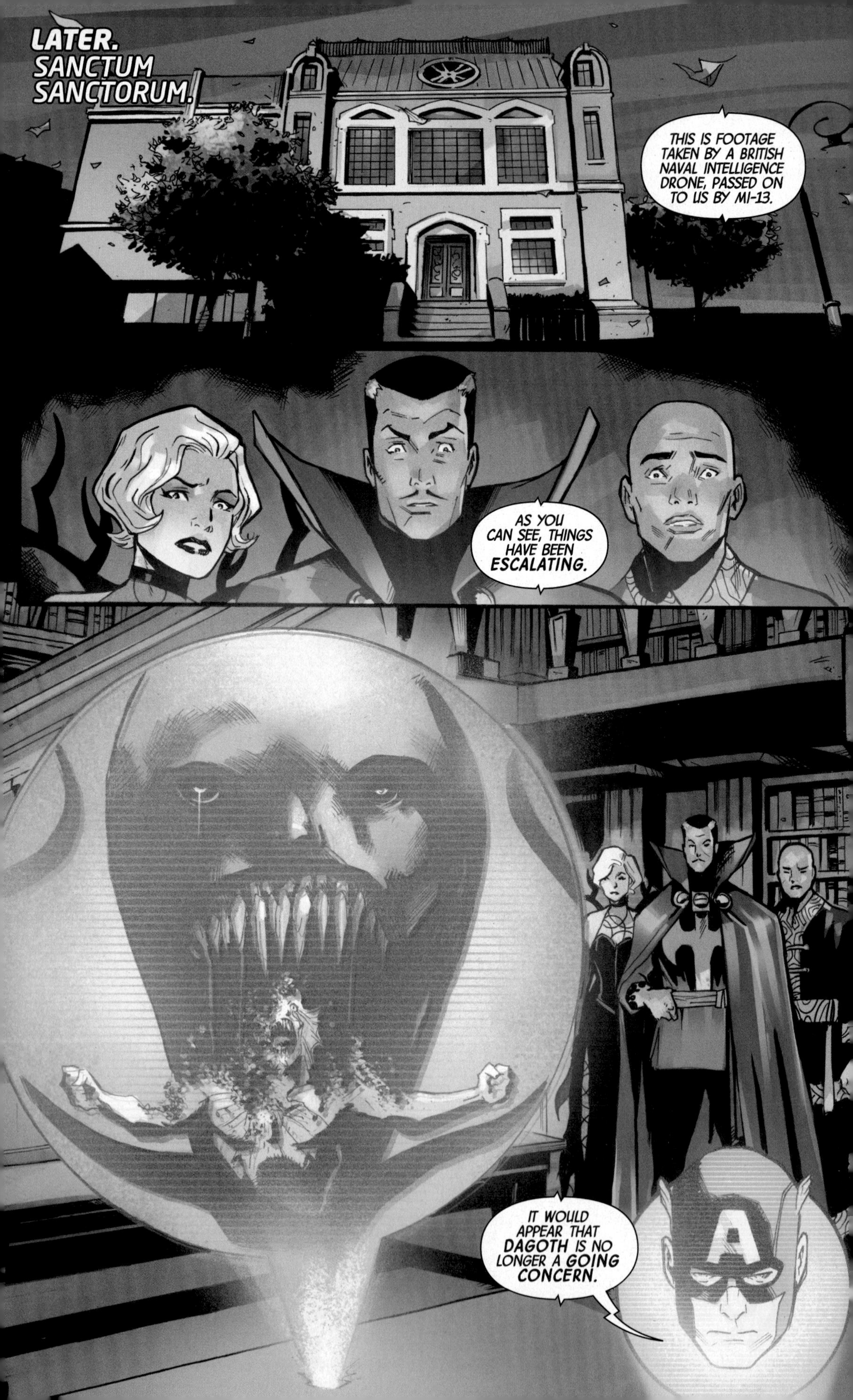
LATER. SANCTUM SANCTORUM.
THIS IS FOOTAGE TAKEN BY A BRITISH NAVAL INTELLIGENCE DRONE, PASSED ON TO US BY MI-13.
AS YOU CAN SEE, THINGS HAVE BEEN ESCALATING.
IT WOULD APPEAR THAT DAGOTH IS NO LONGER A GOING CONCERN.

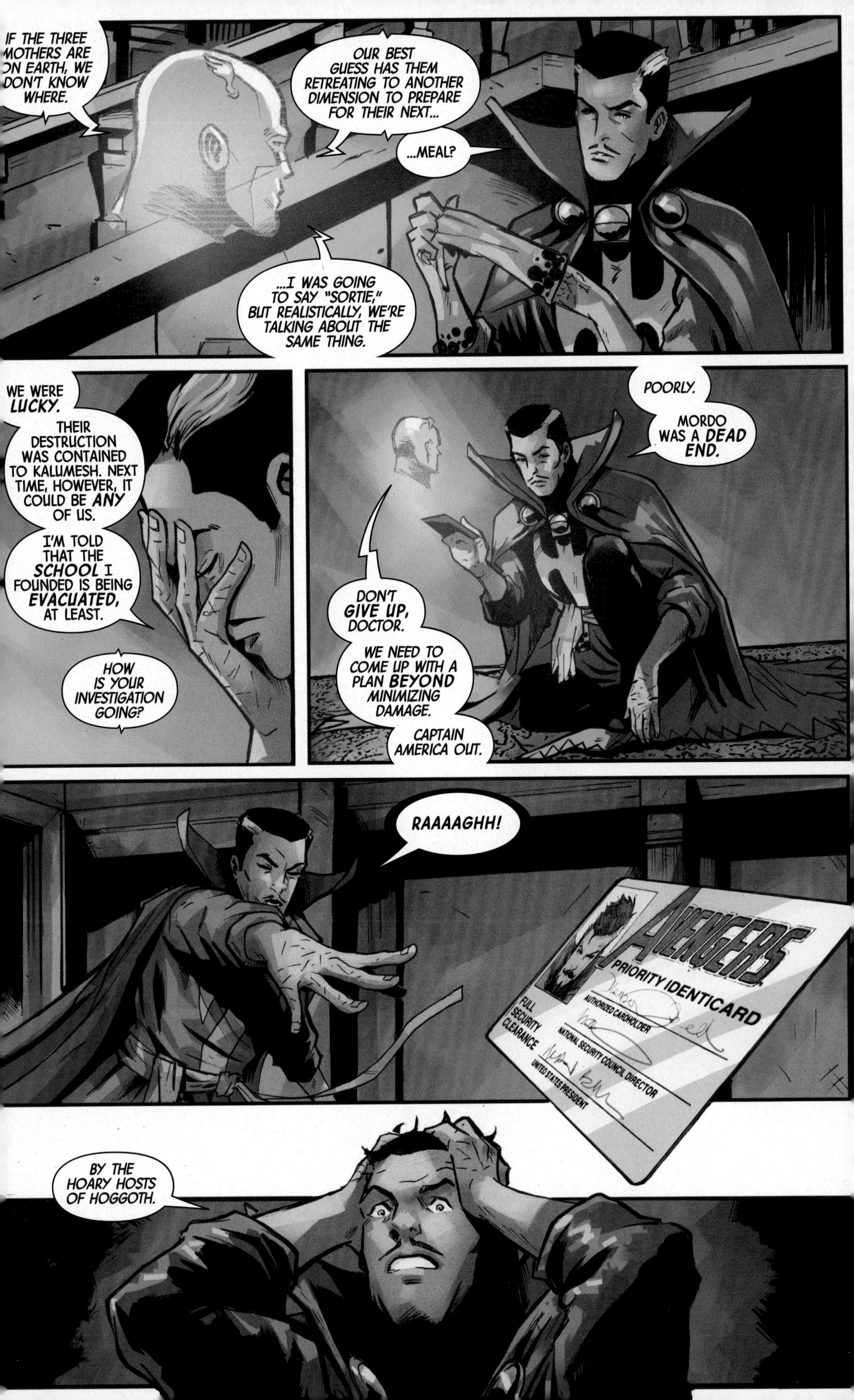

IF THE THREE MOTHERS ARE ON EARTH, WE DON'T KNOW WHERE.
OUR BEST GUESS HAS THEM RETREATING TO ANOTHER DIMENSION TO PREPARE FOR THEIR NEXT...
...MEAL?
...I WAS GOING TO SAY "SORTIE," BUT REALISTICALLY, WE'RE TALKING ABOUT THE SAME THING.
WE WERE LUCKY.
THEIR DESTRUCTION WAS CONTAINED TO KALUMESH. NEXT TIME, HOWEVER, IT COULD BE ANY OF US.
I'M TOLD THAT THE SCHOOL I FOUNDED IS BEING EVACUATED, AT LEAST.
HOW IS YOUR INVESTIGATION GOING?
POORLY.
MORDO WAS A DEAD END.
DON'T GIVE UP, DOCTOR.
WE NEED TO COME UP WITH A PLAN BEYOND MINIMIZING DAMAGE.
CAPTAIN AMERICA OUT.
RAAAAGHH!
AVENGERS
PRIORITY IDENTICARD
AUTHORIZED CARDHOLDER
FULL SECURITY CLEARANCE
NATIONAL SECURITY COUNCIL DIRECTOR
UNITED STATES PRESIDENT
BY THE HOARY HOSTS OF HOGGOTH.

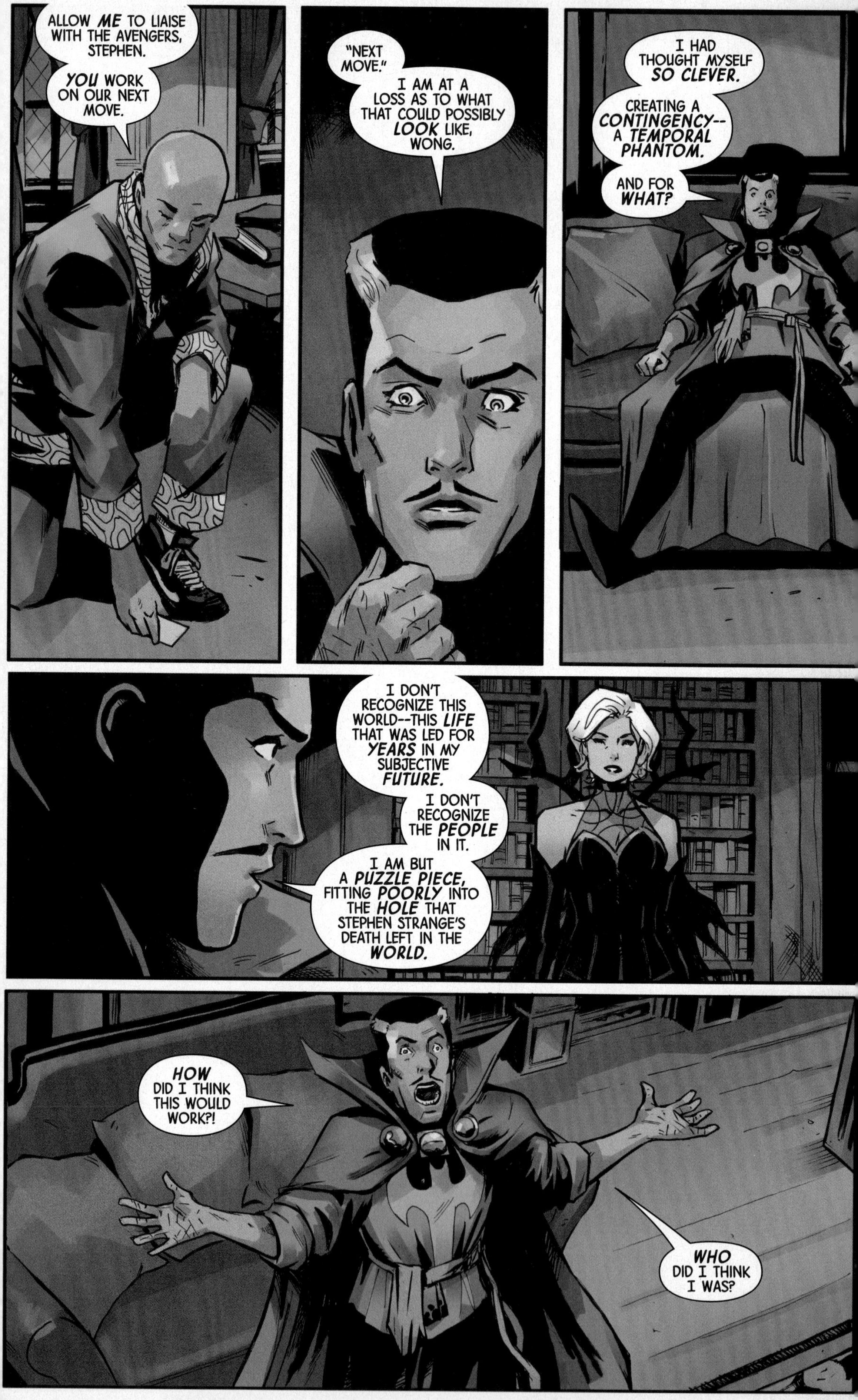
ALLOW ME TO LIAISE WITH THE AVENGERS, STEPHEN.
YOU WORK ON OUR NEXT MOVE.
"NEXT MOVE."
I AM AT A LOSS AS TO WHAT THAT COULD POSSIBLY LOOK LIKE, WONG.
I HAD THOUGHT MYSELF SO CLEVER.
CREATING A CONTINGENCY-- A TEMPORAL PHANTOM.
AND FOR WHAT?
I DON'T RECOGNIZE THIS WORLD--THIS LIFE THAT WAS LED FOR YEARS IN MY SUBJECTIVE FUTURE.
I DON'T RECOGNIZE THE PEOPLE IN IT.
I AM BUT A PUZZLE PIECE, FITTING POORLY INTO THE HOLE THAT STEPHEN STRANGE'S DEATH LEFT IN THE WORLD.
HOW DID I THINK THIS WOULD WORK?!
WHO DID I THINK I WAS?

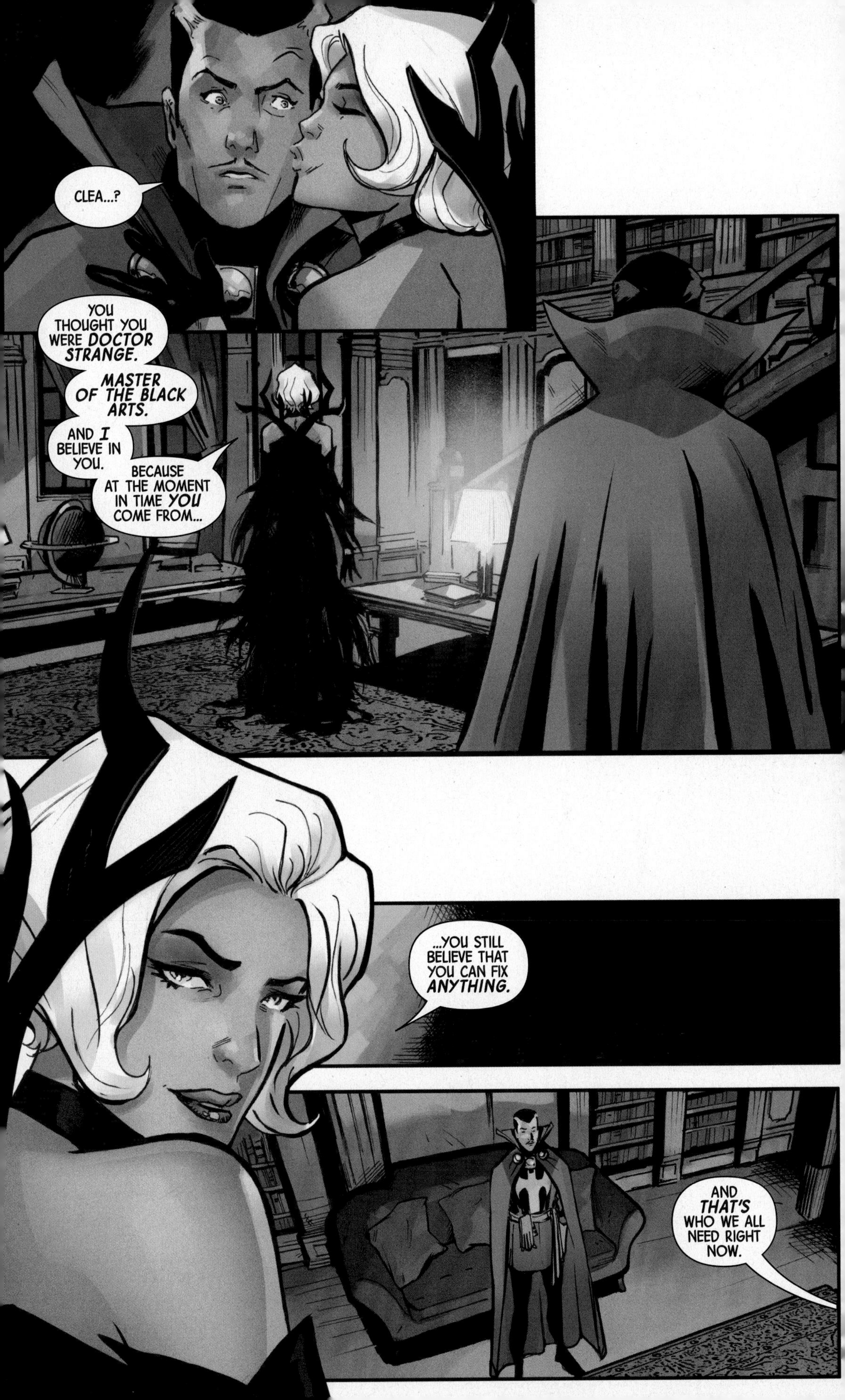

CLEA...?
YOU THOUGHT YOU WERE DOCTOR STRANGE.
MASTER OF THE BLACK ARTS.
AND I BELIEVE IN YOU.
BECAUSE AT THE MOMENT IN TIME YOU COME FROM...
...YOU STILL BELIEVE THAT YOU CAN FIX ANYTHING.
AND THAT'S WHO WE ALL NEED RIGHT NOW.

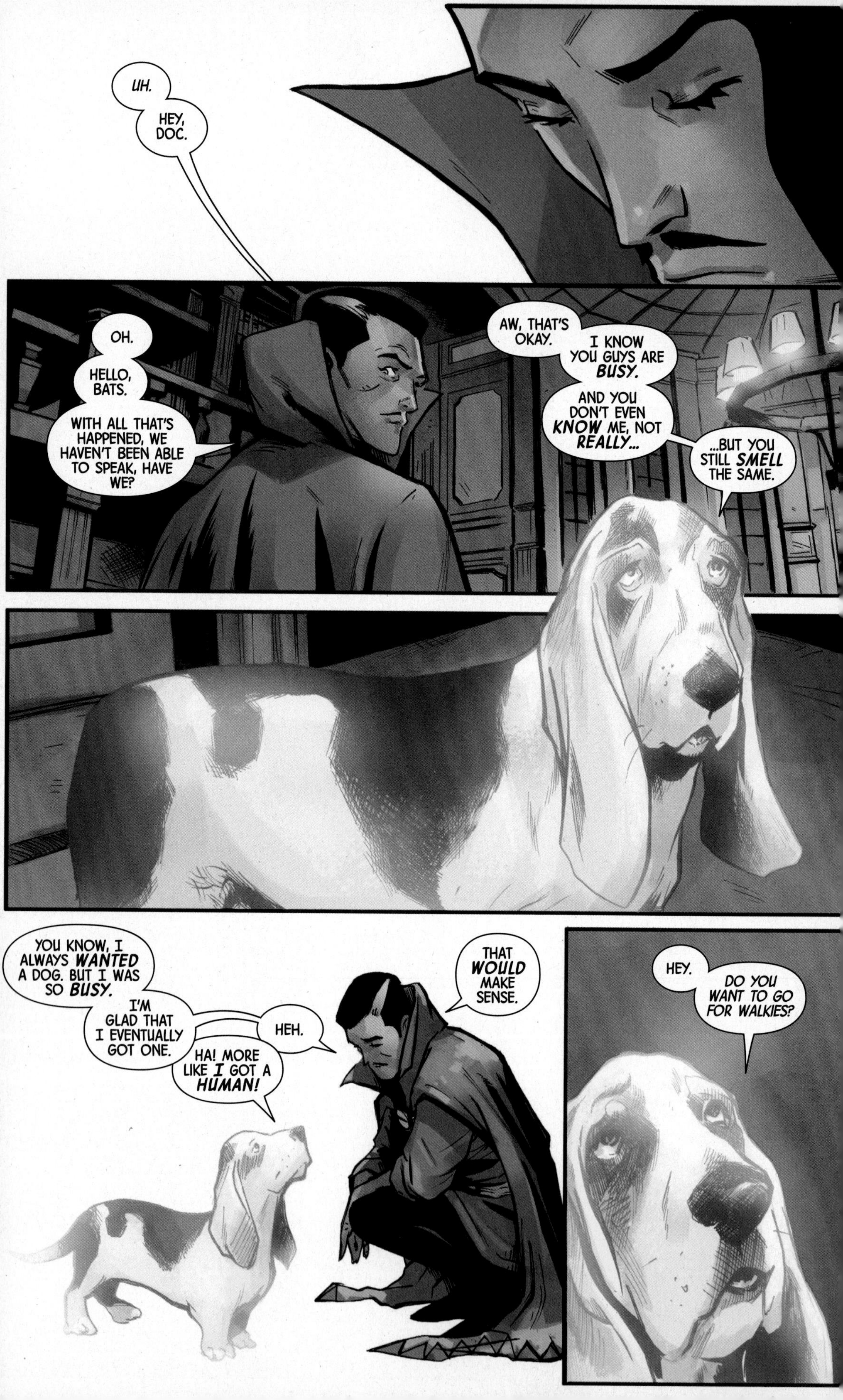
UH.
HEY, DOC.
OH.
HELLO, BATS.
WITH ALL THAT'S HAPPENED, WE HAVEN'T BEEN ABLE TO SPEAK, HAVE WE?
AW, THAT'S OKAY.
I KNOW YOU GUYS ARE BUSY.
AND YOU DON'T EVEN KNOW ME, NOT REALLY...
...BUT YOU STILL SMELL THE SAME.
YOU KNOW, I ALWAYS WANTED A DOG. BUT I WAS SO BUSY.
I'M GLAD THAT I EVENTUALLY GOT ONE.
HEH.
HA! MORE LIKE I GOT A HUMAN!
THAT WOULD MAKE SENSE.
HEY.
DO YOU WANT TO GO FOR WALKIES?

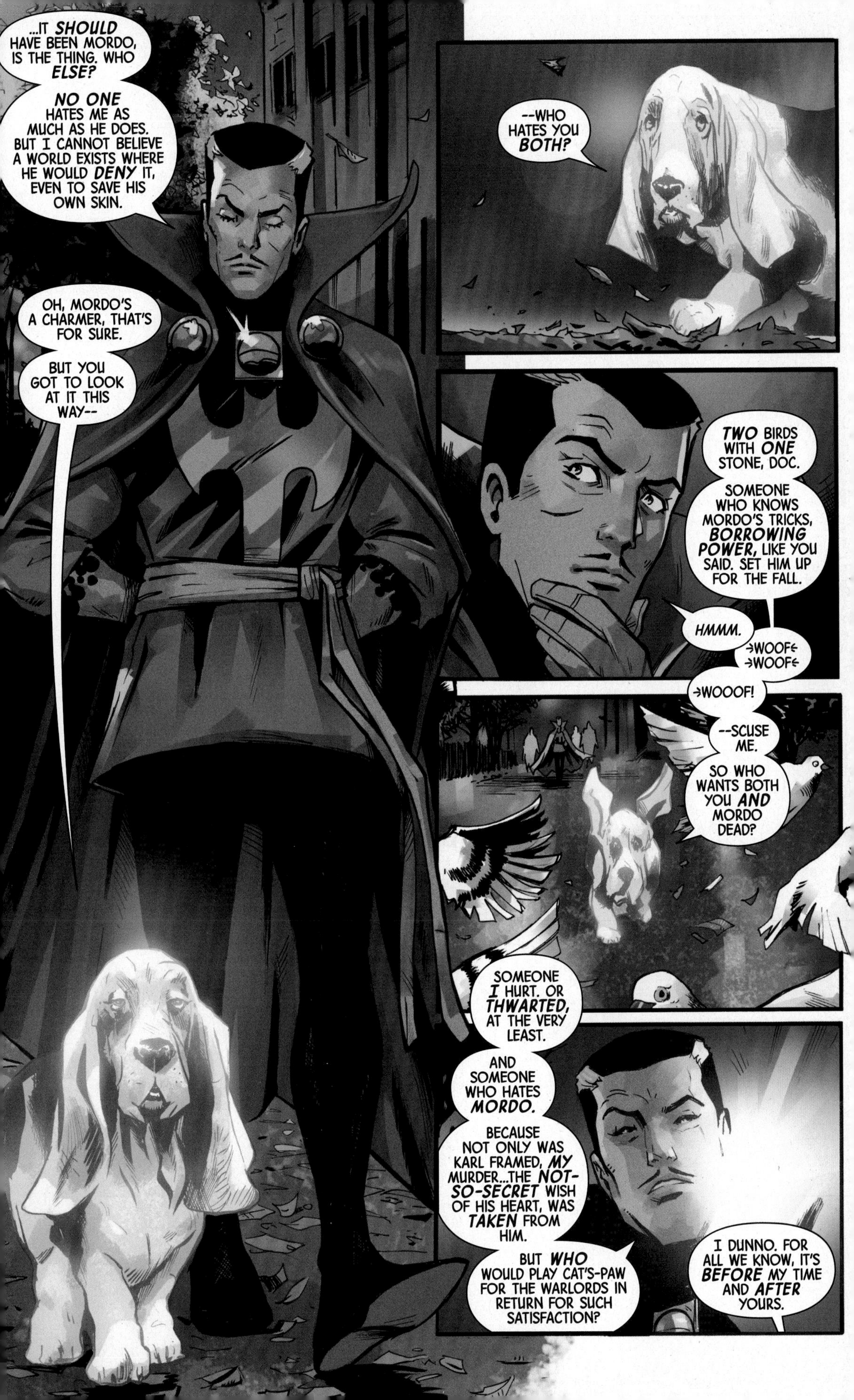

...IT SHOULD HAVE BEEN MORDO, IS THE THING. WHO ELSE?
NO ONE HATES ME AS MUCH AS HE DOES. BUT I CANNOT BELIEVE A WORLD EXISTS WHERE HE WOULD DENY IT, EVEN TO SAVE HIS OWN SKIN.
OH, MORDO'S A CHARMER, THAT'S FOR SURE.
BUT YOU GOT TO LOOK AT IT THIS WAY--
--WHO HATES YOU BOTH?
TWO BIRDS WITH ONE STONE, DOC.
SOMEONE WHO KNOWS MORDO'S TRICKS, BORROWING POWER, LIKE YOU SAID. SET HIM UP FOR THE FALL.
HMMM.
→WOOF← →WOOF←
→WOOOF!
--SCUSE ME.
SO WHO WANTS BOTH YOU AND MORDO DEAD?
SOMEONE I HURT. OR THWARTED, AT THE VERY LEAST.
AND SOMEONE WHO HATES MORDO.
BECAUSE NOT ONLY WAS KARL FRAMED, MY MURDER...THE NOT-SO-SECRET WISH OF HIS HEART, WAS TAKEN FROM HIM.
BUT WHO WOULD PLAY CAT'S-PAW FOR THE WARLORDS IN RETURN FOR SUCH SATISFACTION?
I DUNNO. FOR ALL WE KNOW, IT'S BEFORE MY TIME AND AFTER YOURS.

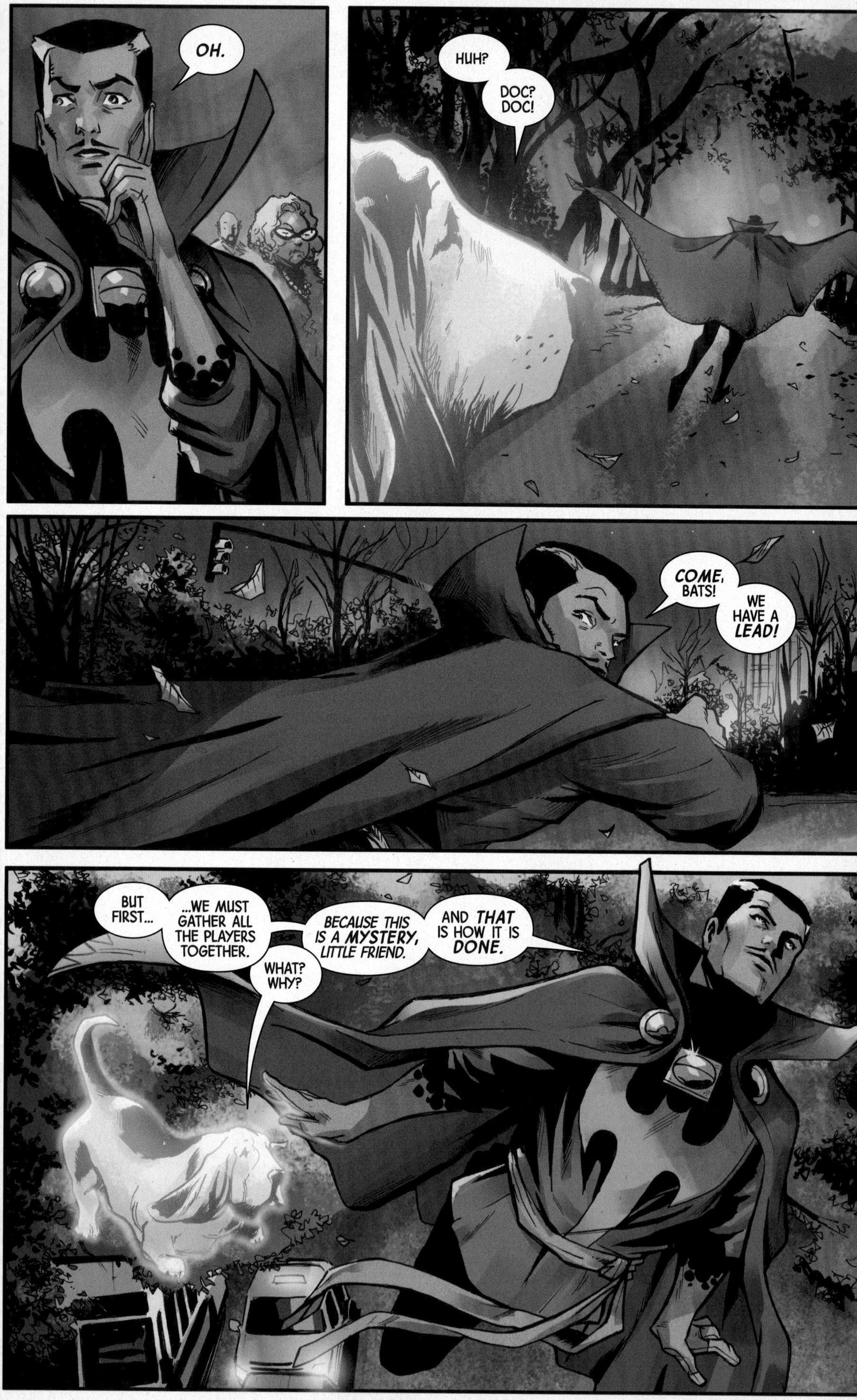
OH.
HUH?
DOC? DOC!
COME, BATS!
WE HAVE A LEAD!
BUT FIRST...
...WE MUST GATHER ALL THE PLAYERS TOGETHER.
WHAT? WHY?
BECAUSE THIS IS A MYSTERY, LITTLE FRIEND.
AND THAT IS HOW IT IS DONE.

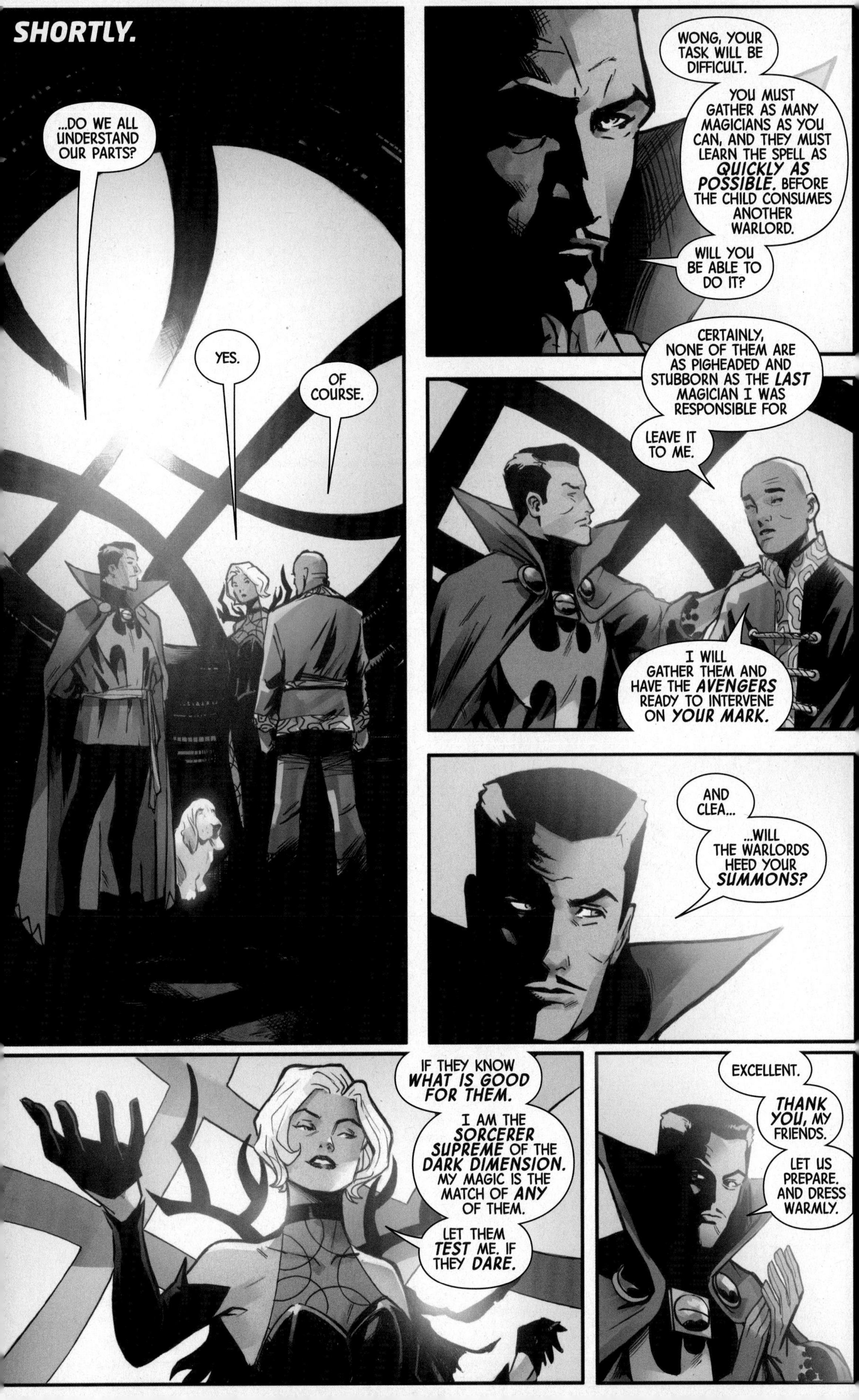
SHORTLY.
...DO WE ALL UNDERSTAND OUR PARTS?
YES.
OF COURSE.
WONG, YOUR TASK WILL BE DIFFICULT.
YOU MUST GATHER AS MANY MAGICIANS AS YOU CAN, AND THEY MUST LEARN THE SPELL AS QUICKLY AS POSSIBLE. BEFORE THE CHILD CONSUMES ANOTHER WARLORD.
WILL YOU BE ABLE TO DO IT?
CERTAINLY, NONE OF THEM ARE AS PIGHEADED AND STUBBORN AS THE LAST MAGICIAN I WAS RESPONSIBLE FOR
LEAVE IT TO ME.
I WILL GATHER THEM AND HAVE THE AVENGERS READY TO INTERVENE ON YOUR MARK.
AND CLEA...
...WILL THE WARLORDS HEED YOUR SUMMONS?
IF THEY KNOW WHAT IS GOOD FOR THEM.
I AM THE SORCERER SUPREME OF THE DARK DIMENSION. MY MAGIC IS THE MATCH OF ANY OF THEM.
LET THEM TEST ME. IF THEY DARE.
EXCELLENT.
THANK YOU, MY FRIENDS.
LET US PREPARE. AND DRESS WARMLY.

CHAPTER TEN

The Drawing Room

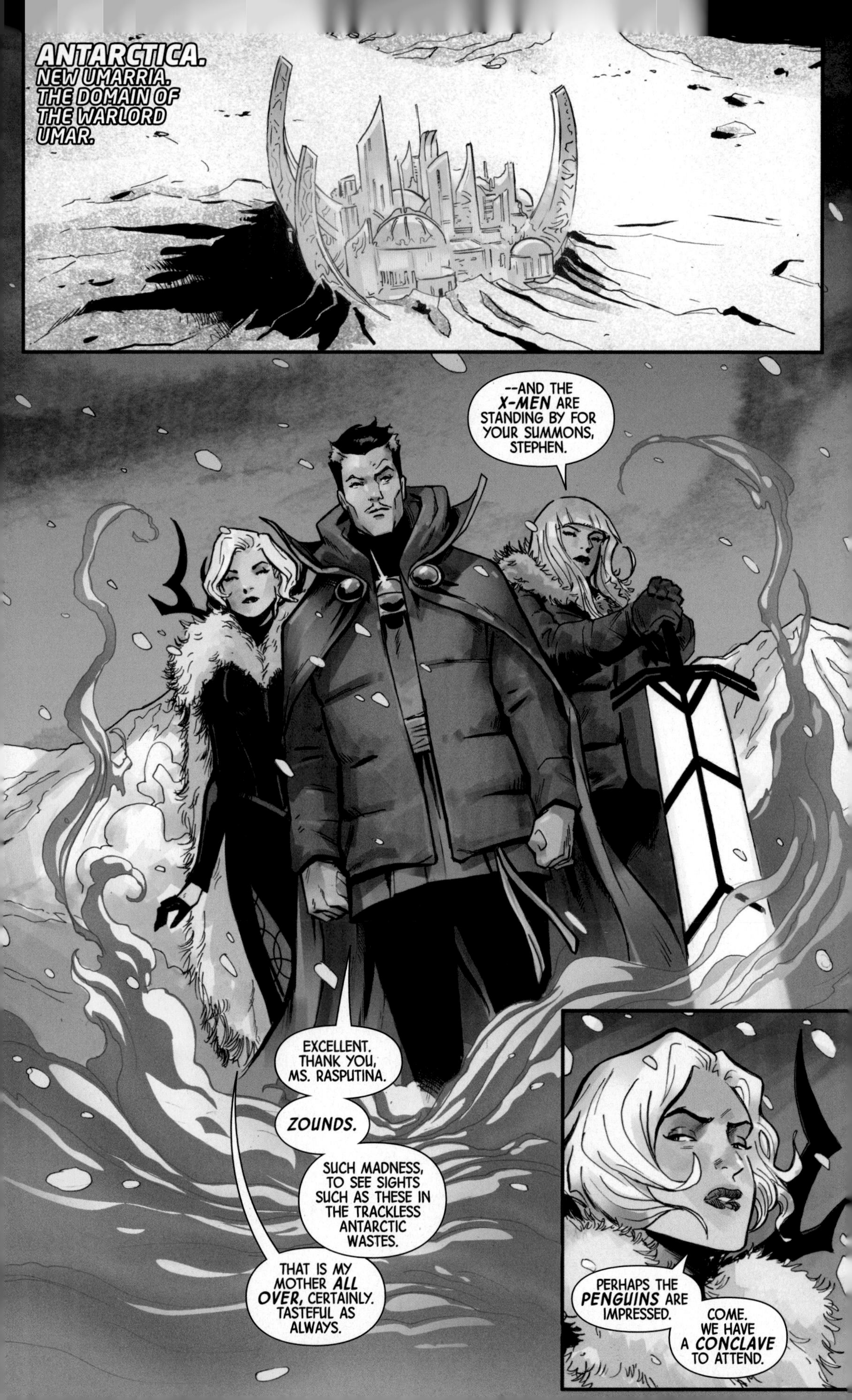
ANTARCTICA.
NEW UMARRIA. THE DOMAIN OF THE WARLORD UMAR.
--AND THE X-MEN ARE STANDING BY FOR YOUR SUMMONS, STEPHEN.
EXCELLENT. THANK YOU, MS. RASPUTINA.
ZOUNDS.
SUCH MADNESS, TO SEE SIGHTS SUCH AS THESE IN THE TRACKLESS ANTARCTIC WASTES.
THAT IS MY MOTHER ALL OVER, CERTAINLY. TASTEFUL AS ALWAYS.
PERHAPS THE PENGUINS ARE IMPRESSED.
COME. WE HAVE A CONCLAVE TO ATTEND.

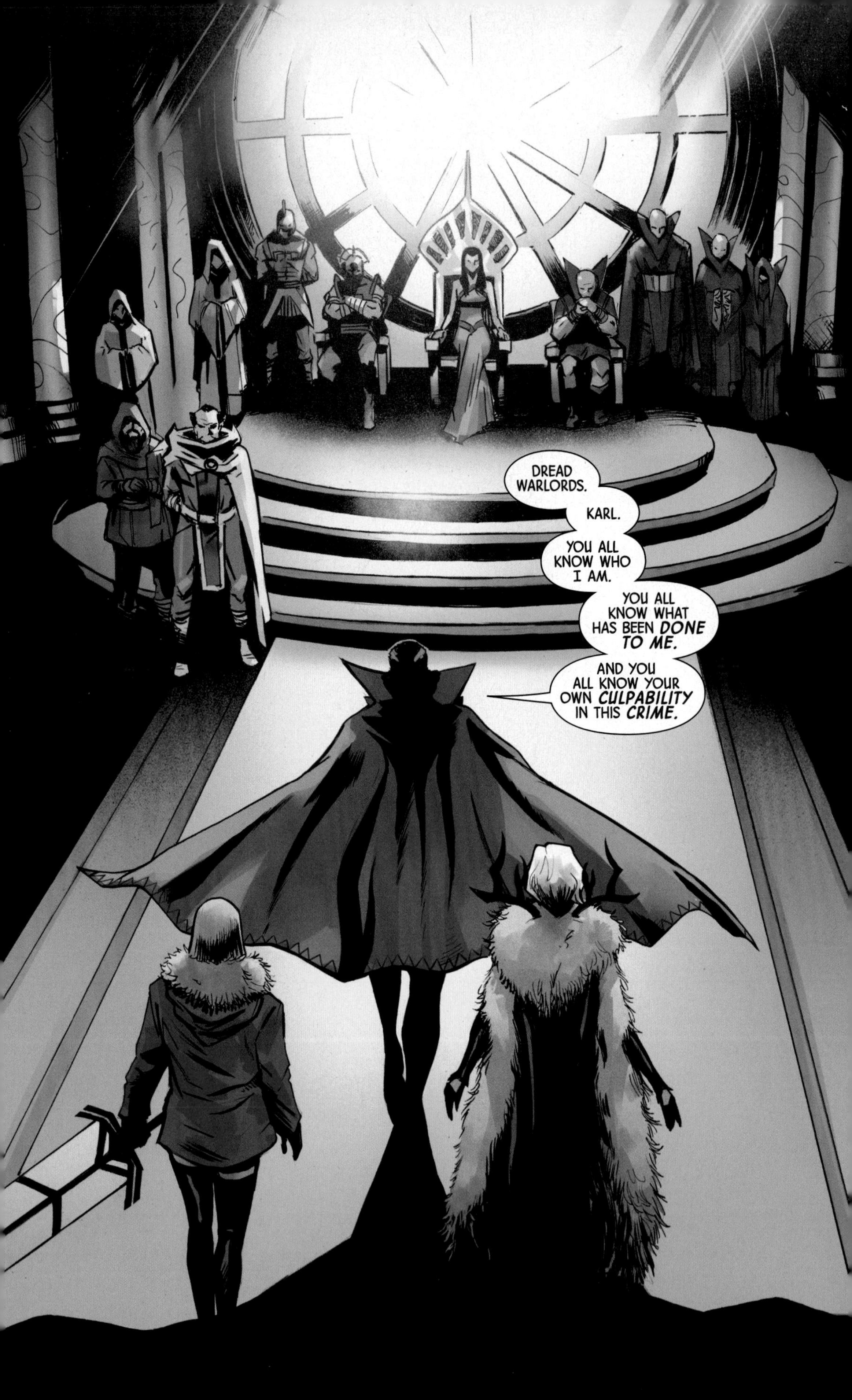
DREAD WARLORDS.
KARL.
YOU ALL KNOW WHO I AM.
YOU ALL KNOW WHAT HAS BEEN DONE TO ME.
AND YOU ALL KNOW YOUR OWN CULPABILITY IN THIS CRIME.

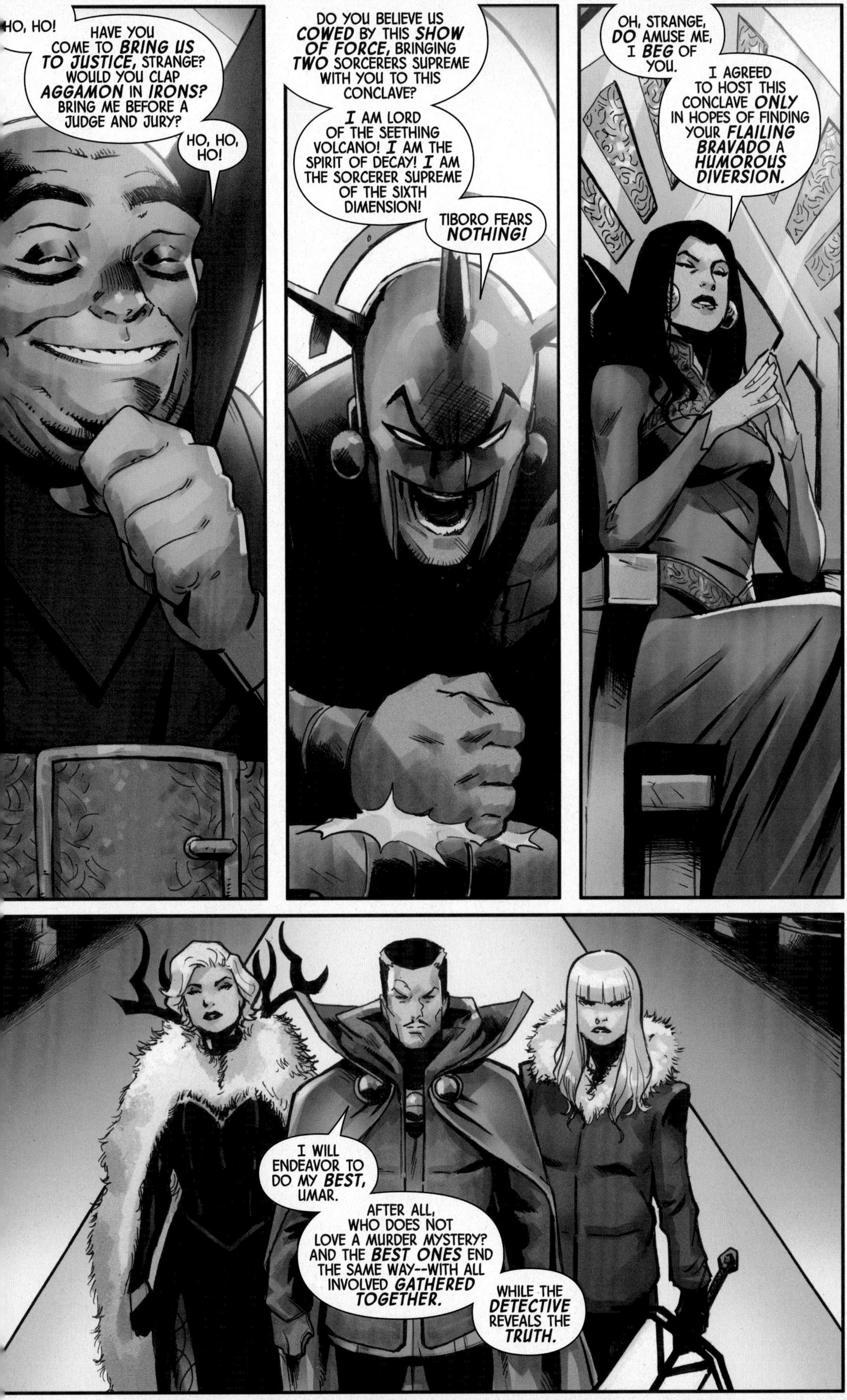

HO, HO!
HAVE YOU COME TO BRING US TO JUSTICE, STRANGE? WOULD YOU CLAP AGGAMON IN IRONS? BRING ME BEFORE A JUDGE AND JURY?
HO, HO, HO!
DO YOU BELIEVE US COWED BY THIS SHOW OF FORCE, BRINGING TWO SORCERERS SUPREME WITH YOU TO THIS CONCLAVE?
I AM LORD OF THE SEETHING VOLCANO! I AM THE SPIRIT OF DECAY! I AM THE SORCERER SUPREME OF THE SIXTH DIMENSION!
TIBORO FEARS NOTHING!
OH, STRANGE, DO AMUSE ME, I BEG OF YOU.
I AGREED TO HOST THIS CONCLAVE ONLY IN HOPES OF FINDING YOUR FLAILING BRAVADO A HUMOROUS DIVERSION.
I WILL ENDEAVOR TO DO MY BEST, UMAR.
AFTER ALL, WHO DOES NOT LOVE A MURDER MYSTERY? AND THE BEST ONES END THE SAME WAY--WITH ALL INVOLVED GATHERED TOGETHER.
WHILE THE DETECTIVE REVEALS THE TRUTH.

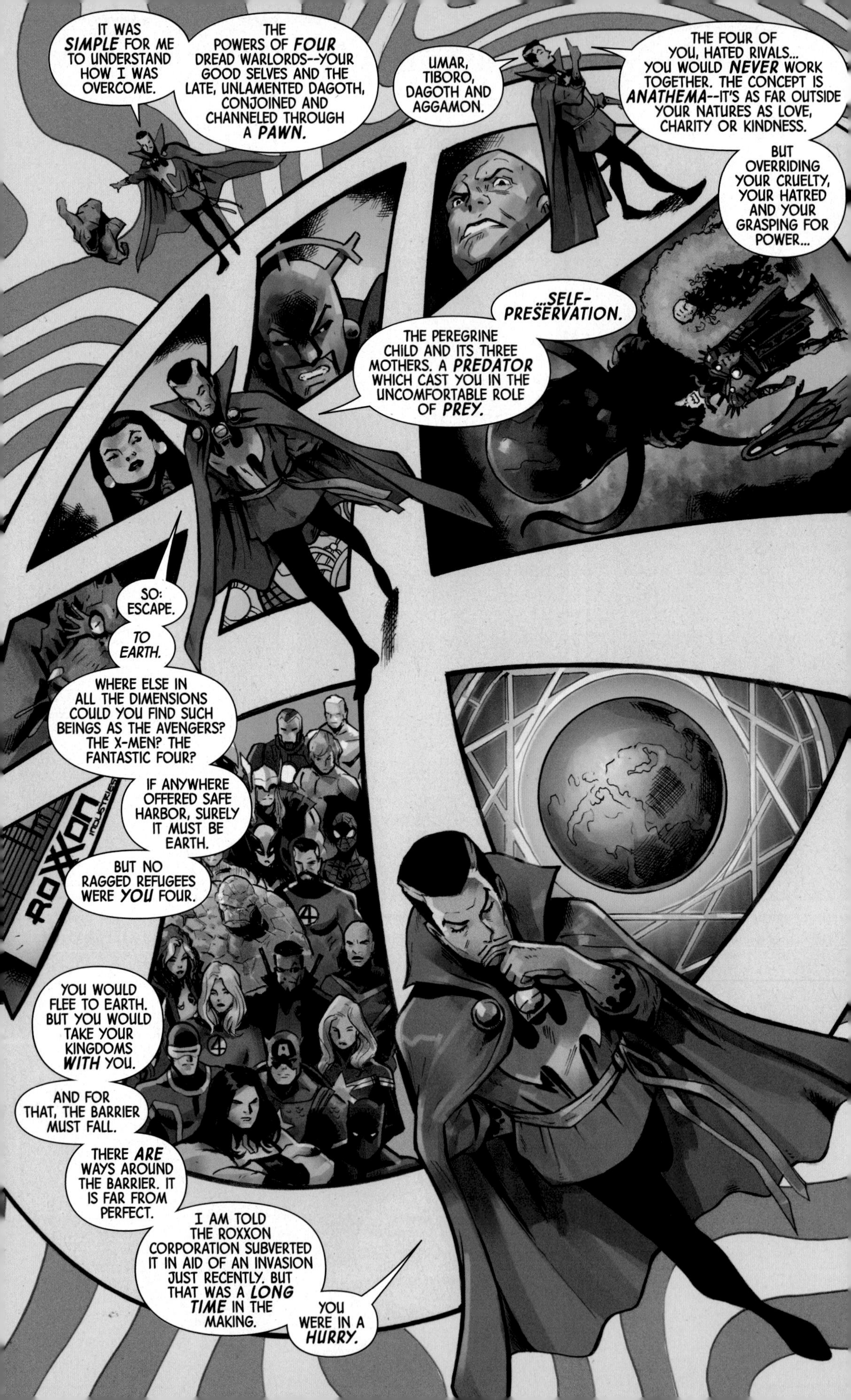
IT WAS SIMPLE FOR ME TO UNDERSTAND HOW I WAS OVERCOME.
THE POWERS OF FOUR DREAD WARLORDS--YOUR GOOD SELVES AND THE LATE, UNLAMENTED DAGOTH, CONJOINED AND CHANNELED THROUGH A PAWN.
UMAR, TIBORO, DAGOTH AND AGGAMON.
THE FOUR OF YOU, HATED RIVALS... YOU WOULD NEVER WORK TOGETHER. THE CONCEPT IS ANATHEMA--IT'S AS FAR OUTSIDE YOUR NATURES AS LOVE, CHARITY OR KINDNESS.
BUT OVERRIDING YOUR CRUELTY, YOUR HATRED AND YOUR GRASPING FOR POWER...
...SELF-PRESERVATION.
THE PEREGRINE CHILD AND ITS THREE MOTHERS. A PREDATOR WHICH CAST YOU IN THE UNCOMFORTABLE ROLE OF PREY.
SO: ESCAPE.
TO EARTH.
WHERE ELSE IN ALL THE DIMENSIONS COULD YOU FIND SUCH BEINGS AS THE AVENGERS? THE X-MEN? THE FANTASTIC FOUR?
IF ANYWHERE OFFERED SAFE HARBOR, SURELY IT MUST BE EARTH.
BUT NO RAGGED REFUGEES WERE YOU FOUR.
ROXXON INDUSTRIES
YOU WOULD FLEE TO EARTH. BUT YOU WOULD TAKE YOUR KINGDOMS WITH YOU.
AND FOR THAT, THE BARRIER MUST FALL.
THERE ARE WAYS AROUND THE BARRIER. IT IS FAR FROM PERFECT.
I AM TOLD THE ROXXON CORPORATION SUBVERTED IT IN AID OF AN INVASION JUST RECENTLY. BUT THAT WAS A LONG TIME IN THE MAKING.
YOU WERE IN A HURRY.

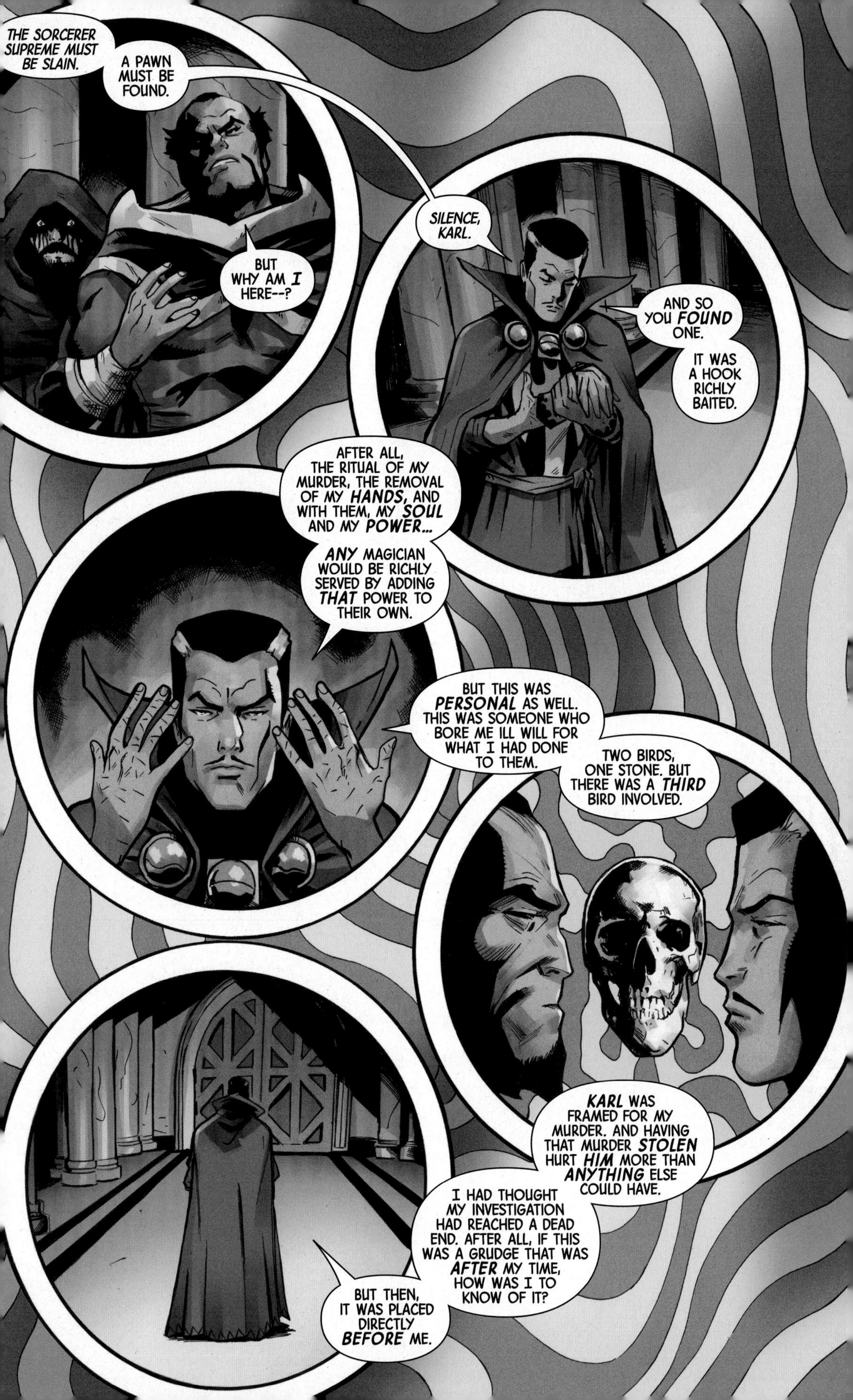
THE SORCERER SUPREME MUST BE SLAIN.
A PAWN MUST BE FOUND.
BUT WHY AM I HERE--?
SILENCE, KARL.
AND SO YOU FOUND ONE.
IT WAS A HOOK RICHLY BAITED.
AFTER ALL, THE RITUAL OF MY MURDER, THE REMOVAL OF MY HANDS, AND WITH THEM, MY SOUL AND MY POWER...
ANY MAGICIAN WOULD BE RICHLY SERVED BY ADDING THAT POWER TO THEIR OWN.
BUT THIS WAS PERSONAL AS WELL. THIS WAS SOMEONE WHO BORE ME ILL WILL FOR WHAT I HAD DONE TO THEM.
TWO BIRDS, ONE STONE. BUT THERE WAS A THIRD BIRD INVOLVED.
KARL WAS FRAMED FOR MY MURDER. AND HAVING THAT MURDER STOLEN HURT HIM MORE THAN ANYTHING ELSE COULD HAVE.
I HAD THOUGHT MY INVESTIGATION HAD REACHED A DEAD END. AFTER ALL, IF THIS WAS A GRUDGE THAT WAS AFTER MY TIME, HOW WAS I TO KNOW OF IT?
BUT THEN, IT WAS PLACED DIRECTLY BEFORE ME.

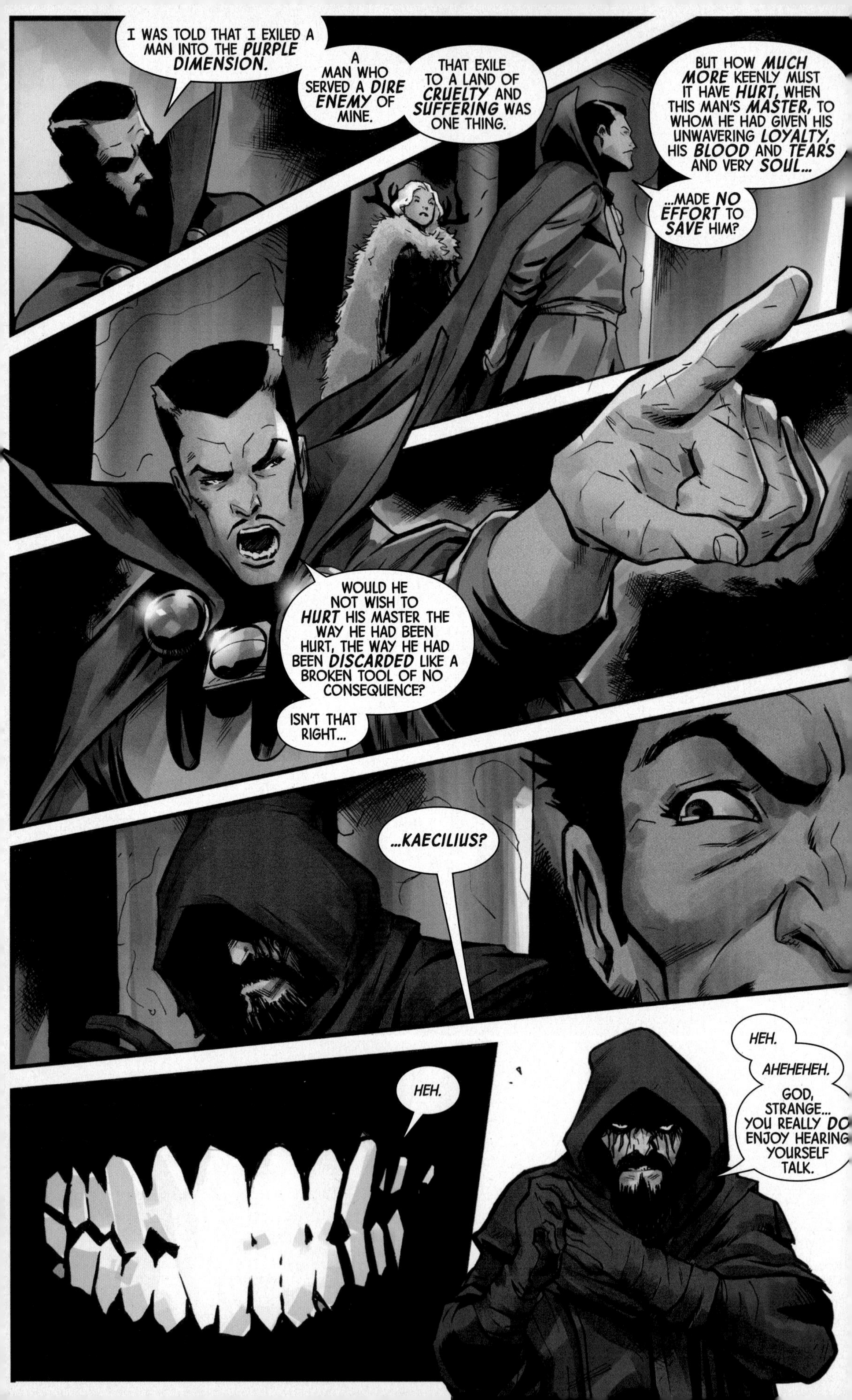

I WAS TOLD THAT I EXILED A MAN INTO THE PURPLE DIMENSION.
A MAN WHO SERVED A DIRE ENEMY OF MINE.
THAT EXILE TO A LAND OF CRUELTY AND SUFFERING WAS ONE THING.
BUT HOW MUCH MORE KEENLY MUST IT HAVE HURT, WHEN THIS MAN'S MASTER, TO WHOM HE HAD GIVEN HIS UNWAVERING LOYALTY, HIS BLOOD AND TEARS AND VERY SOUL...
...MADE NO EFFORT TO SAVE HIM?
WOULD HE NOT WISH TO HURT HIS MASTER THE WAY HE HAD BEEN HURT, THE WAY HE HAD BEEN DISCARDED LIKE A BROKEN TOOL OF NO CONSEQUENCE?
ISN'T THAT RIGHT...
...KAECILIUS?
HEH.
HEH.
AHEHEHEH.
GOD, STRANGE... YOU REALLY DO ENJOY HEARING YOURSELF TALK.

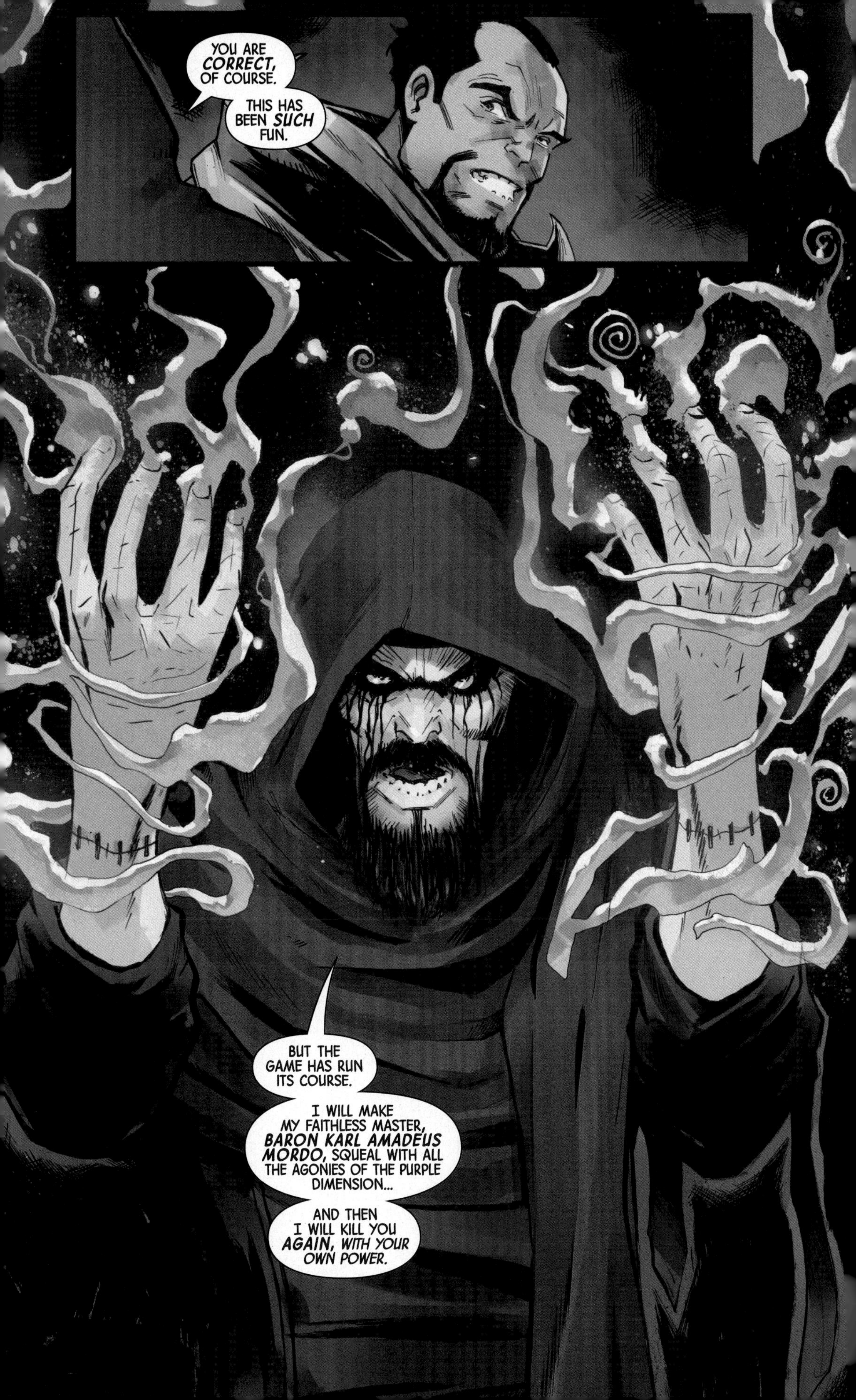
YOU ARE CORRECT, OF COURSE.
THIS HAS BEEN SUCH FUN.
BUT THE GAME HAS RUN ITS COURSE.
I WILL MAKE MY FAITHLESS MASTER, BARON KARL AMADEUS MORDO, SQUEAL WITH ALL THE AGONIES OF THE PURPLE DIMENSION...
AND THEN I WILL KILL YOU AGAIN, WITH YOUR OWN POWER.

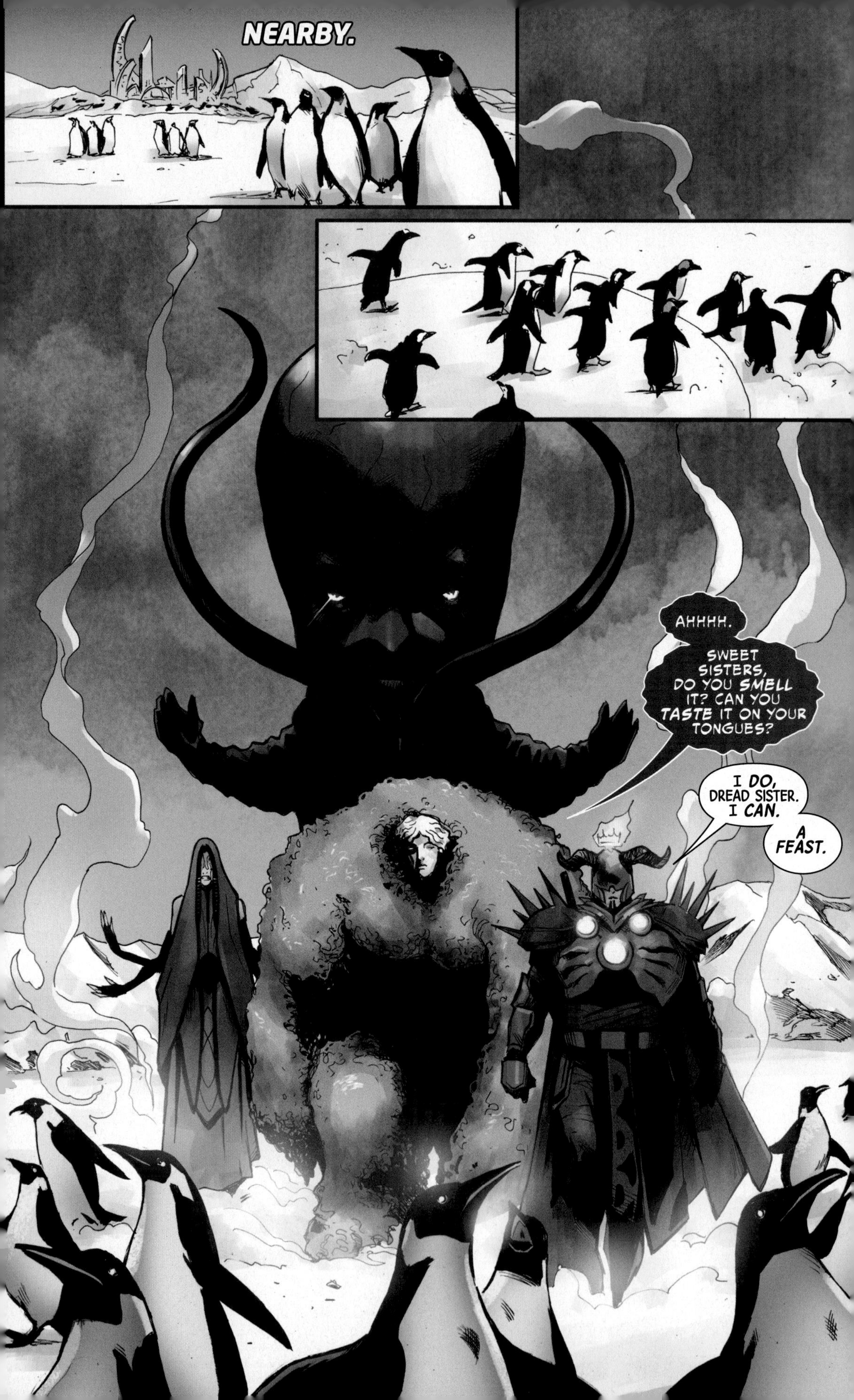
NEARBY.
AHHHH.
SWEET SISTERS, DO YOU SMELL IT? CAN YOU TASTE IT ON YOUR TONGUES?
I DO, DREAD SISTER. I CAN.
A FEAST.

CHAPTER ELEVEN

Physician, heal Thyself

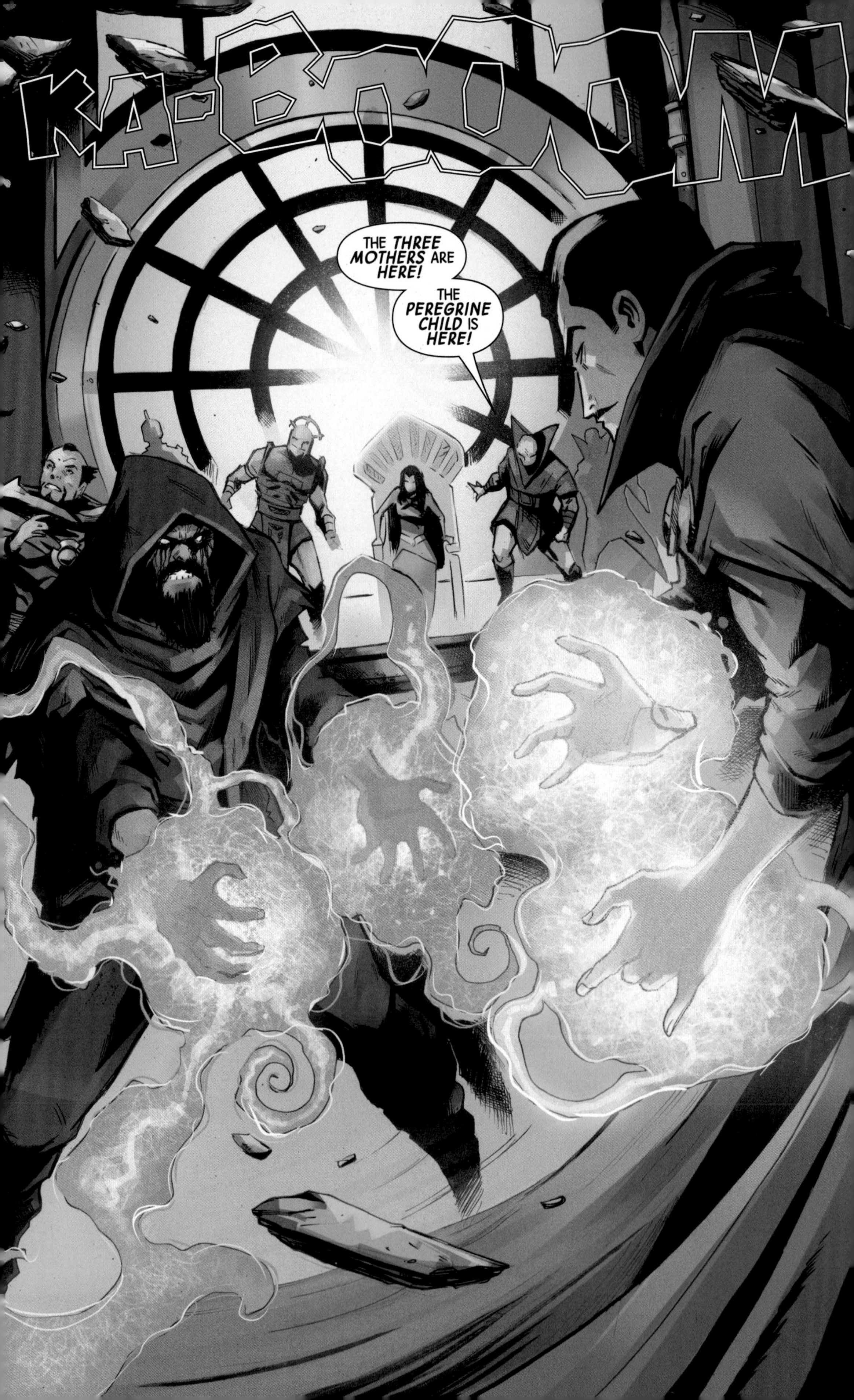
KA-BOOOM!
THE THREE MOTHERS ARE HERE!
THE PEREGRINE CHILD IS HERE!

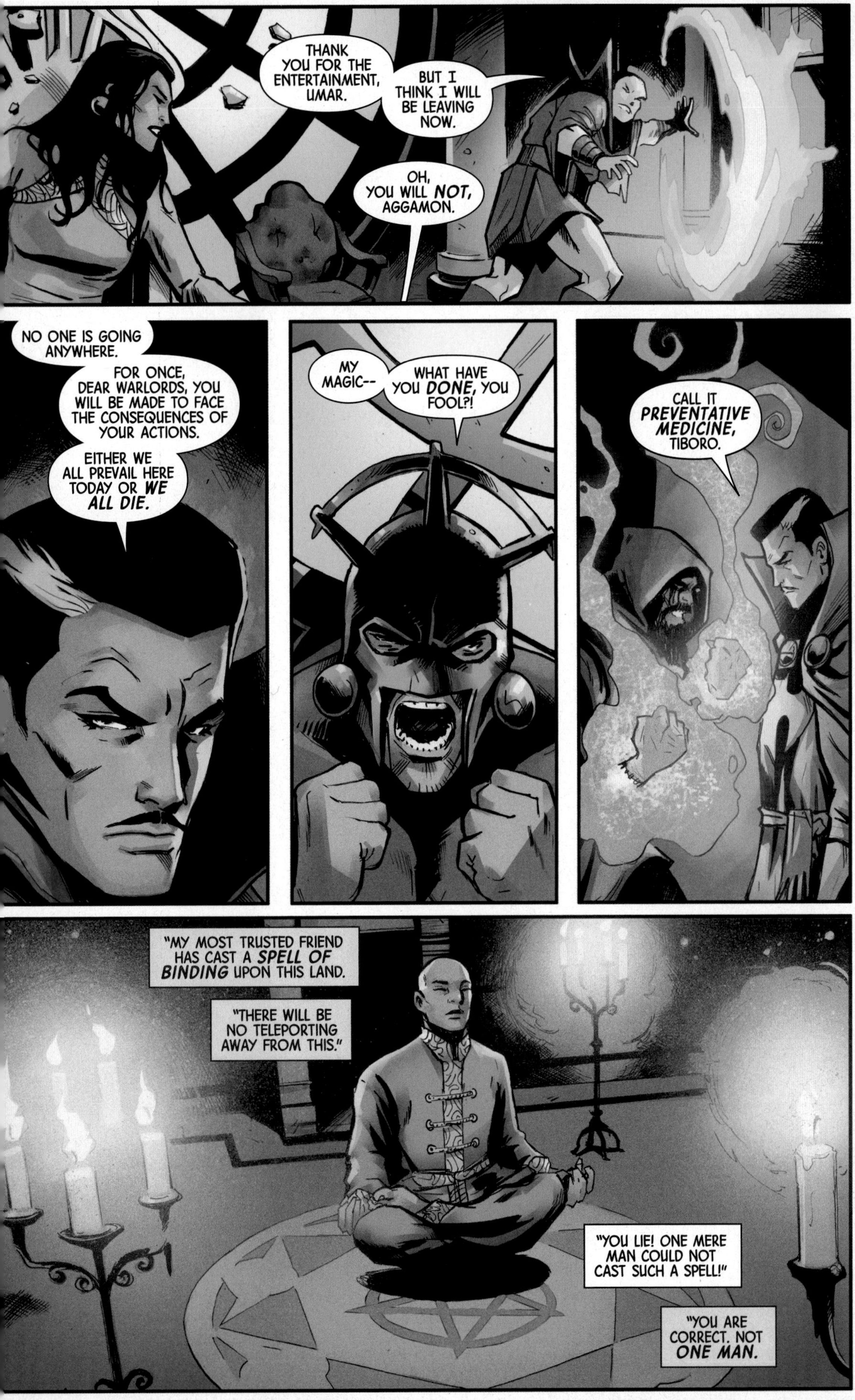
THANK YOU FOR THE ENTERTAINMENT, UMAR.
BUT I THINK I WILL BE LEAVING NOW.
OH, YOU WILL NOT, AGGAMON.
NO ONE IS GOING ANYWHERE.
FOR ONCE, DEAR WARLORDS, YOU WILL BE MADE TO FACE THE CONSEQUENCES OF YOUR ACTIONS.
EITHER WE ALL PREVAIL HERE TODAY OR WE ALL DIE.
MY MAGIC--
WHAT HAVE YOU DONE, YOU FOOL?!
CALL IT PREVENTATIVE MEDICINE, TIBORO.
"MY MOST TRUSTED FRIEND HAS CAST A SPELL OF BINDING UPON THIS LAND.
"THERE WILL BE NO TELEPORTING AWAY FROM THIS."
"YOU LIE! ONE MERE MAN COULD NOT CAST SUCH A SPELL!"
"YOU ARE CORRECT. NOT ONE MAN.

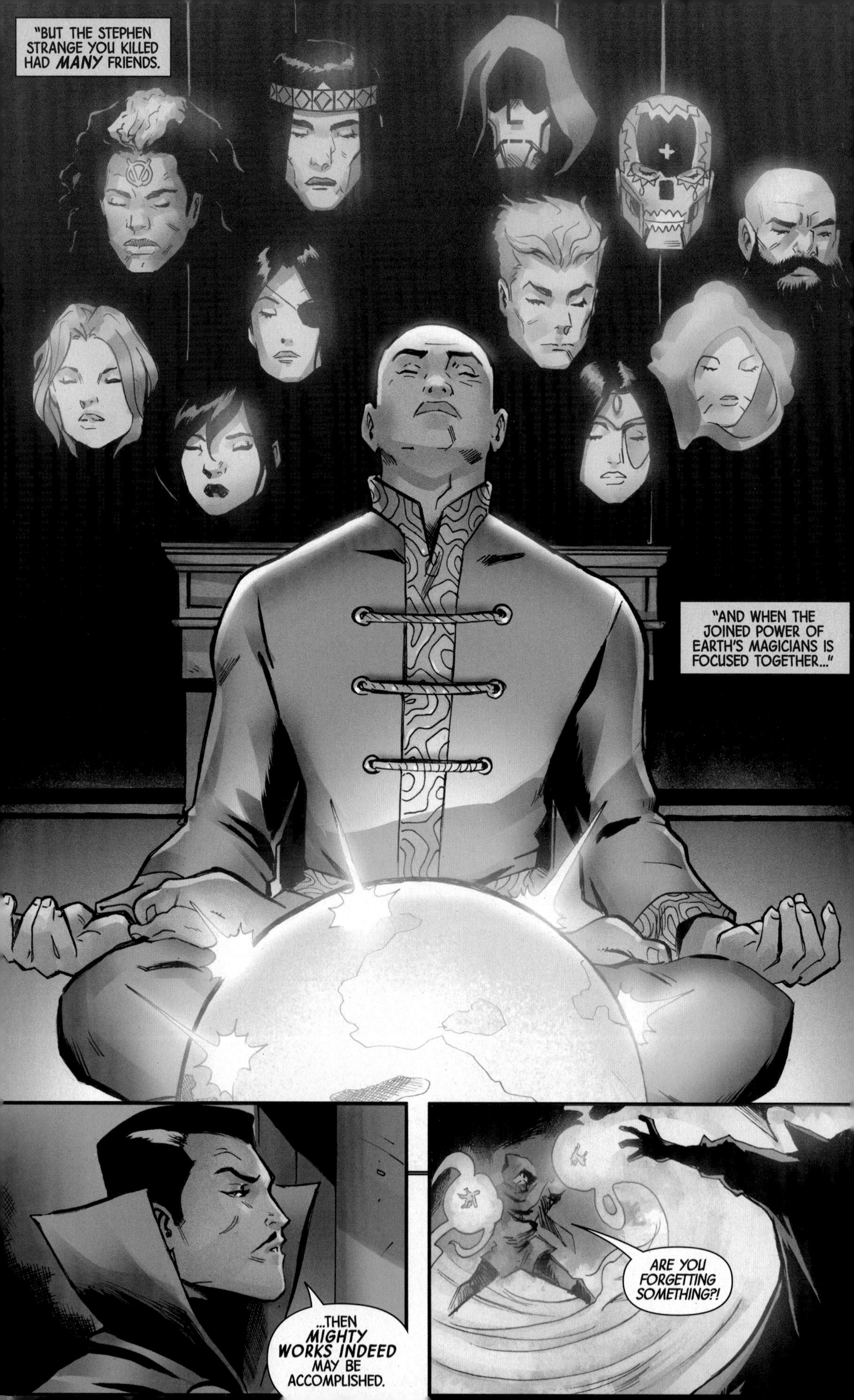
"BUT THE STEPHEN STRANGE YOU KILLED HAD MANY FRIENDS.
"AND WHEN THE JOINED POWER OF EARTH'S MAGICIANS IS FOCUSED TOGETHER..."
...THEN MIGHTY WORKS INDEED MAY BE ACCOMPLISHED.
ARE YOU FORGETTING SOMETHING?!

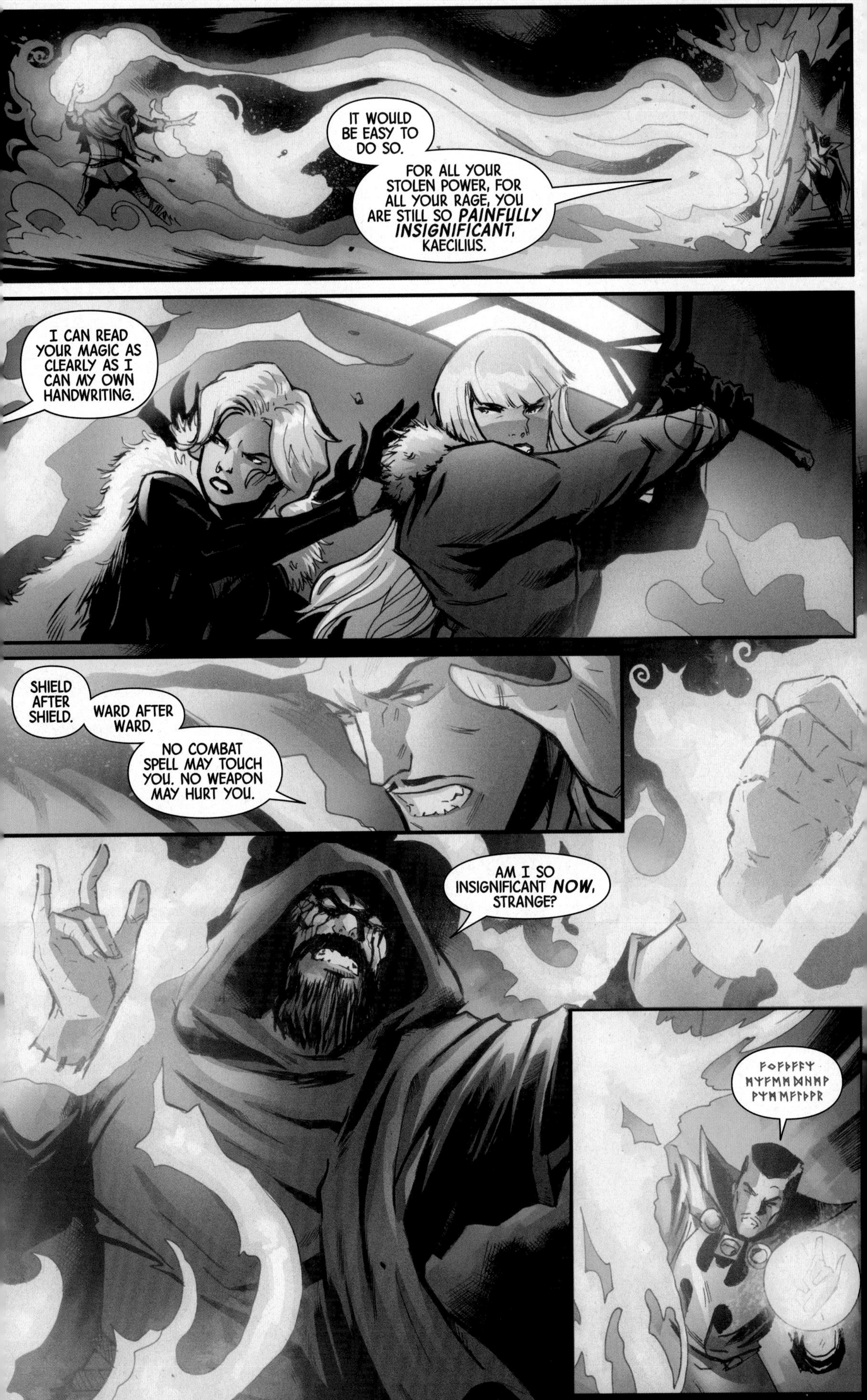
IT WOULD BE EASY TO DO SO.
FOR ALL YOUR STOLEN POWER, FOR ALL YOUR RAGE, YOU ARE STILL SO *PAINFULLY INSIGNIFICANT*, KAECILIUS.
I CAN READ YOUR MAGIC AS CLEARLY AS I CAN MY OWN HANDWRITING.
SHIELD AFTER SHIELD.
WARD AFTER WARD.
NO COMBAT SPELL MAY TOUCH YOU. NO WEAPON MAY HURT YOU.
AM I SO INSIGNIFICANT *NOW*, STRANGE?

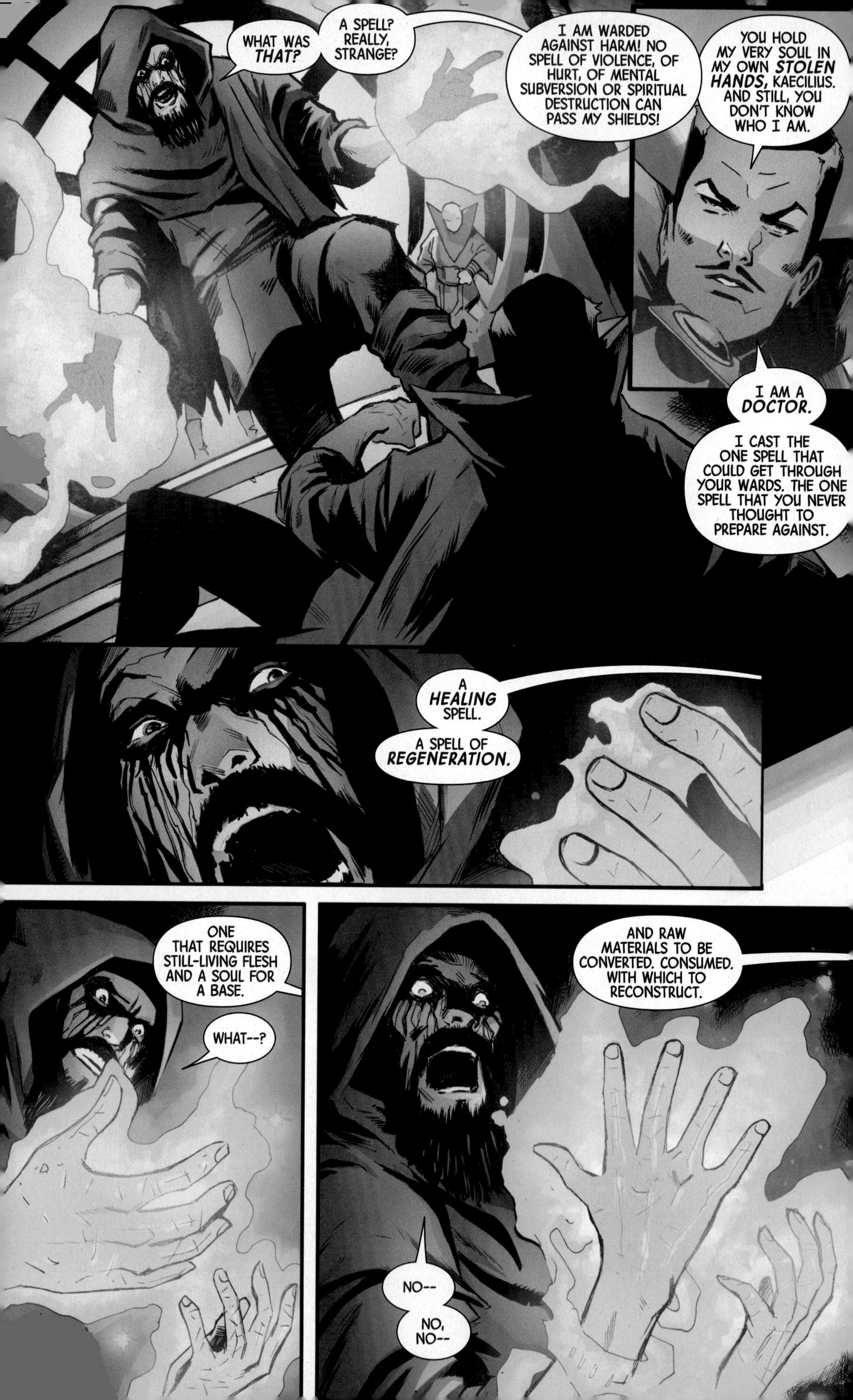
WHAT WAS THAT?
A SPELL? REALLY, STRANGE?
I AM WARDED AGAINST HARM! NO SPELL OF VIOLENCE, OF HURT, OF MENTAL SUBVERSION OR SPIRITUAL DESTRUCTION CAN PASS MY SHIELDS!
YOU HOLD MY VERY SOUL IN MY OWN STOLEN HANDS, KAECILIUS. AND STILL, YOU DON'T KNOW WHO I AM.
I AM A DOCTOR.
I CAST THE ONE SPELL THAT COULD GET THROUGH YOUR WARDS. THE ONE SPELL THAT YOU NEVER THOUGHT TO PREPARE AGAINST.
A HEALING SPELL.
A SPELL OF REGENERATION.
ONE THAT REQUIRES STILL-LIVING FLESH AND A SOUL FOR A BASE.
WHAT--?
AND RAW MATERIALS TO BE CONVERTED. CONSUMED. WITH WHICH TO RECONSTRUCT.
NO--
NO, NO--

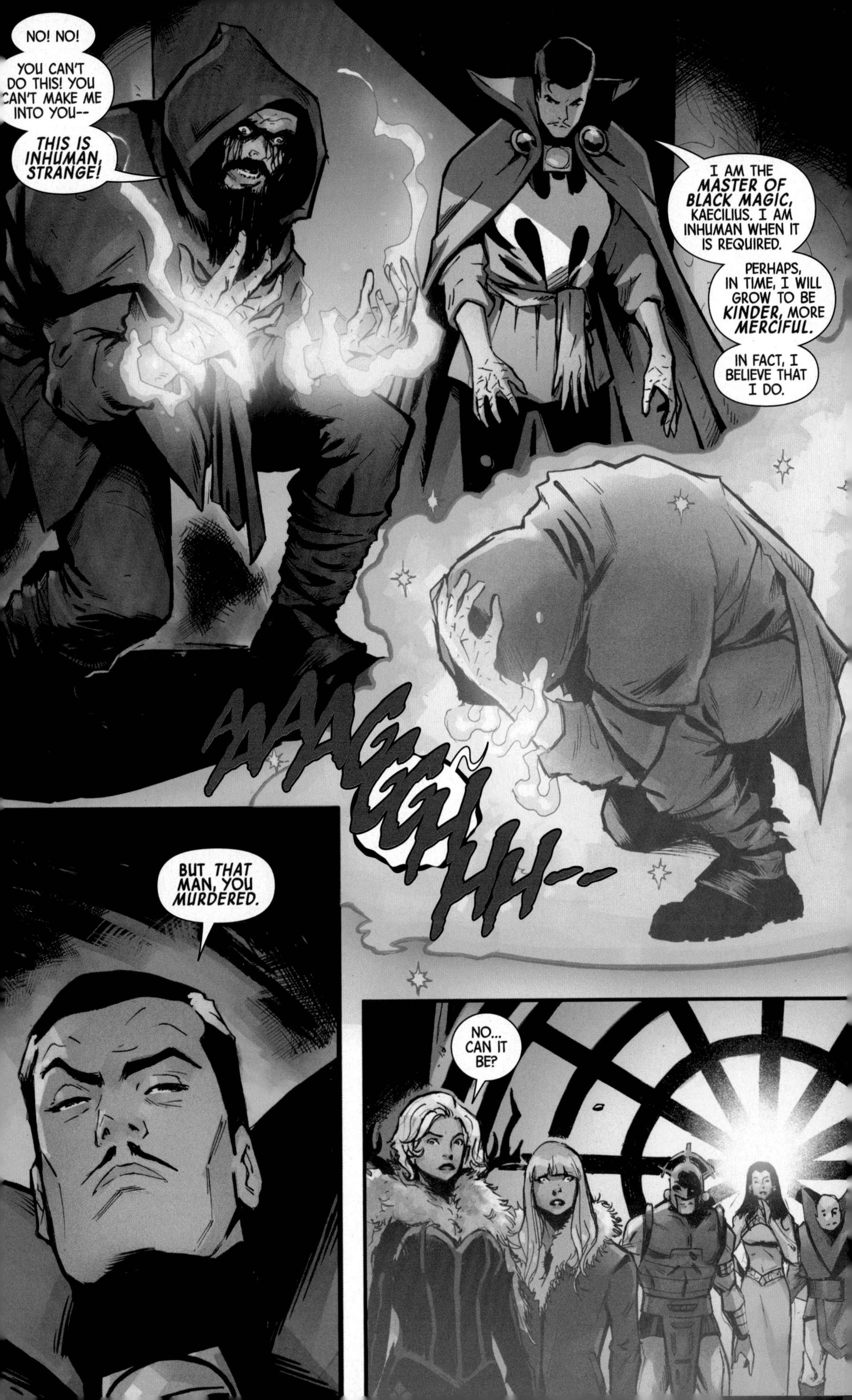
NO! NO!
YOU CAN'T DO THIS! YOU CAN'T MAKE ME INTO YOU--
THIS IS INHUMAN, STRANGE!
I AM THE MASTER OF BLACK MAGIC, KAECILIUS. I AM INHUMAN WHEN IT IS REQUIRED.
PERHAPS, IN TIME, I WILL GROW TO BE KINDER, MORE MERCIFUL.
IN FACT, I BELIEVE THAT I DO.
AAAGGGHHH--
BUT THAT MAN, YOU MURDERED.
NO... CAN IT BE?

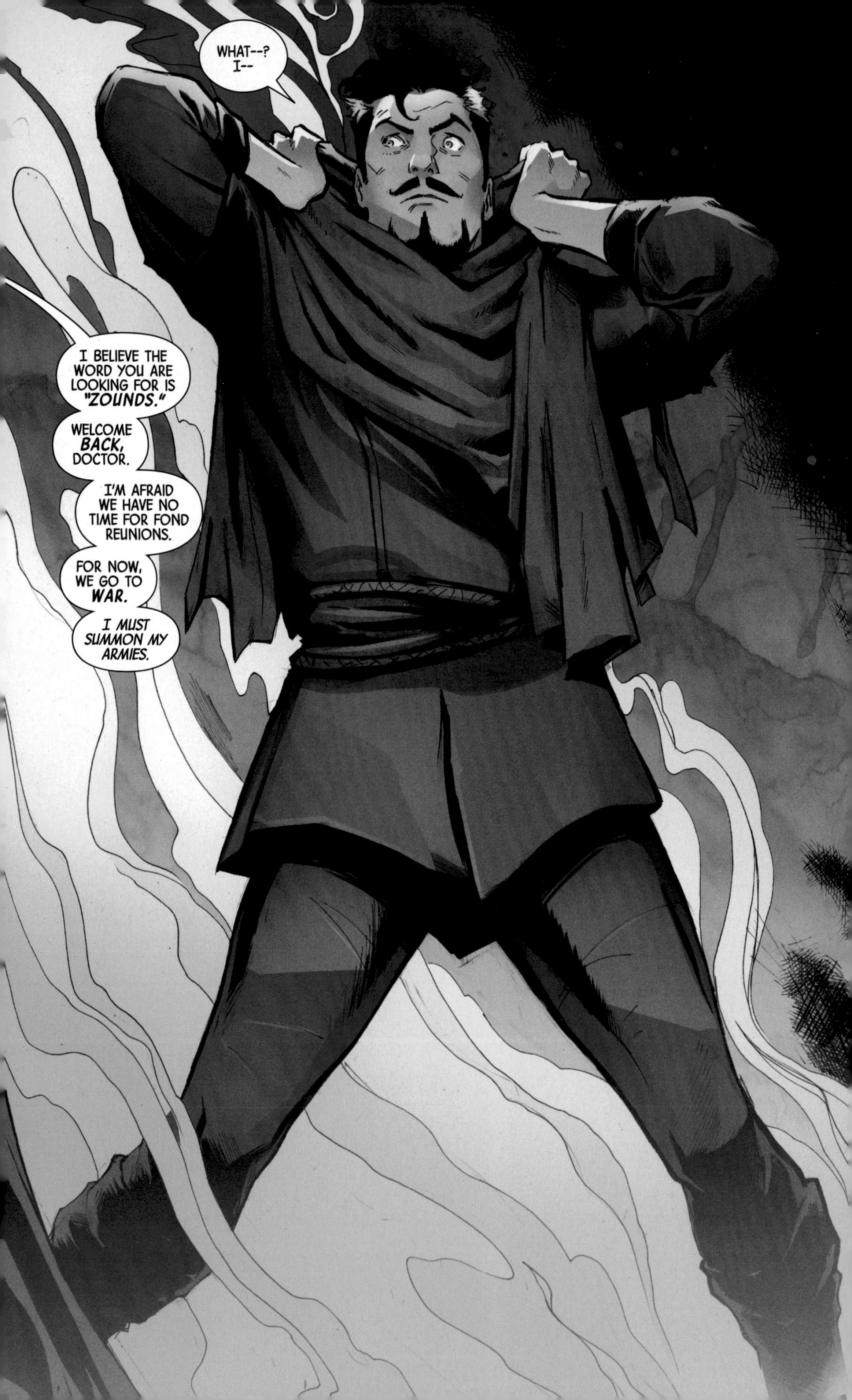
WHAT--? I--
I BELIEVE THE WORD YOU ARE LOOKING FOR IS "ZOUNDS."
WELCOME BACK, DOCTOR.
I'M AFRAID WE HAVE NO TIME FOR FOND REUNIONS.
FOR NOW, WE GO TO WAR.
I MUST SUMMON MY ARMIES.

CHAPTER TWELVE

The Battle of Antarctica

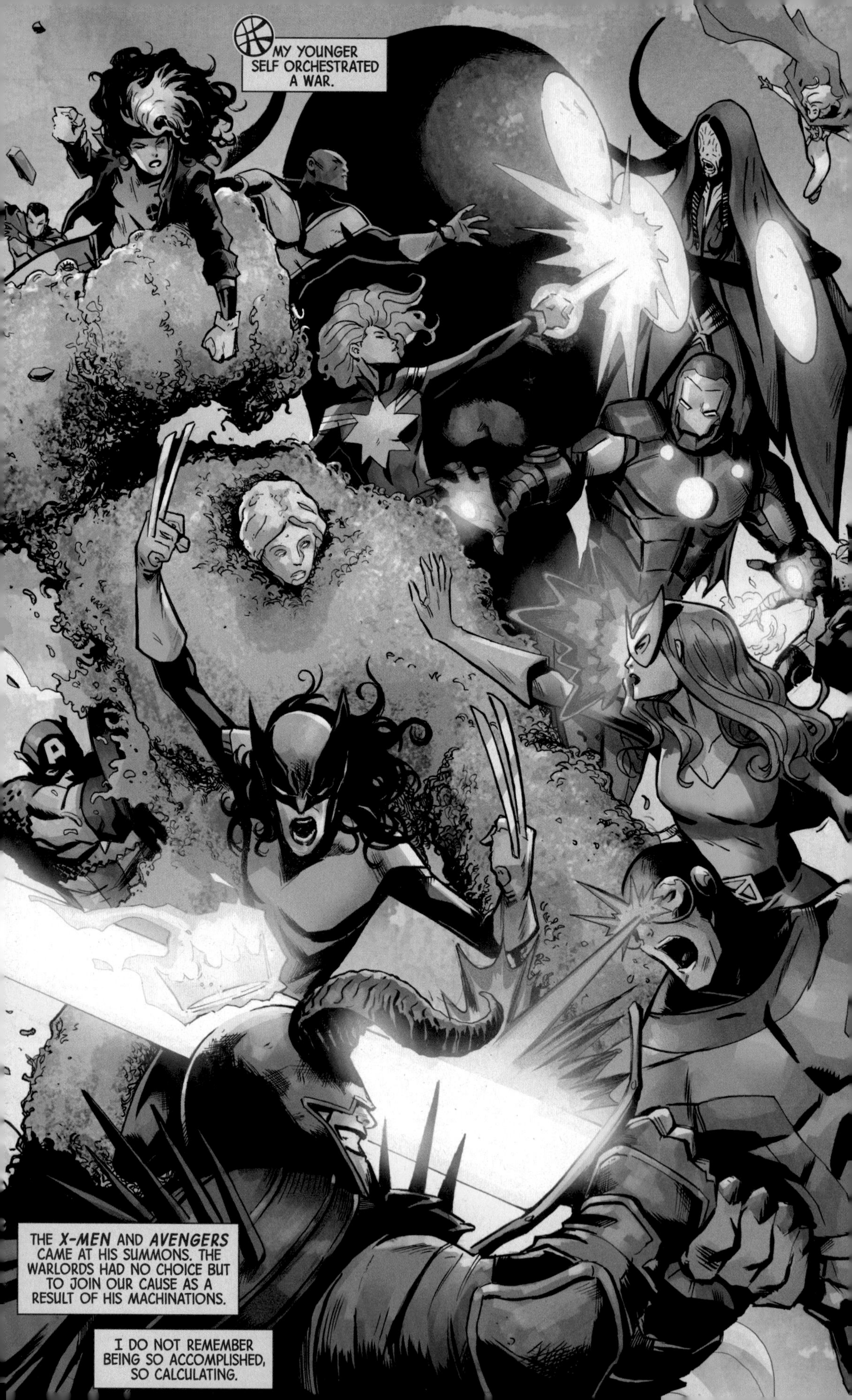
MY YOUNGER SELF ORCHESTRATED A WAR.
THE X-MEN AND AVENGERS CAME AT HIS SUMMONS. THE WARLORDS HAD NO CHOICE BUT TO JOIN OUR CAUSE AS A RESULT OF HIS MACHINATIONS.
I DO NOT REMEMBER BEING SO ACCOMPLISHED, SO CALCULATING.

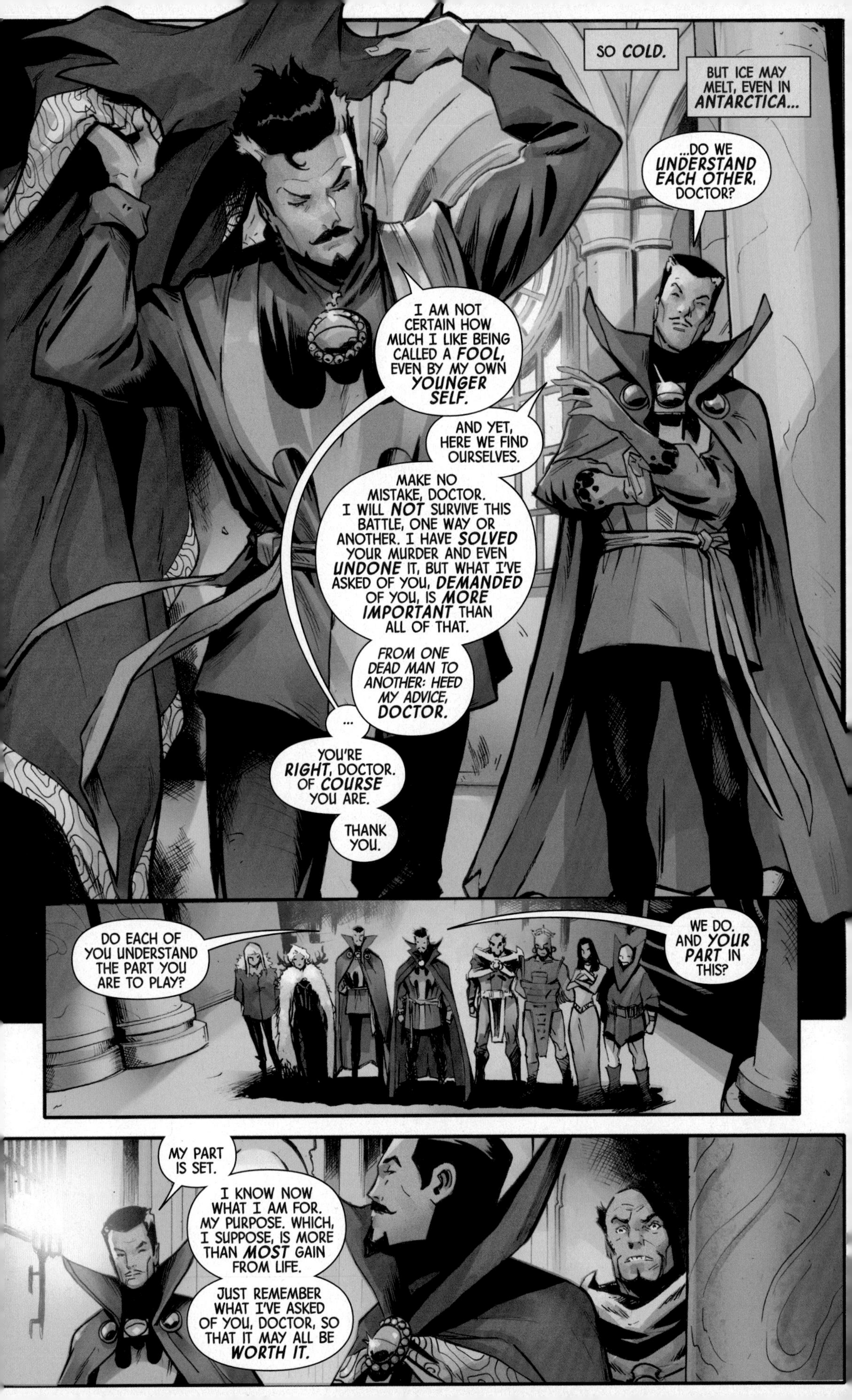
SO COLD.
BUT ICE MAY MELT, EVEN IN ANTARCTICA...
...DO WE UNDERSTAND EACH OTHER, DOCTOR?
I AM NOT CERTAIN HOW MUCH I LIKE BEING CALLED A FOOL, EVEN BY MY OWN YOUNGER SELF.
AND YET, HERE WE FIND OURSELVES.
MAKE NO MISTAKE, DOCTOR. I WILL NOT SURVIVE THIS BATTLE, ONE WAY OR ANOTHER. I HAVE SOLVED YOUR MURDER AND EVEN UNDONE IT, BUT WHAT I'VE ASKED OF YOU, DEMANDED OF YOU, IS MORE IMPORTANT THAN ALL OF THAT.
FROM ONE DEAD MAN TO ANOTHER: HEED MY ADVICE, DOCTOR.
...
YOU'RE RIGHT, DOCTOR. OF COURSE YOU ARE.
THANK YOU.
DO EACH OF YOU UNDERSTAND THE PART YOU ARE TO PLAY?
WE DO. AND YOUR PART IN THIS?
MY PART IS SET.
I KNOW NOW WHAT I AM FOR. MY PURPOSE. WHICH, I SUPPOSE, IS MORE THAN MOST GAIN FROM LIFE.
JUST REMEMBER WHAT I'VE ASKED OF YOU, DOCTOR, SO THAT IT MAY ALL BE WORTH IT.

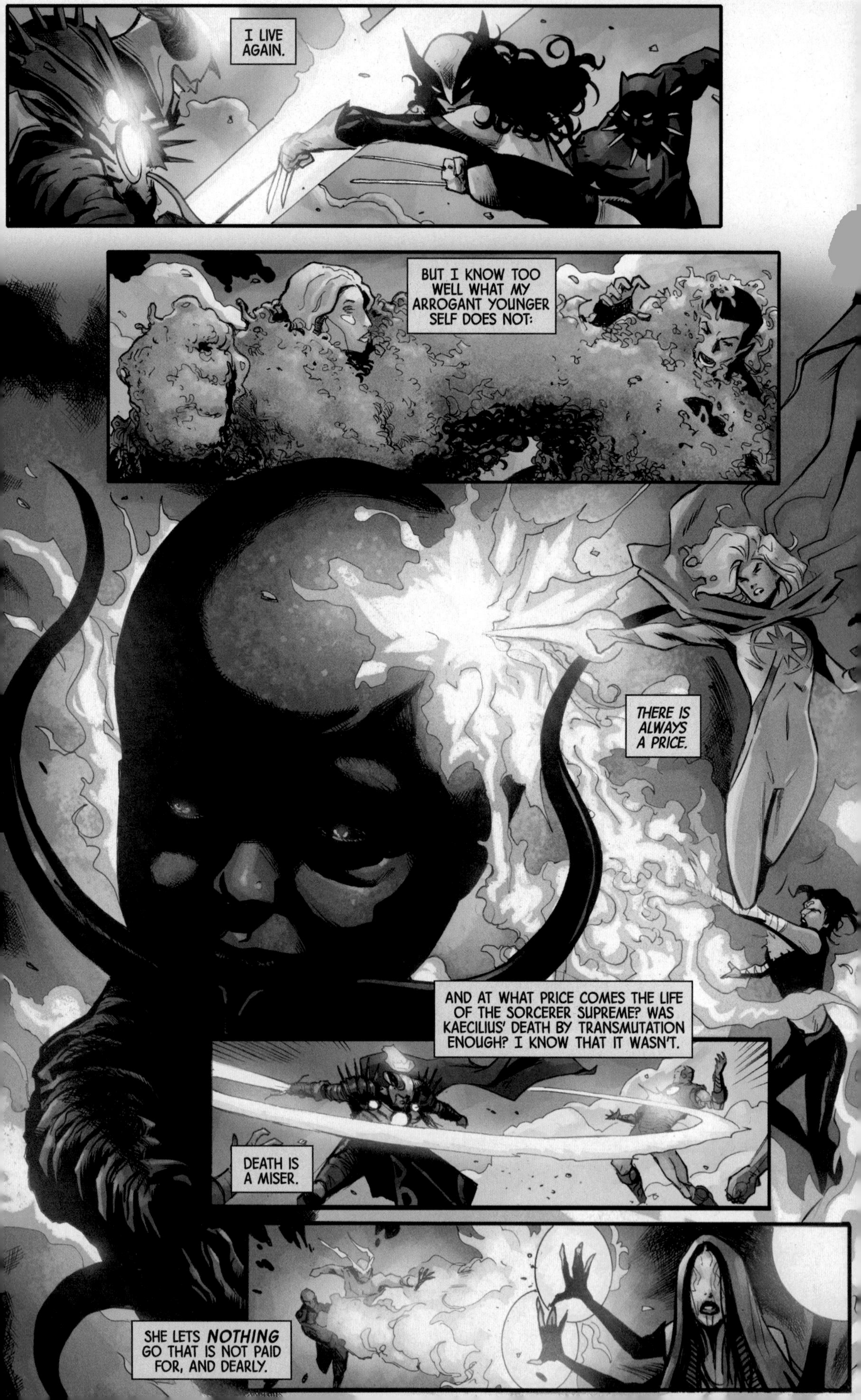
I LIVE AGAIN.
BUT I KNOW TOO WELL WHAT MY ARROGANT YOUNGER SELF DOES NOT:
THERE IS ALWAYS A PRICE.
AND AT WHAT PRICE COMES THE LIFE OF THE SORCERER SUPREME? WAS KAECILIUS' DEATH BY TRANSMUTATION ENOUGH? I KNOW THAT IT WASN'T.
DEATH IS A MISER.
SHE LETS *NOTHING* GO THAT IS NOT PAID FOR, AND DEARLY.

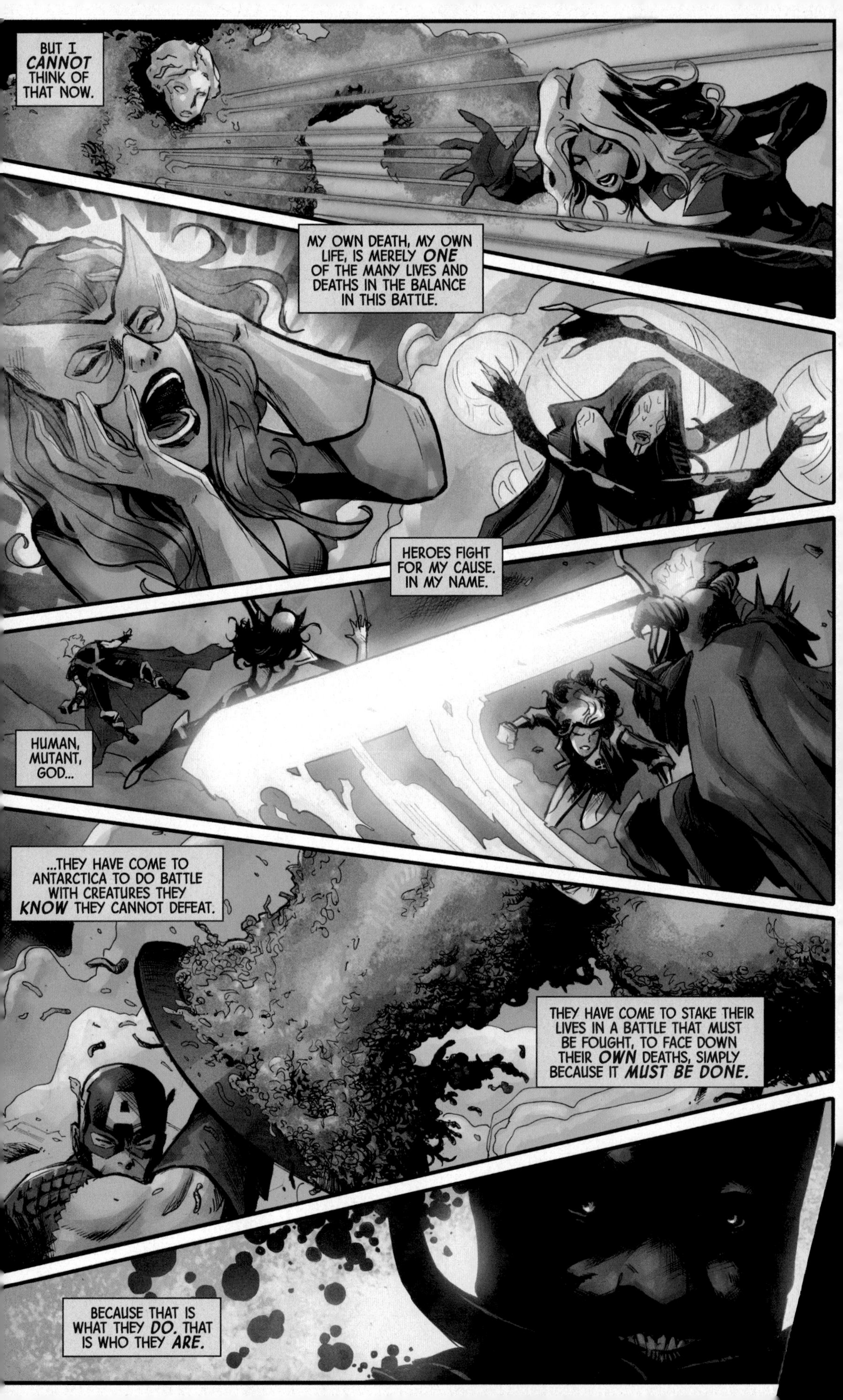

BUT I CANNOT THINK OF THAT NOW.
MY OWN DEATH, MY OWN LIFE, IS MERELY ONE OF THE MANY LIVES AND DEATHS IN THE BALANCE IN THIS BATTLE.
HEROES FIGHT FOR MY CAUSE. IN MY NAME.
HUMAN, MUTANT, GOD...
...THEY HAVE COME TO ANTARCTICA TO DO BATTLE WITH CREATURES THEY KNOW THEY CANNOT DEFEAT.
THEY HAVE COME TO STAKE THEIR LIVES IN A BATTLE THAT MUST BE FOUGHT, TO FACE DOWN THEIR OWN DEATHS, SIMPLY BECAUSE IT MUST BE DONE.
BECAUSE THAT IS WHAT THEY DO. THAT IS WHO THEY ARE.

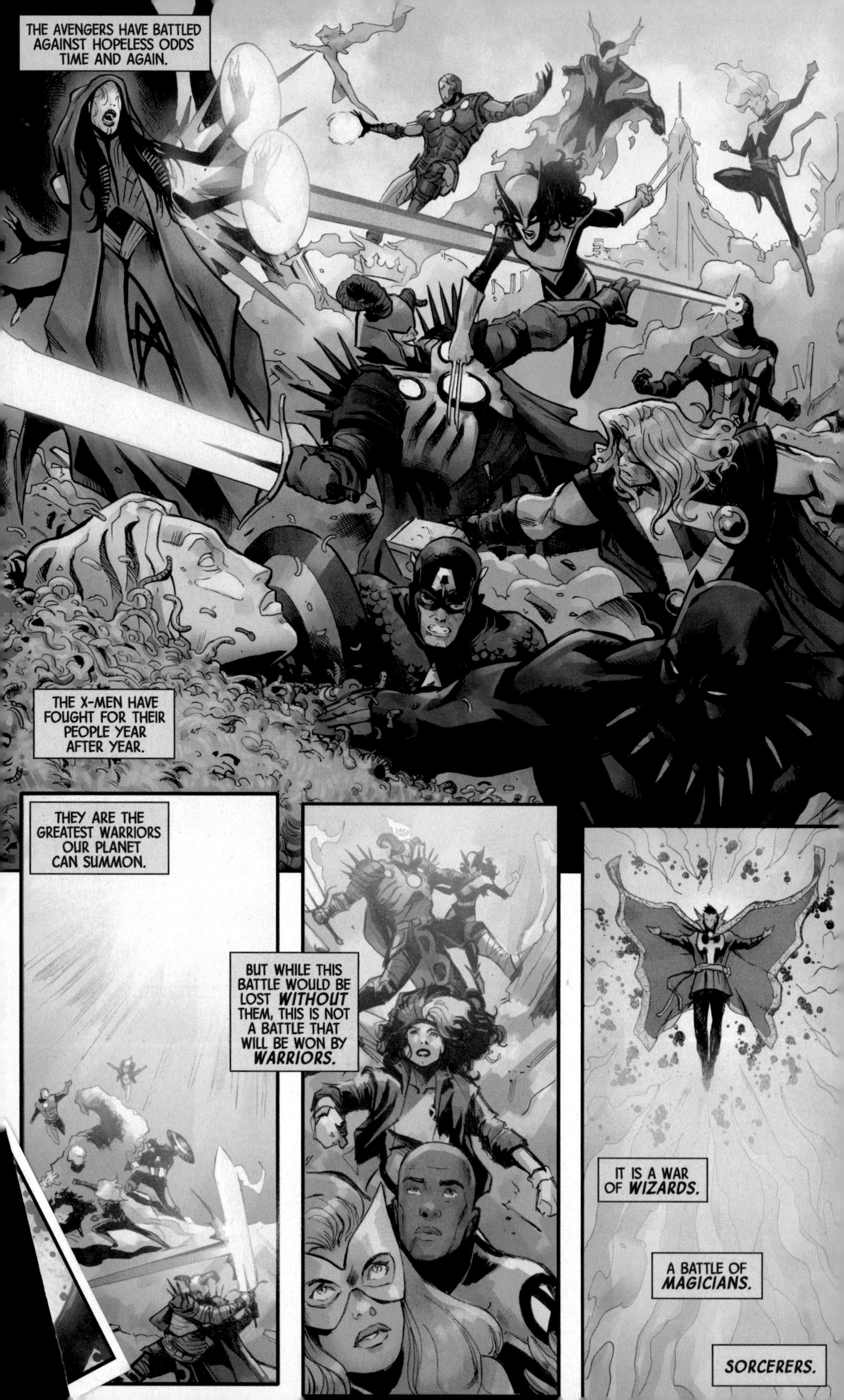
THE AVENGERS HAVE BATTLED AGAINST HOPELESS ODDS TIME AND AGAIN.
THE X-MEN HAVE FOUGHT FOR THEIR PEOPLE YEAR AFTER YEAR.
THEY ARE THE GREATEST WARRIORS OUR PLANET CAN SUMMON.
BUT WHILE THIS BATTLE WOULD BE LOST *WITHOUT* THEM, THIS IS NOT A BATTLE THAT WILL BE WON BY *WARRIORS*.
IT IS A WAR OF *WIZARDS*.
A BATTLE OF *MAGICIANS*.
SORCERERS.

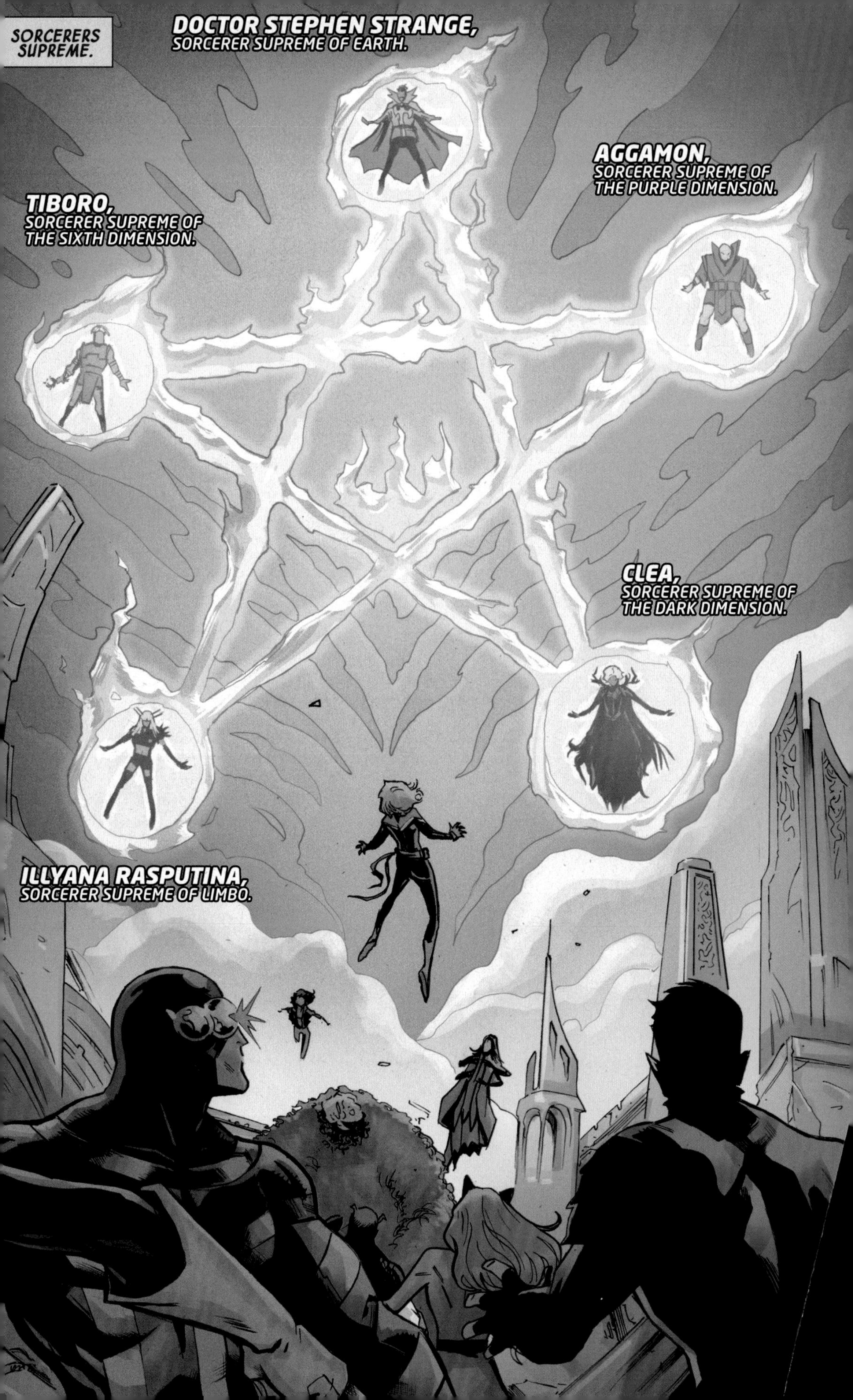
SORCERERS SUPREME.
DOCTOR STEPHEN STRANGE,
SORCERER SUPREME OF EARTH.
AGGAMON,
SORCERER SUPREME OF THE PURPLE DIMENSION.
TIBORO,
SORCERER SUPREME OF THE SIXTH DIMENSION.
CLEA,
SORCERER SUPREME OF THE DARK DIMENSION.
ILLYANA RASPUTINA,
SORCERER SUPREME OF LIMBO.

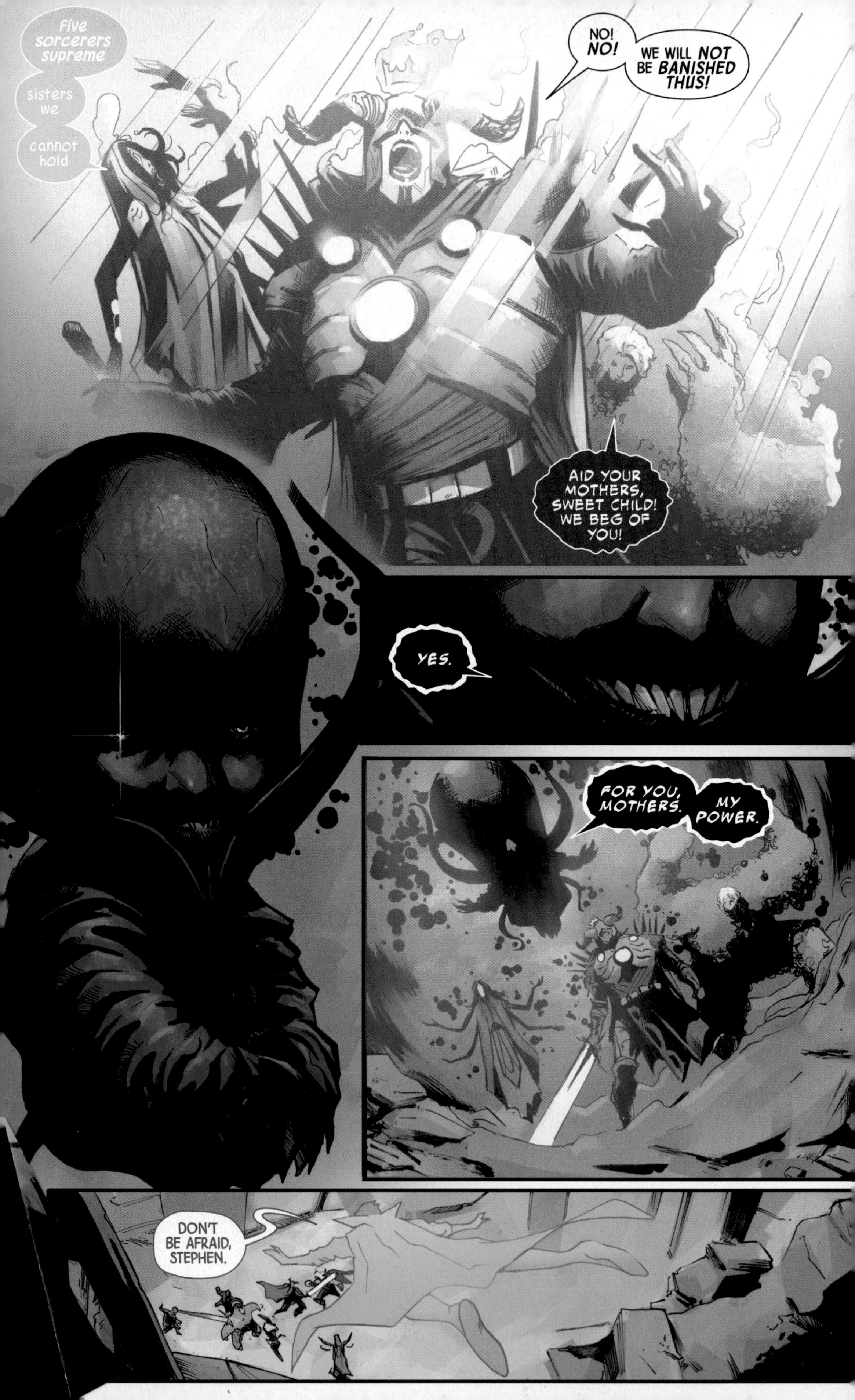
five sorcerers supreme
sisters we
cannot hold
NO! NO!
WE WILL NOT BE BANISHED THUS!
AID YOUR MOTHERS, SWEET CHILD! WE BEG OF YOU!
YES.
FOR YOU, MOTHERS.
MY POWER.
DON'T BE AFRAID, STEPHEN.

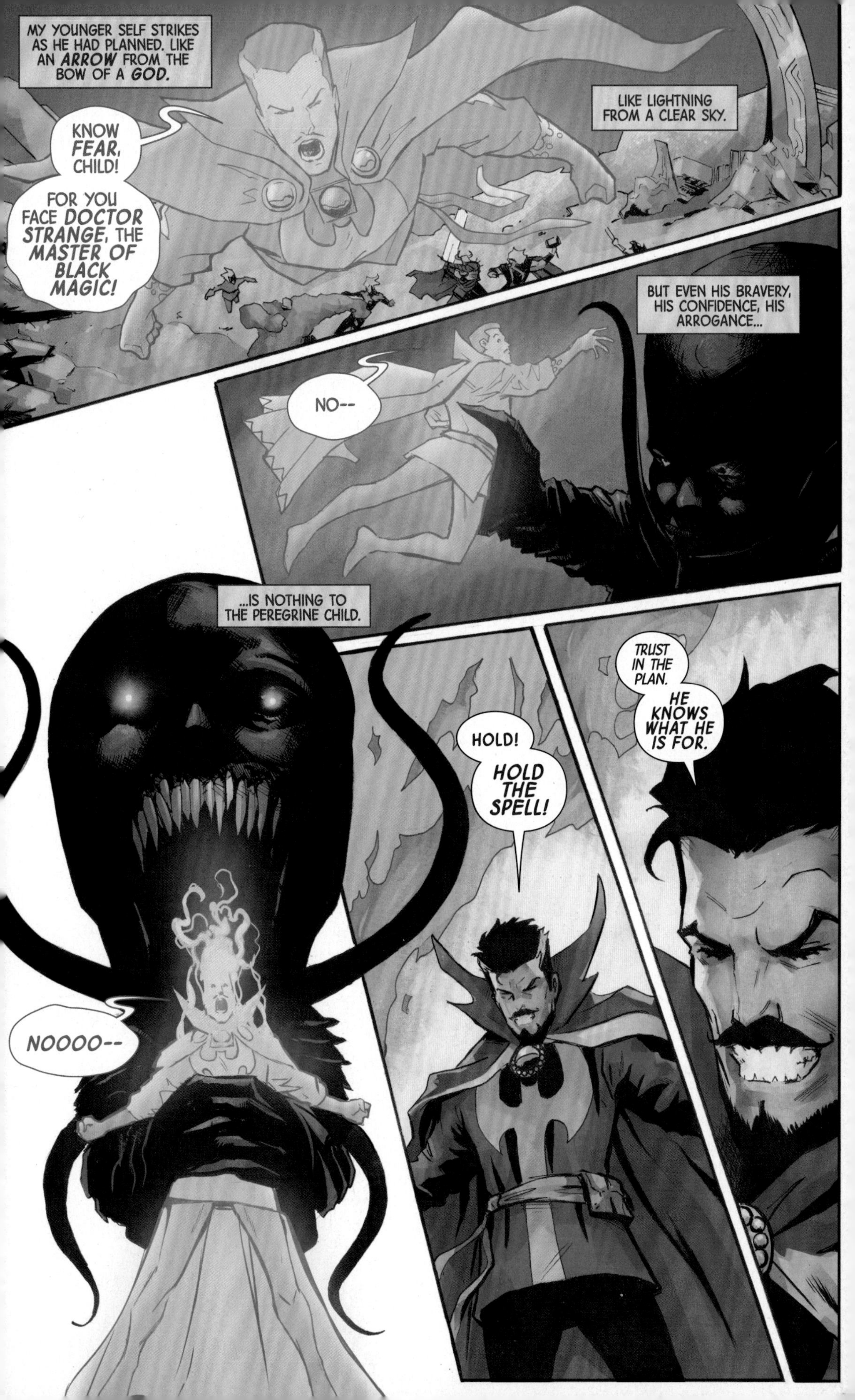
MY YOUNGER SELF STRIKES AS HE HAD PLANNED. LIKE AN ARROW FROM THE BOW OF A GOD.
KNOW FEAR, CHILD!
FOR YOU FACE DOCTOR STRANGE, THE MASTER OF BLACK MAGIC!
LIKE LIGHTNING FROM A CLEAR SKY.
BUT EVEN HIS BRAVERY, HIS CONFIDENCE, HIS ARROGANCE...
NO--
...IS NOTHING TO THE PEREGRINE CHILD.
NOOOO--
HOLD!
HOLD THE SPELL!
TRUST IN THE PLAN.
HE KNOWS WHAT HE IS FOR.

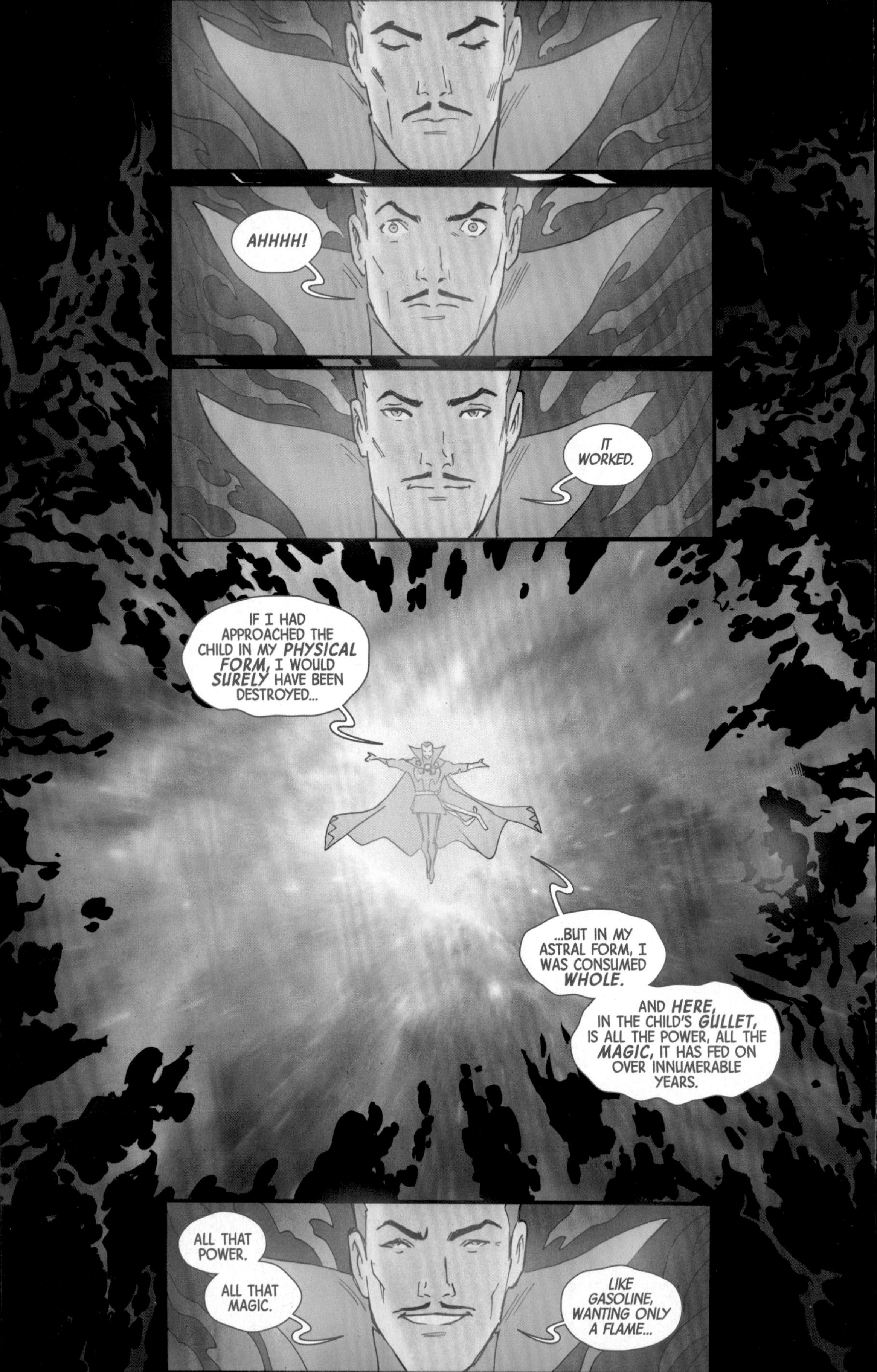
AHHHH!
IT WORKED.
IF I HAD APPROACHED THE CHILD IN MY PHYSICAL FORM, I WOULD SURELY HAVE BEEN DESTROYED...
...BUT IN MY ASTRAL FORM, I WAS CONSUMED WHOLE.
AND HERE, IN THE CHILD'S GULLET, IS ALL THE POWER, ALL THE MAGIC, IT HAS FED ON OVER INNUMERABLE YEARS.
ALL THAT POWER.
ALL THAT MAGIC.
LIKE GASOLINE, WANTING ONLY A FLAME...

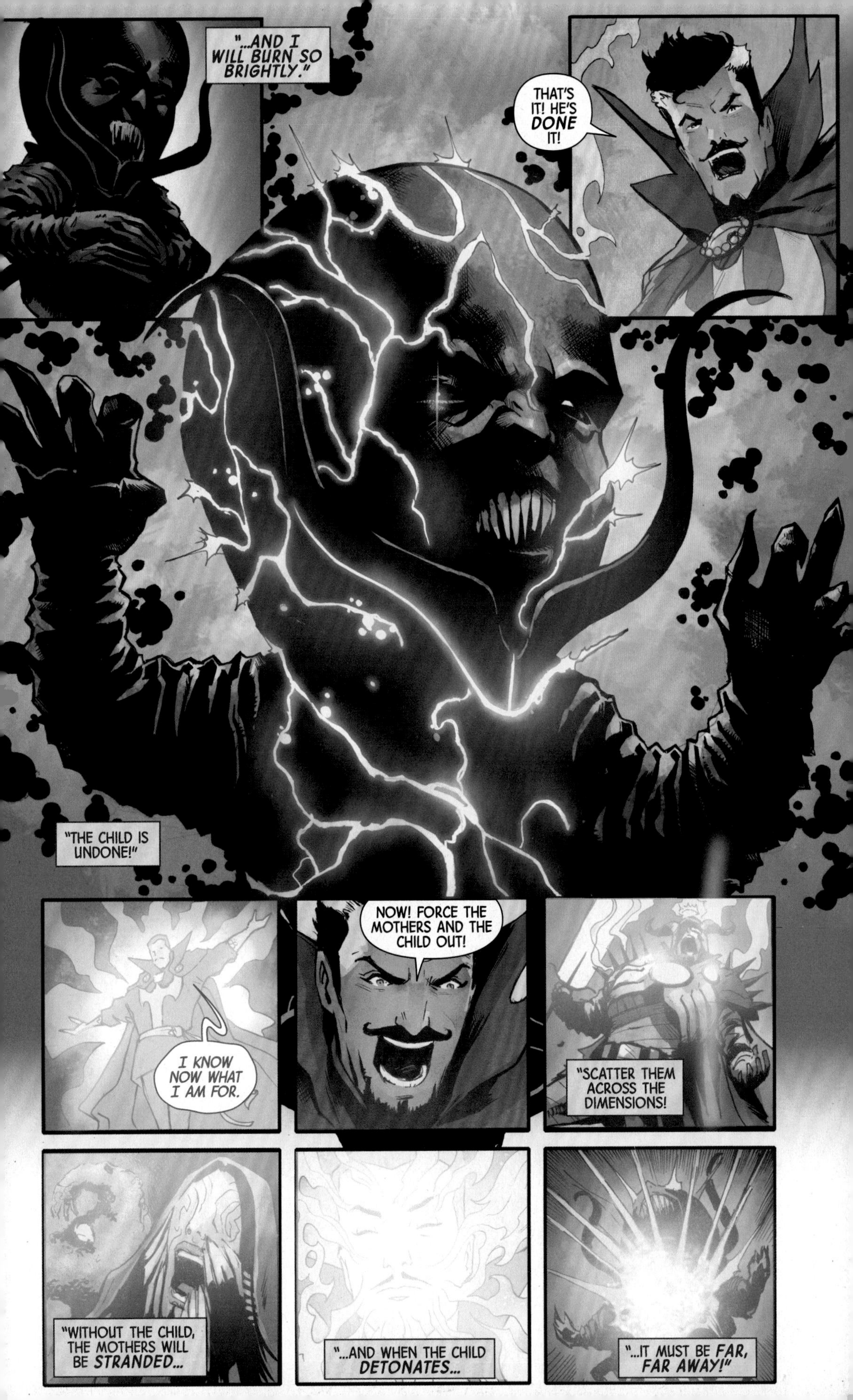
"...AND I WILL BURN SO BRIGHTLY."
THAT'S IT! HE'S DONE IT!
"THE CHILD IS UNDONE!"
I KNOW NOW WHAT I AM FOR.
NOW! FORCE THE MOTHERS AND THE CHILD OUT!
"SCATTER THEM ACROSS THE DIMENSIONS!
"WITHOUT THE CHILD, THE MOTHERS WILL BE STRANDED...
"...AND WHEN THE CHILD DETONATES...
"...IT MUST BE FAR, FAR AWAY!"

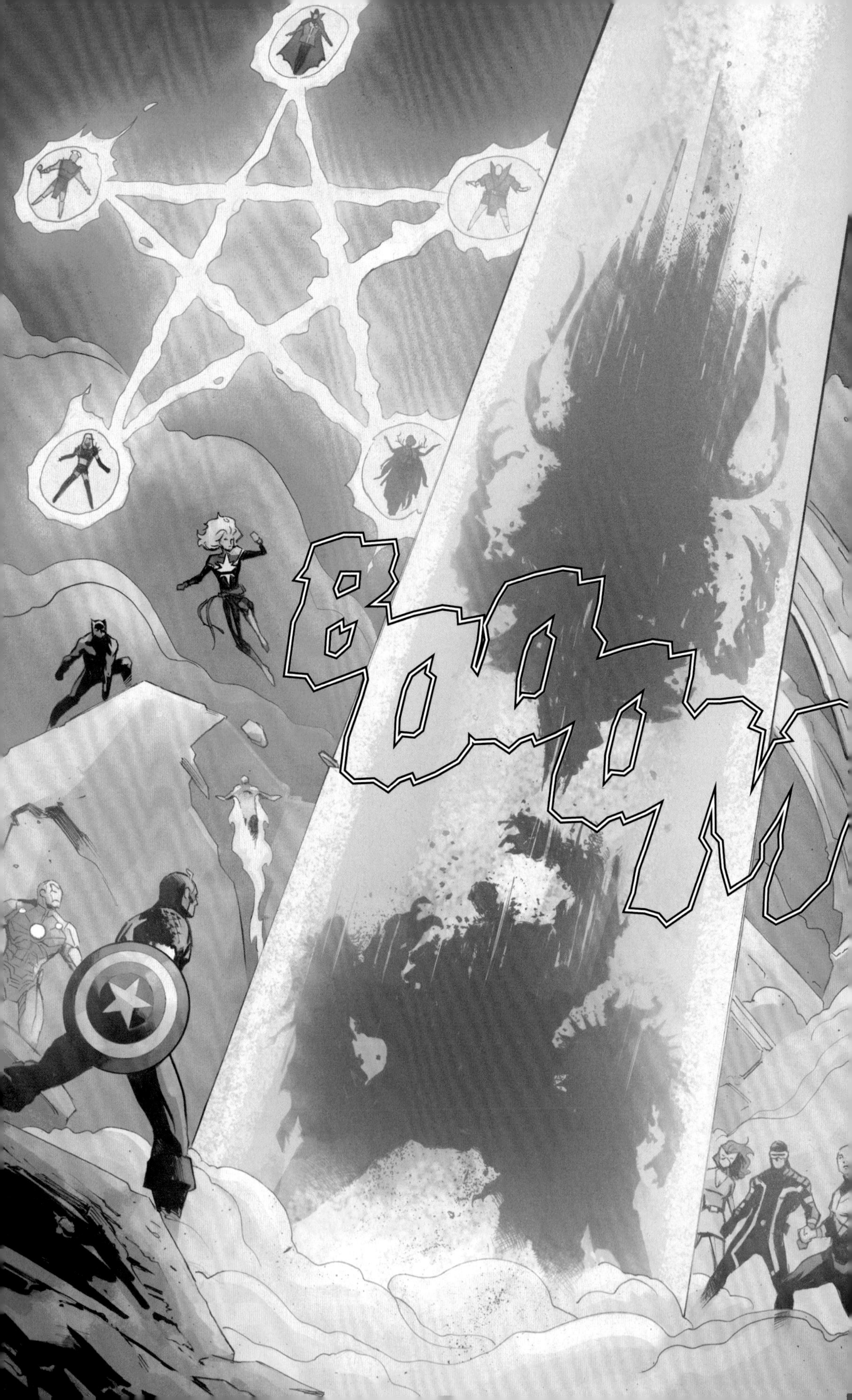
BOOOOM

CHAPTER THIRTEEN

The Death of Doctor Strange

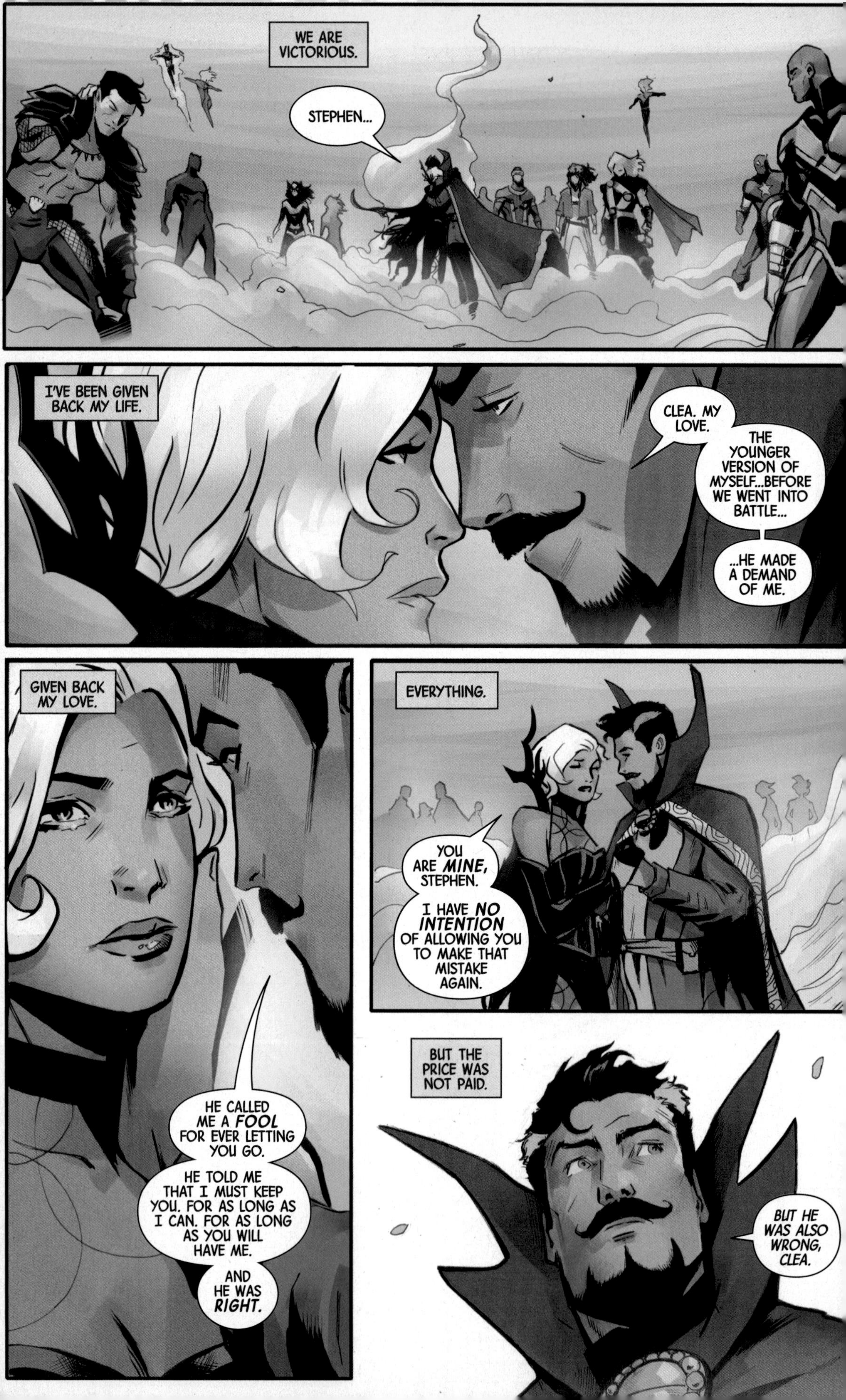
WE ARE VICTORIOUS.
STEPHEN...
I'VE BEEN GIVEN BACK MY LIFE.
CLEA. MY LOVE.
THE YOUNGER VERSION OF MYSELF...BEFORE WE WENT INTO BATTLE...
...HE MADE A DEMAND OF ME.
GIVEN BACK MY LOVE.
HE CALLED ME A FOOL FOR EVER LETTING YOU GO.
HE TOLD ME THAT I MUST KEEP YOU. FOR AS LONG AS I CAN. FOR AS LONG AS YOU WILL HAVE ME.
AND HE WAS RIGHT.
EVERYTHING.
YOU ARE MINE, STEPHEN.
I HAVE NO INTENTION OF ALLOWING YOU TO MAKE THAT MISTAKE AGAIN.
BUT THE PRICE WAS NOT PAID.
BUT HE WAS ALSO WRONG, CLEA.

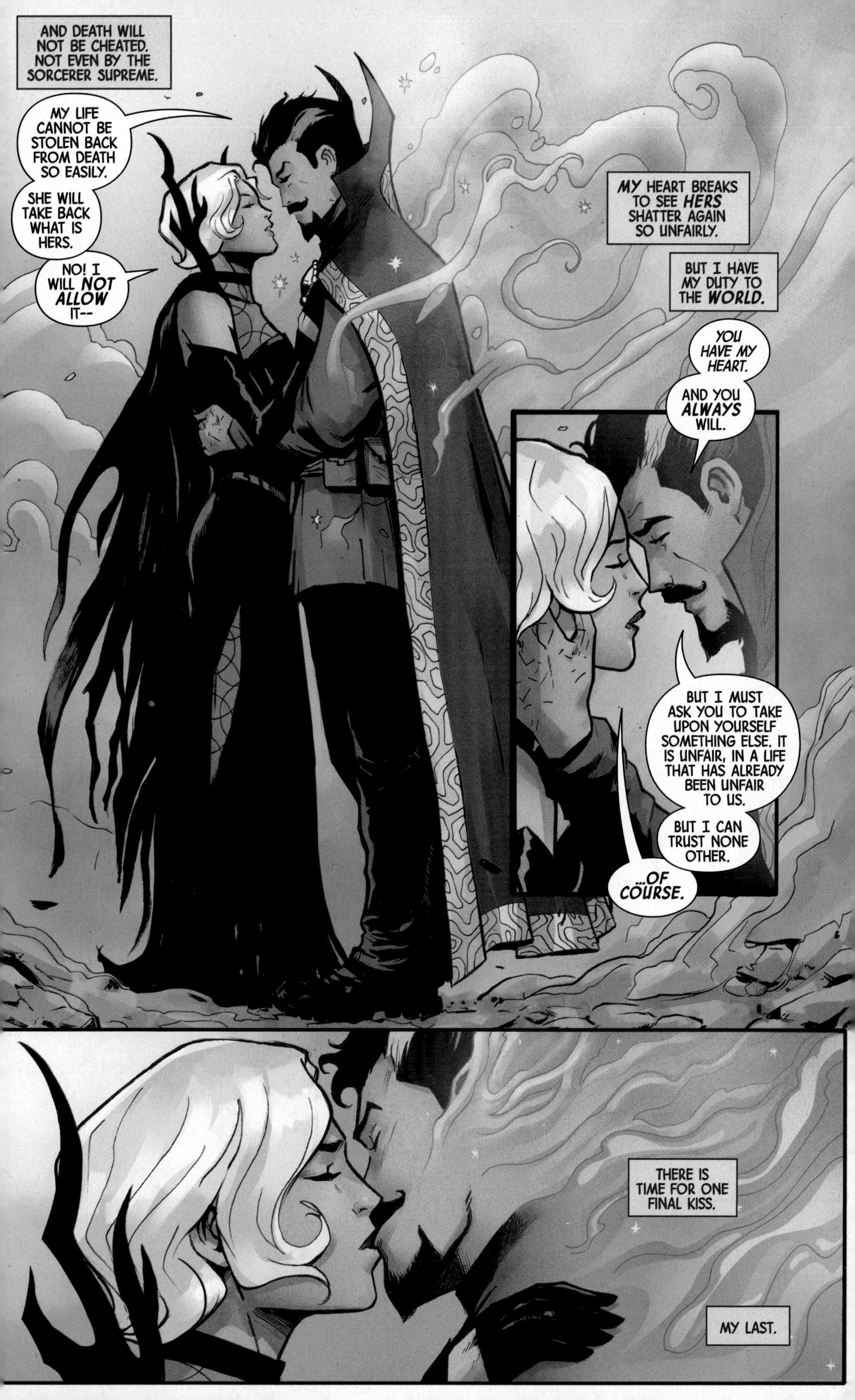
AND DEATH WILL NOT BE CHEATED. NOT EVEN BY THE SORCERER SUPREME.
MY LIFE CANNOT BE STOLEN BACK FROM DEATH SO EASILY.
SHE WILL TAKE BACK WHAT IS HERS.
NO! I WILL NOT ALLOW IT--
MY HEART BREAKS TO SEE HERS SHATTER AGAIN SO UNFAIRLY.
BUT I HAVE MY DUTY TO THE WORLD.
YOU HAVE MY HEART.
AND YOU ALWAYS WILL.
BUT I MUST ASK YOU TO TAKE UPON YOURSELF SOMETHING ELSE. IT IS UNFAIR, IN A LIFE THAT HAS ALREADY BEEN UNFAIR TO US.
BUT I CAN TRUST NONE OTHER.
...OF COURSE.
THERE IS TIME FOR ONE FINAL KISS.
MY LAST.

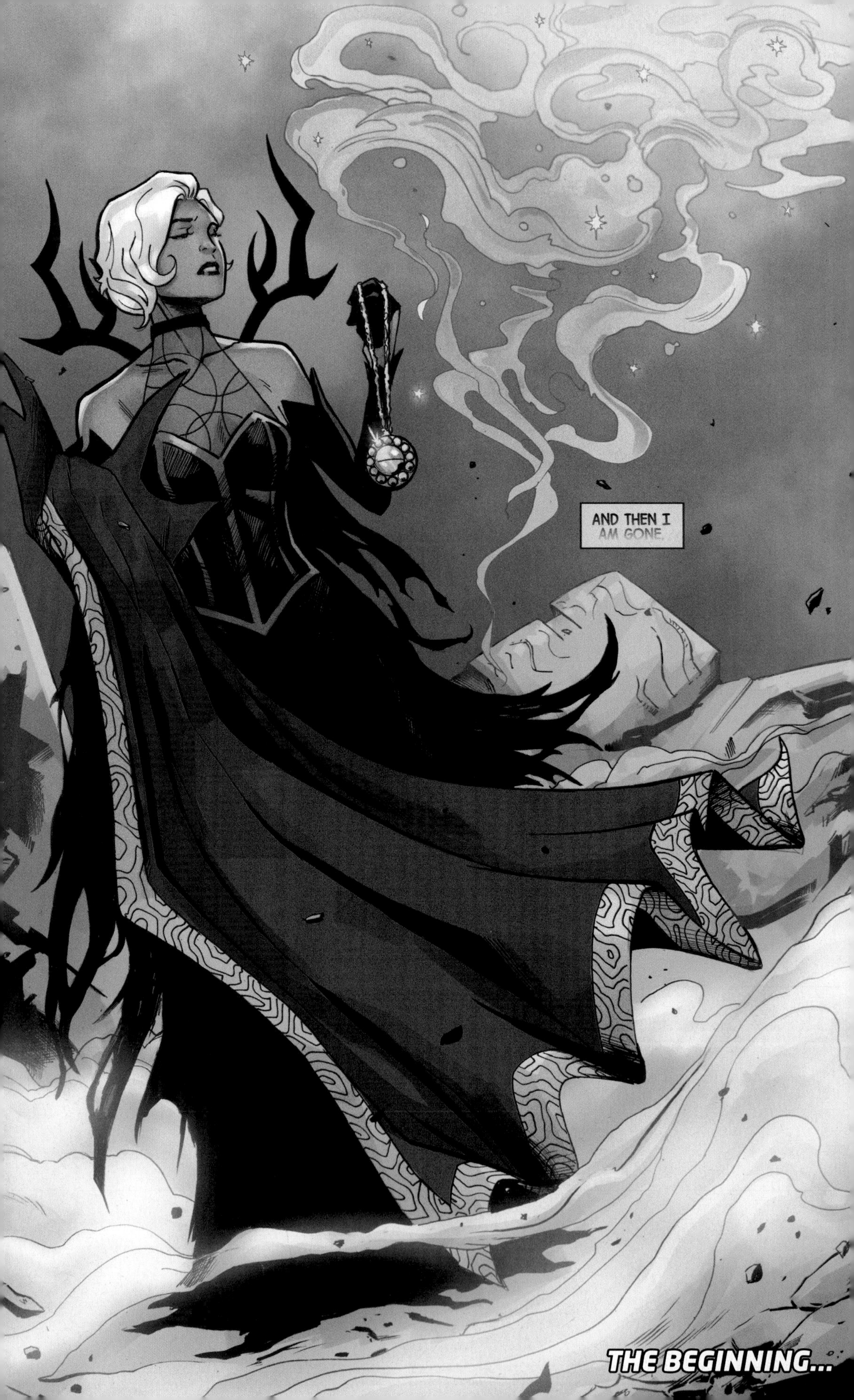
AND THEN I AM GONE.
THE BEGINNING...

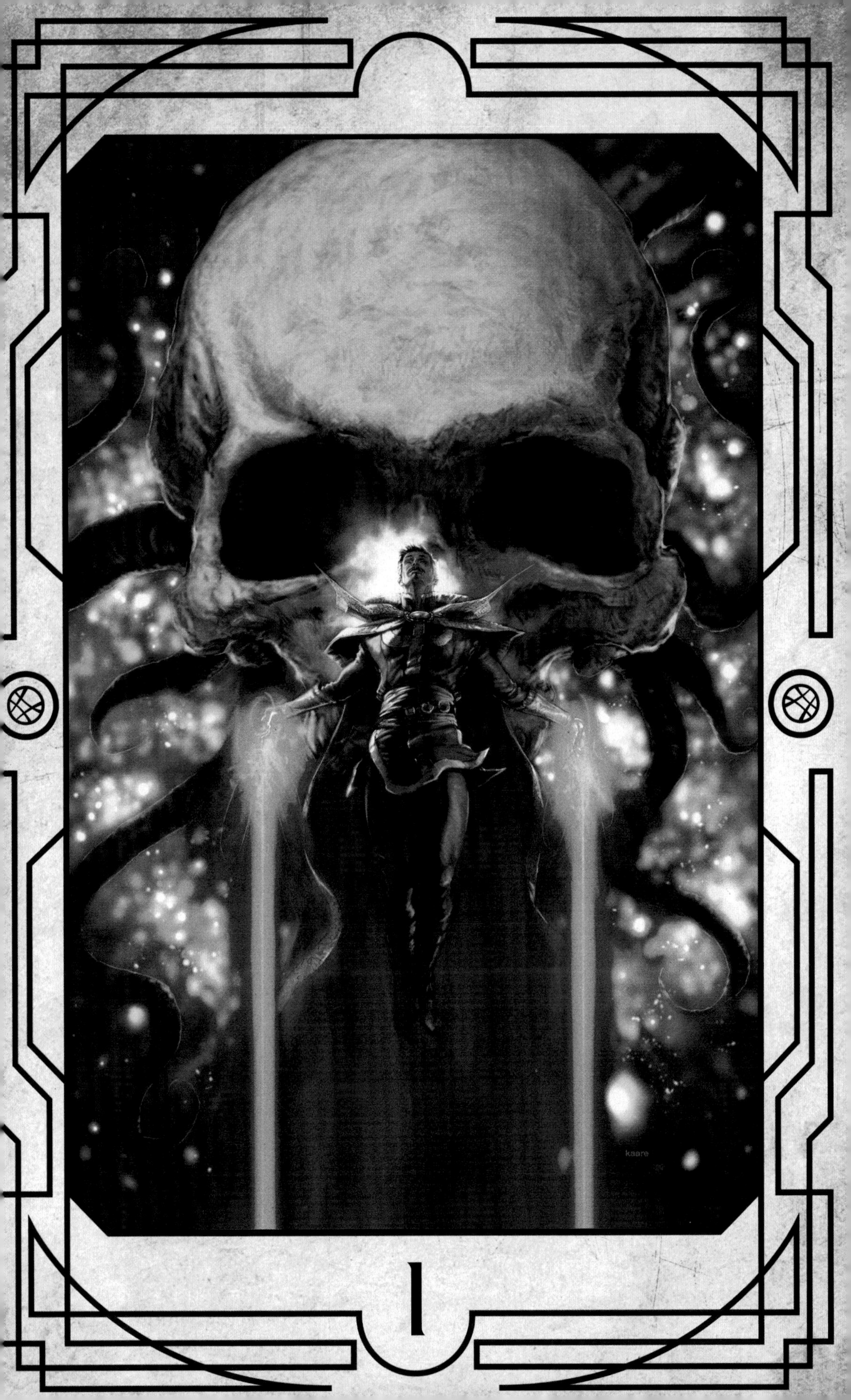
kaare
I

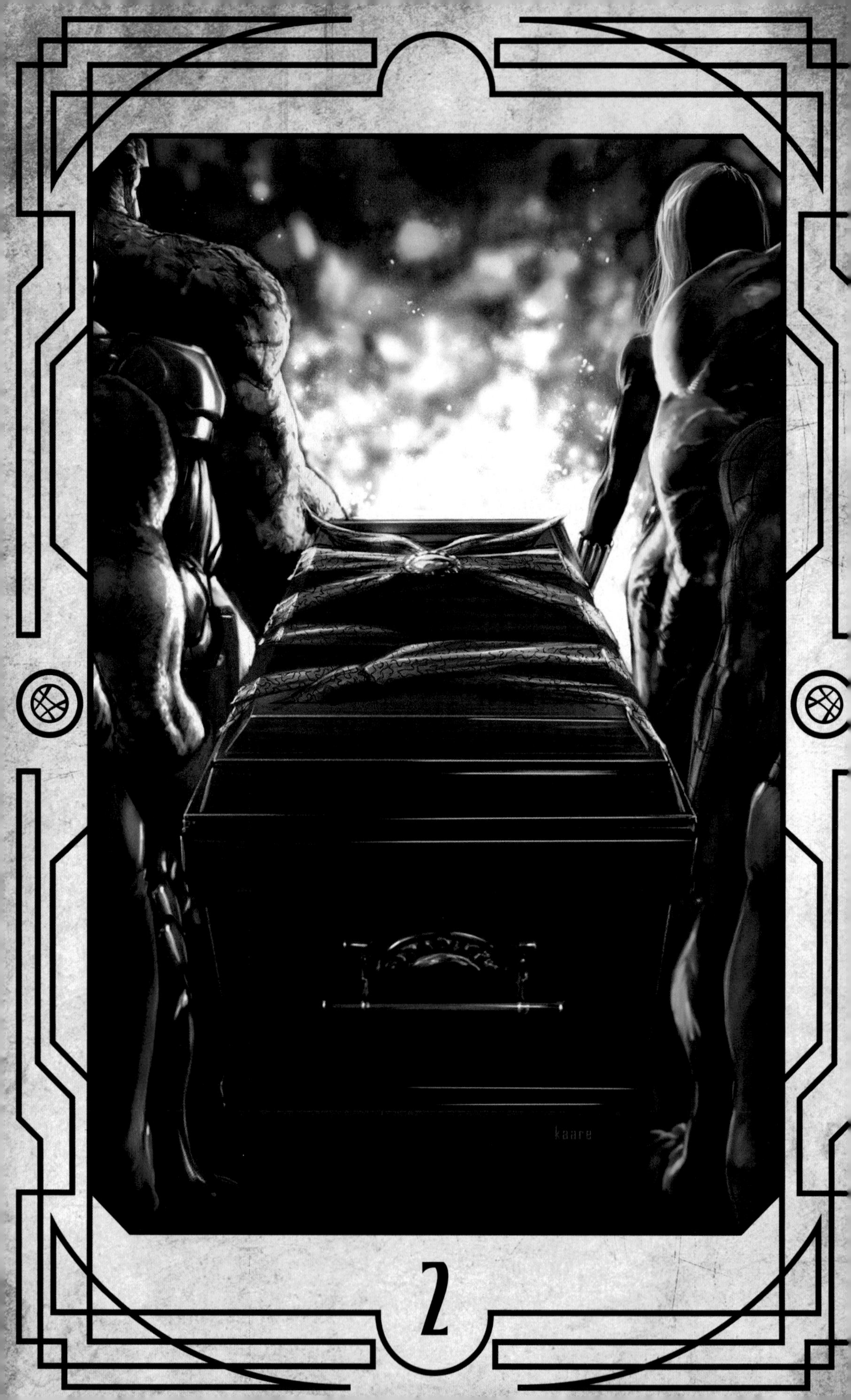
kaare
2

HERE LIES
STEPHEN
STRANGE

3

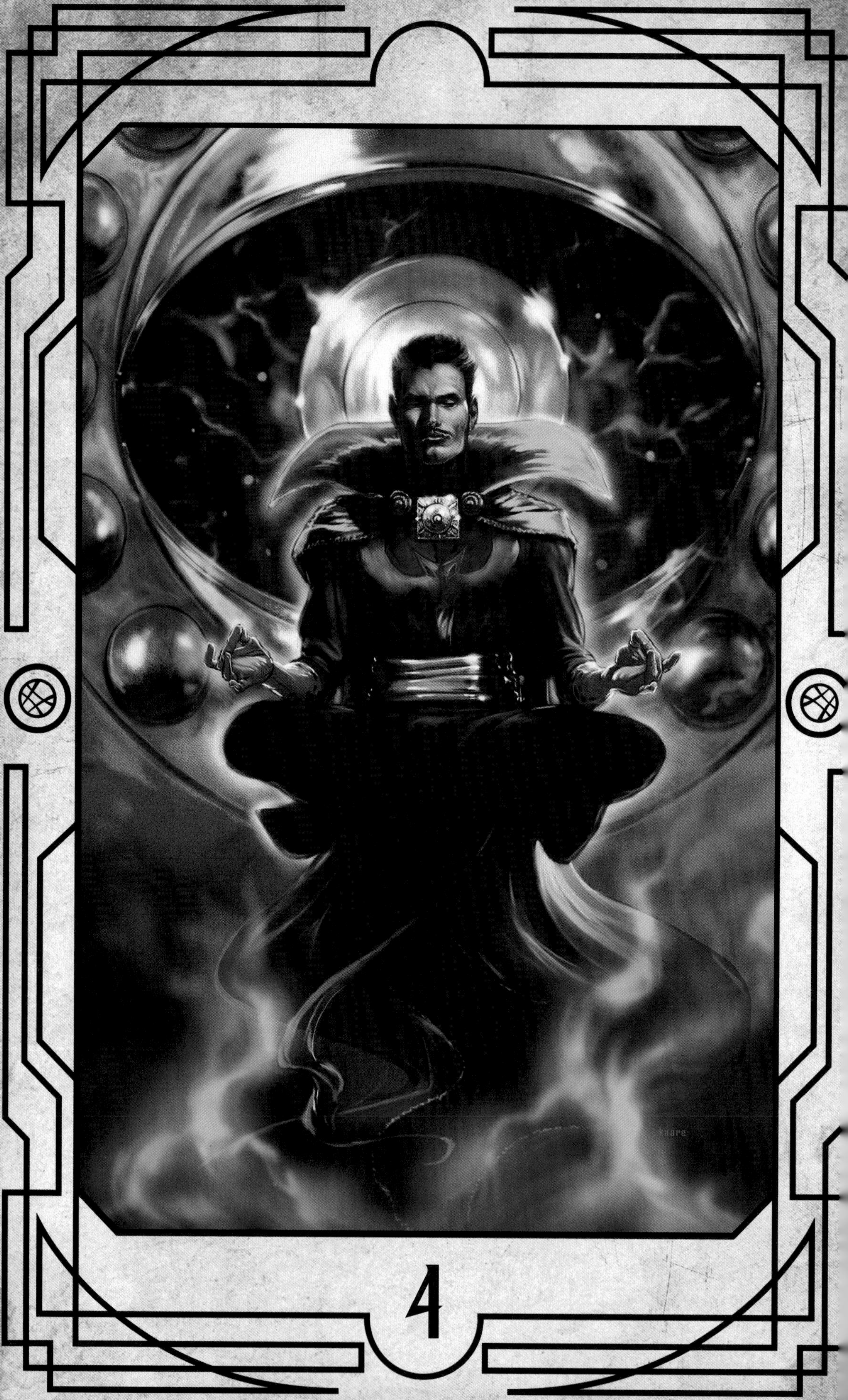
4

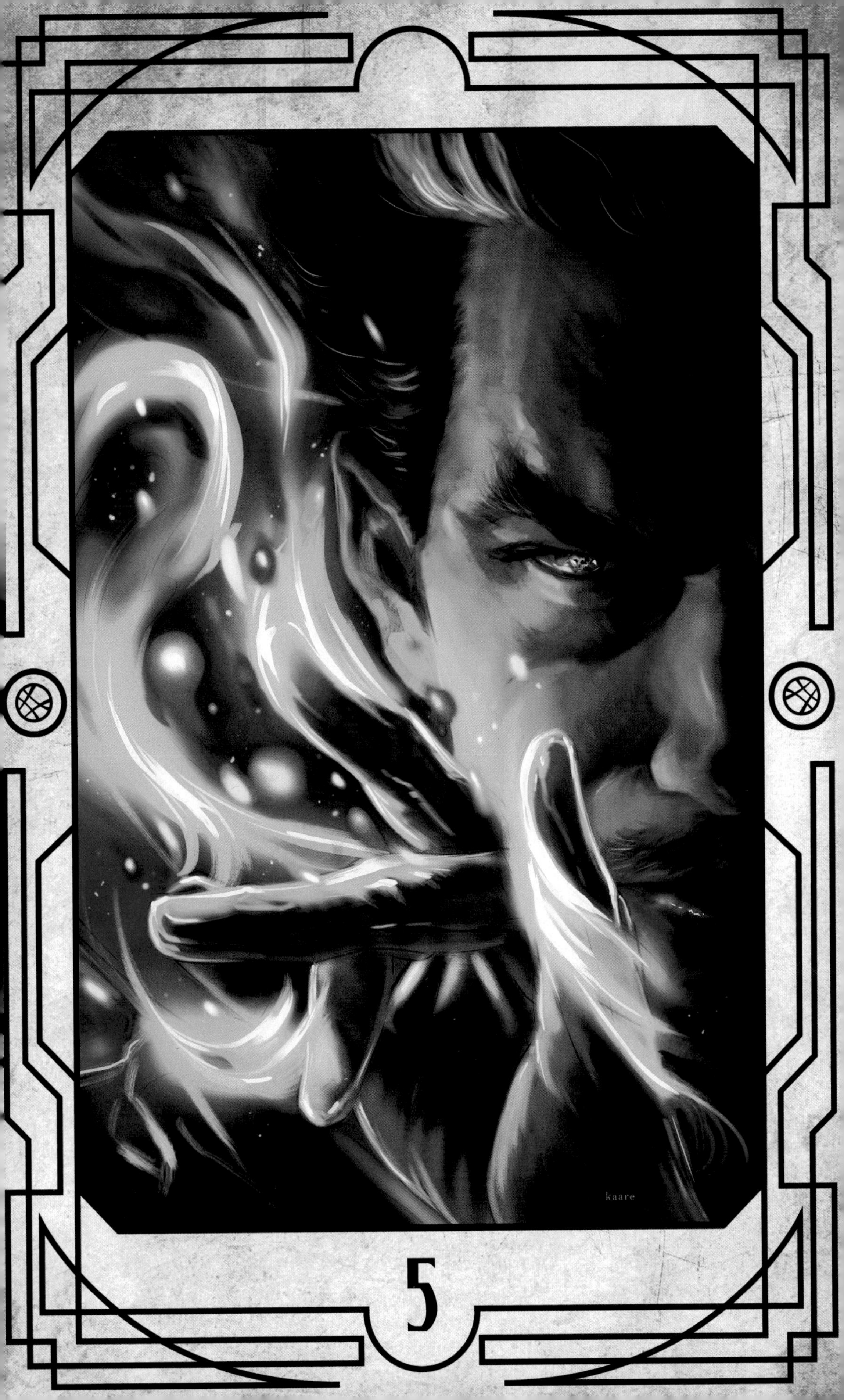
kaare

5

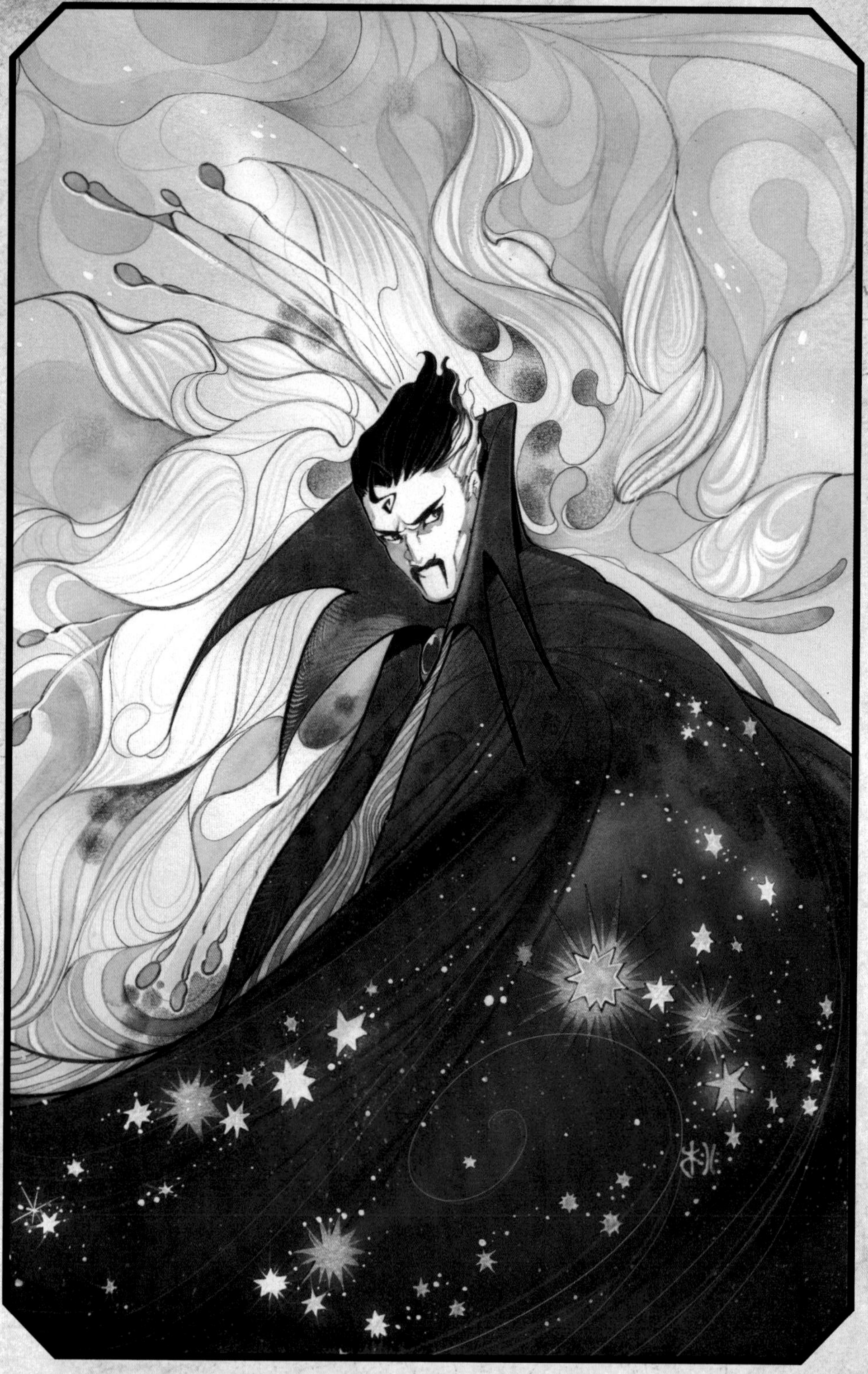

Peach Momoko

#1 VARIANT

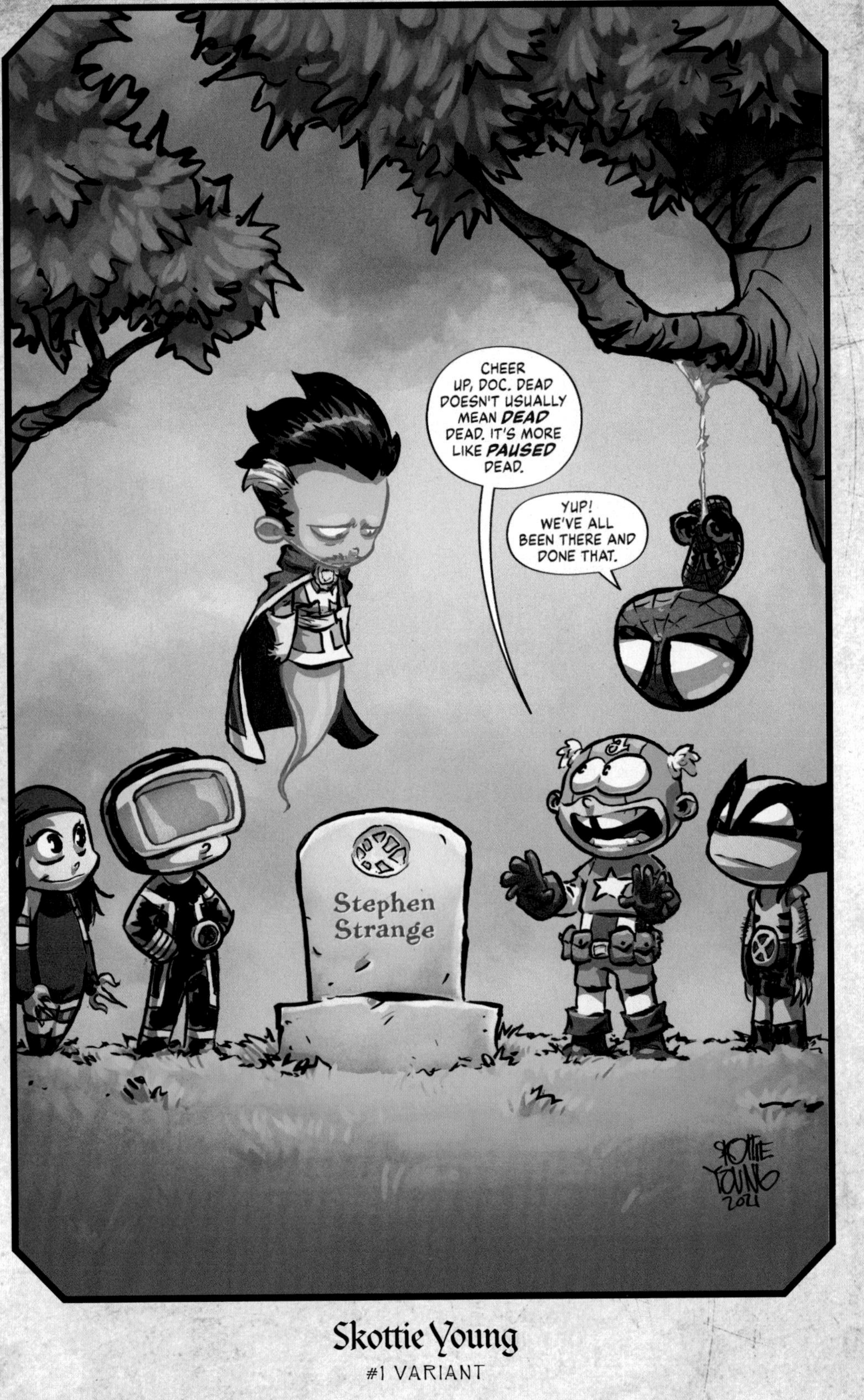
CHEER UP, DOC. DEAD DOESN'T USUALLY MEAN DEAD DEAD. IT'S MORE LIKE PAUSED DEAD.
YUP! WE'VE ALL BEEN THERE AND DONE THAT.
Stephen Strange
SKOTTIE YOUNG 2021

Skottie Young

#1 VARIANT

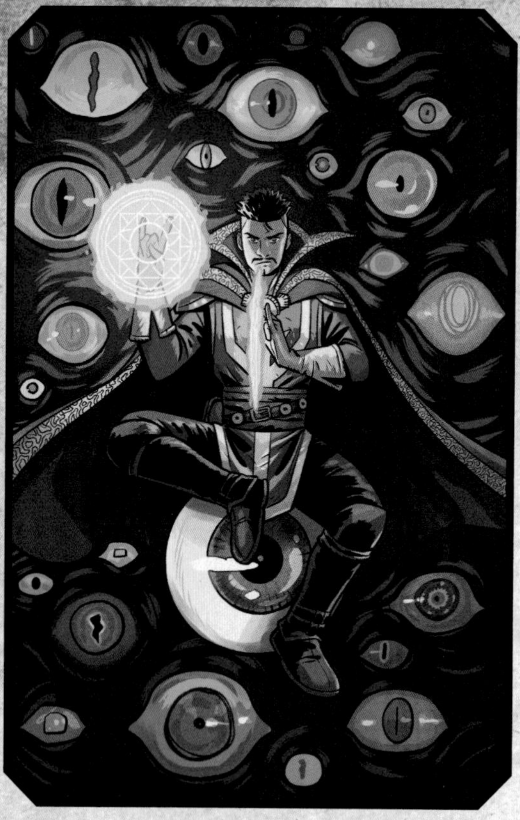

Natacha Bustos
#1 STORMBREAKERS VARIANT

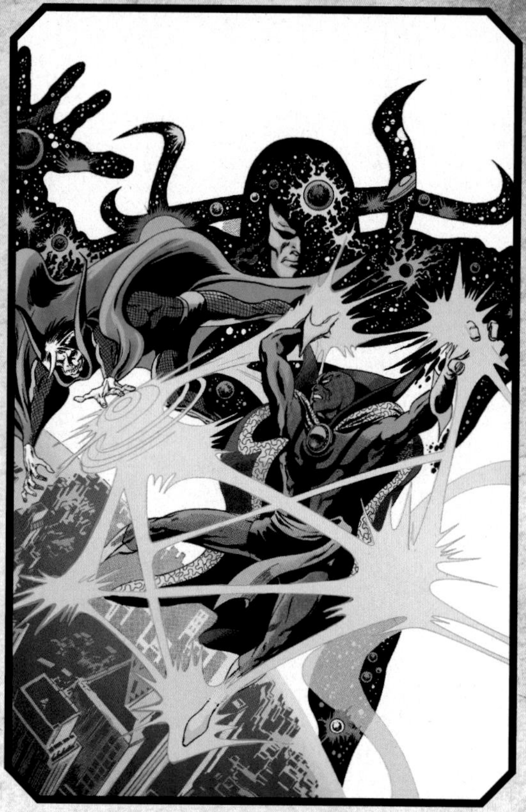

Gene Colan
#1 HIDDEN GEM VARIANT

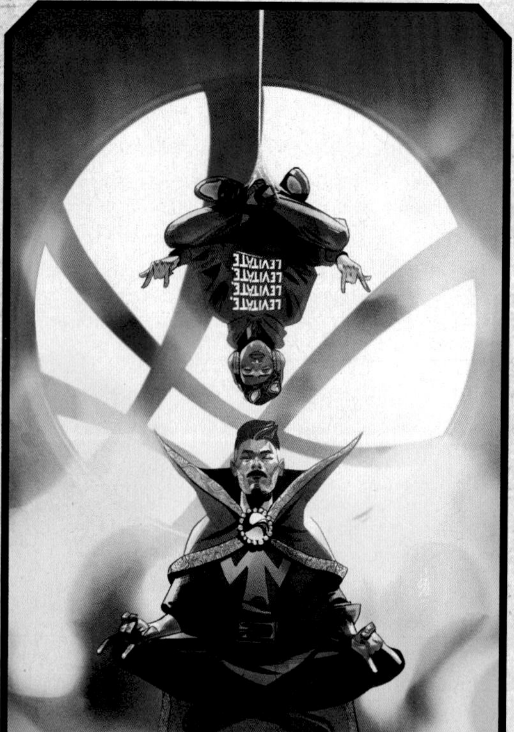

Mike Del Mundo
#1 MILES MORALES 10TH ANNIVERSARY VARIANT

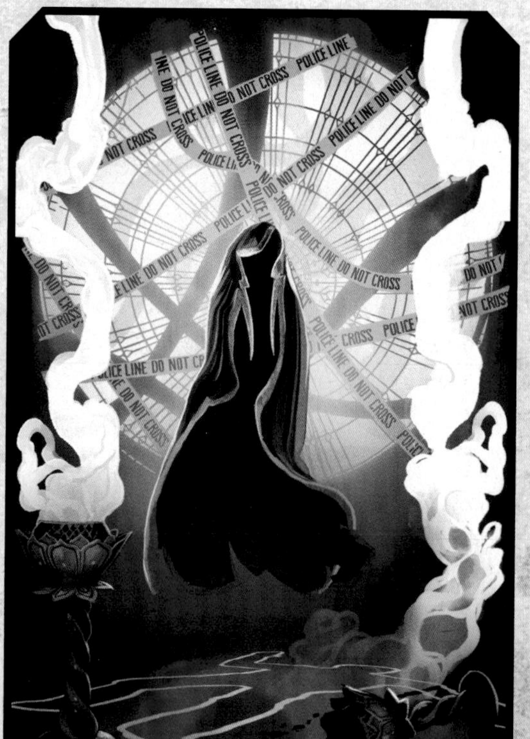
POLICE LINE DO NOT CROSS

Stephanie Hans
#1 VARIANT

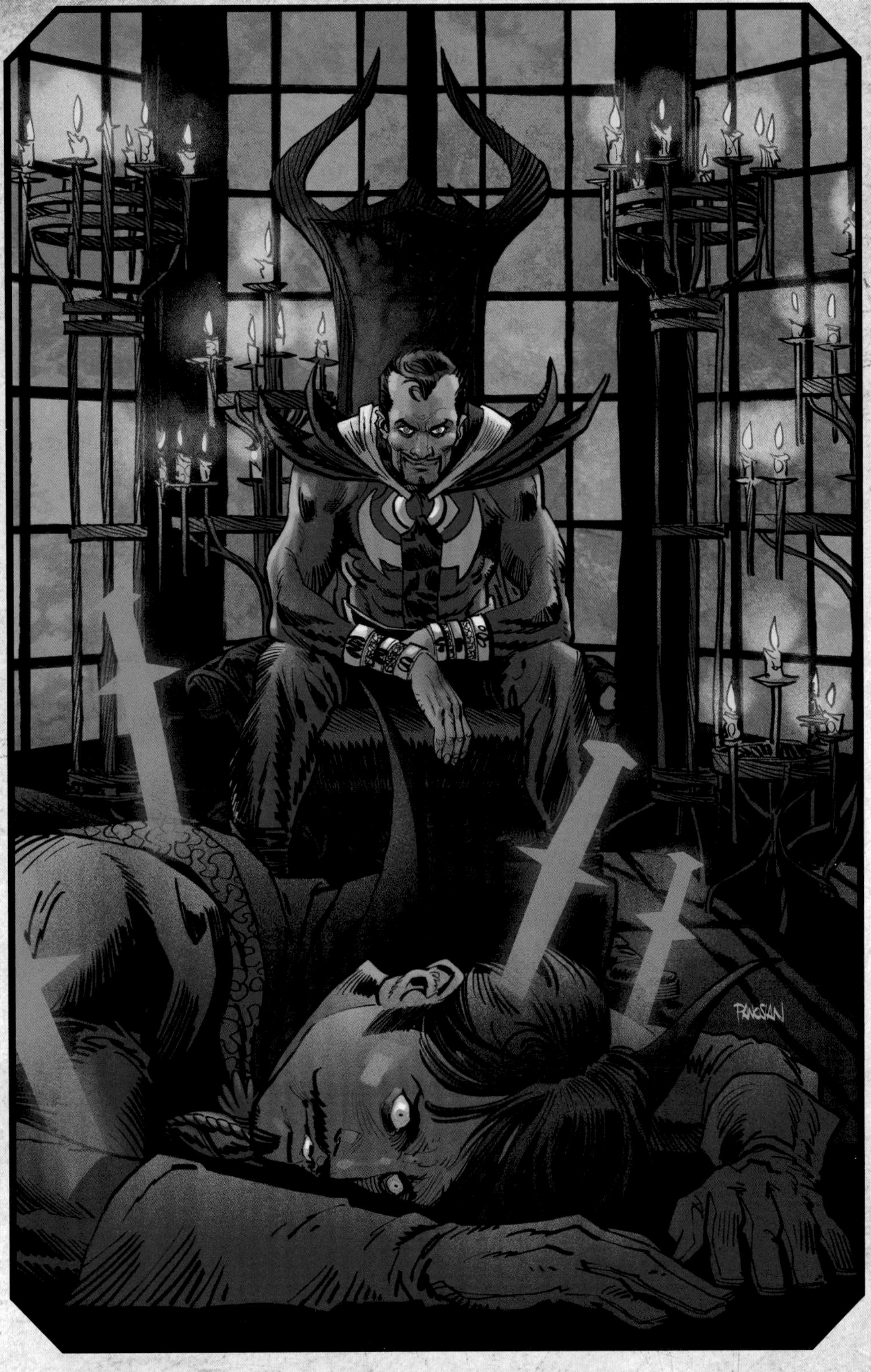
PANOSIAN

Dan Panosian

#2 VARIANT

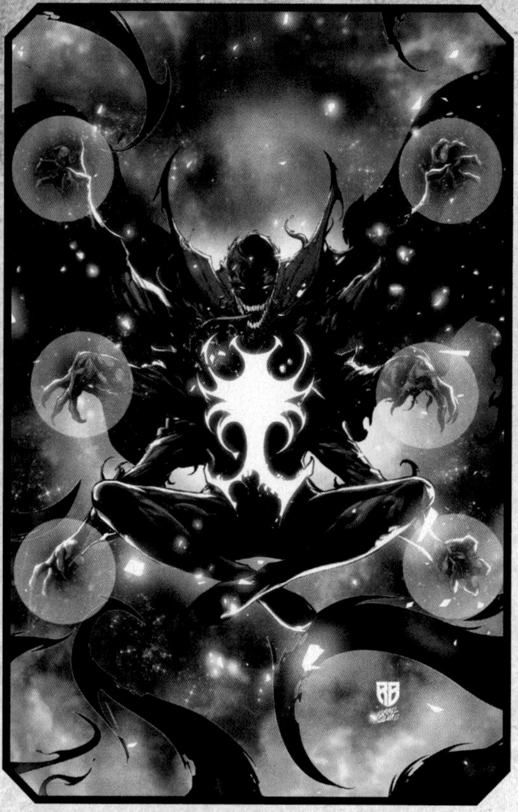

R.B. Silva & Israel Silva

#2 STORMBREAKERS VARIANT

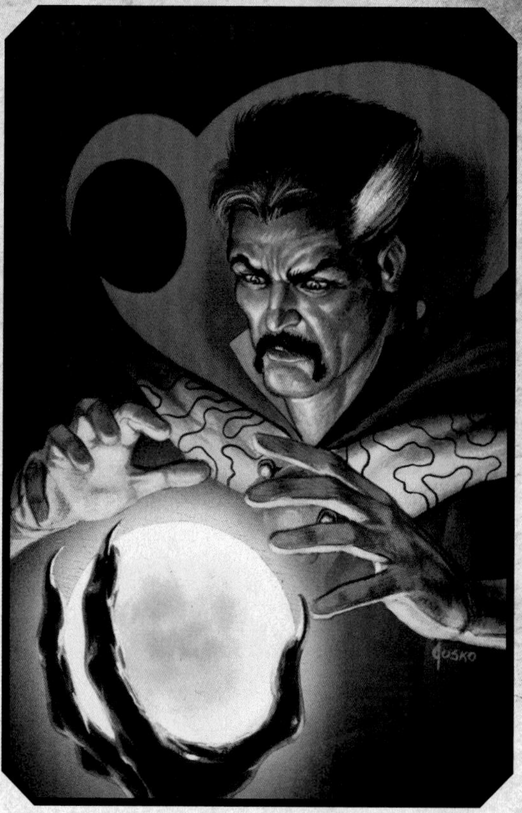

Joe Jusko

#2 MARVEL MASTERPIECES VARIANT

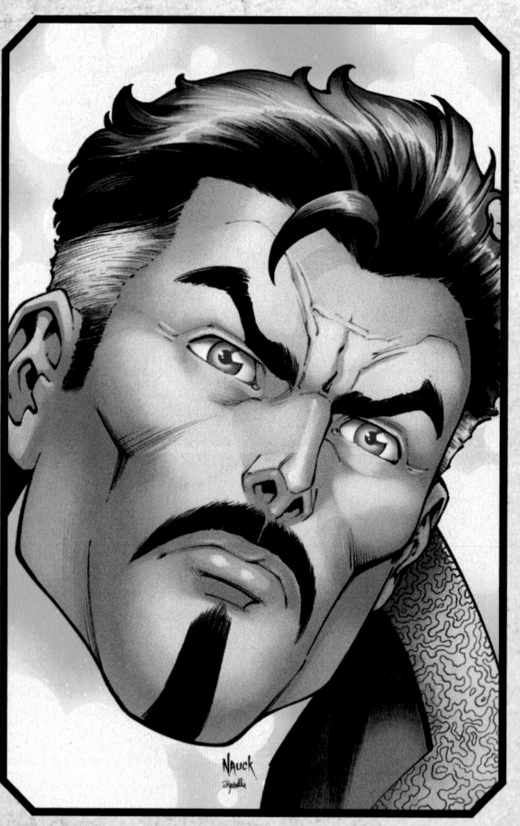

Todd Nauck & Rachelle Rosenberg

#2 HEADSHOT VARIANT

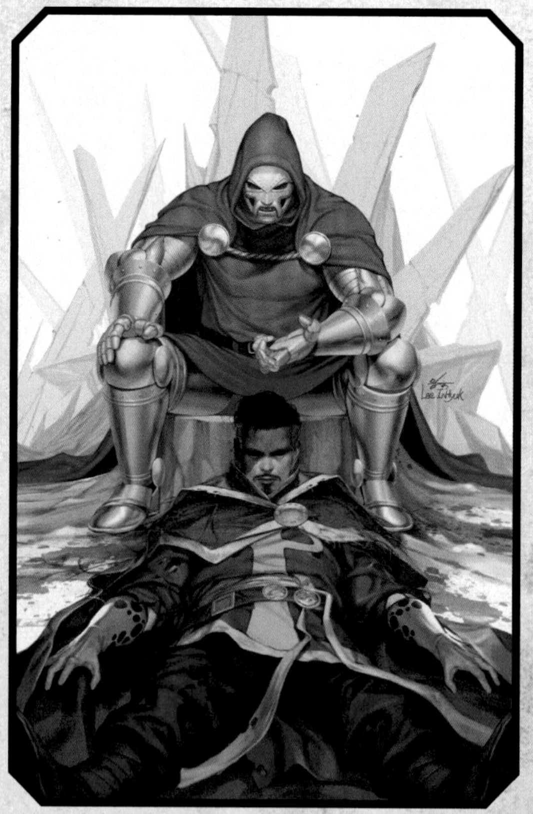

InHyuk Lee

#3 VARIANT

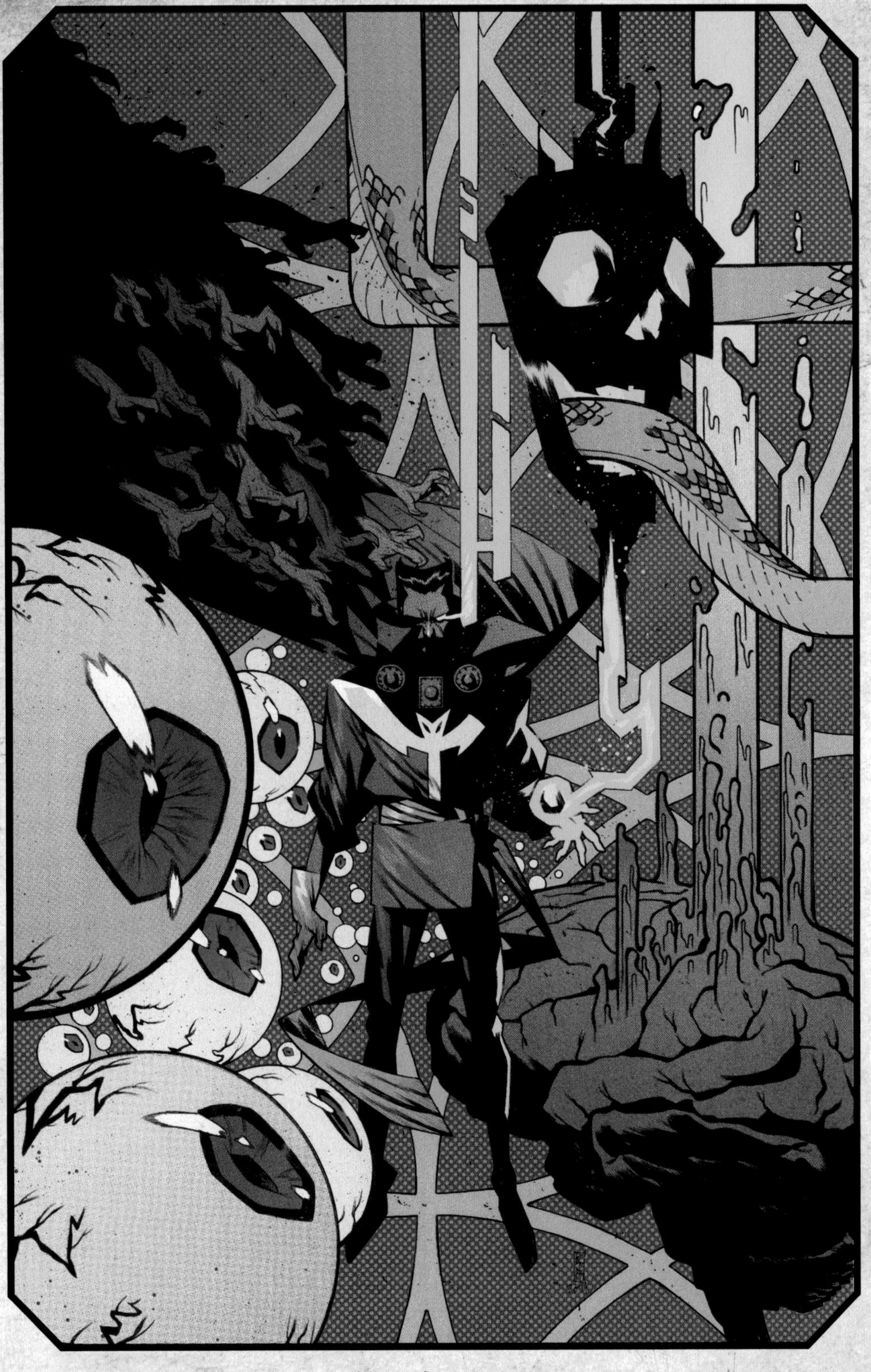

Kim Jacinto

#3 VARIANT

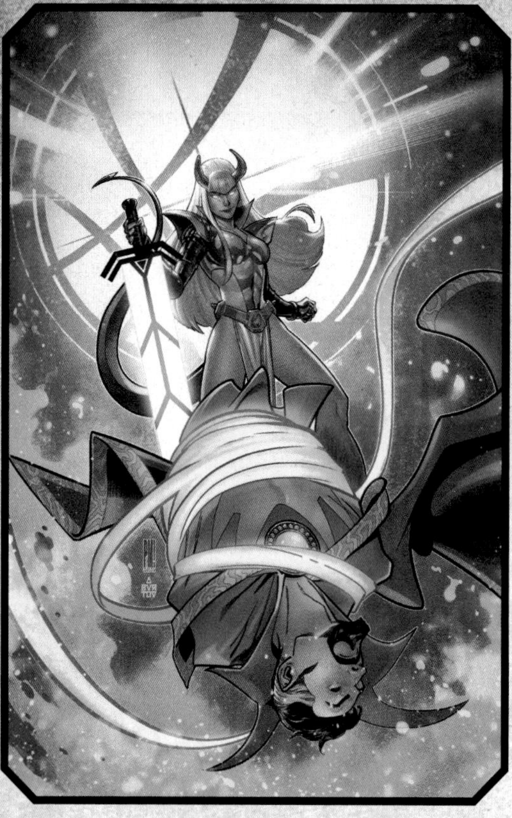

Paco Medina & Jesus Aburtov

#4 VARIANT

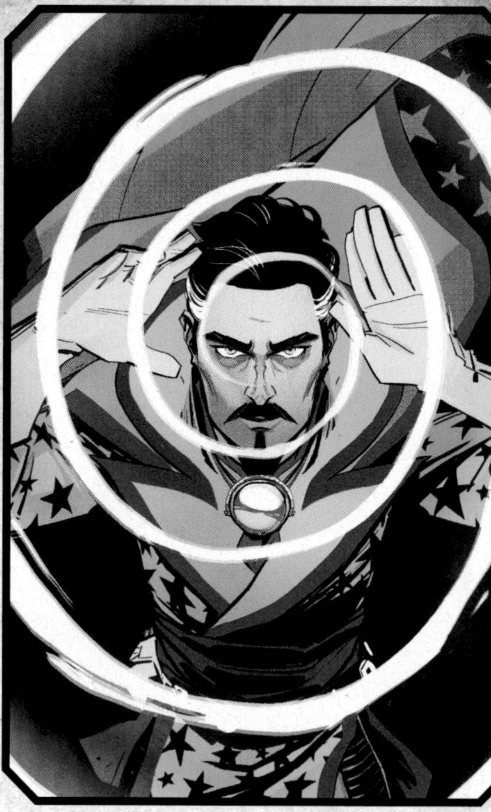

Annie Wu

#4 DEVIL'S REIGN VARIANT

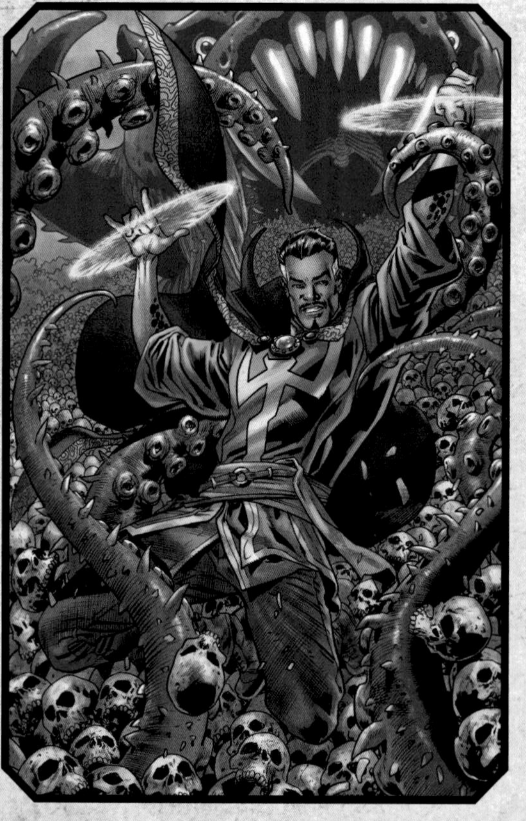

Bryan Hitch & Alex Sinclair

#5 VARIANT

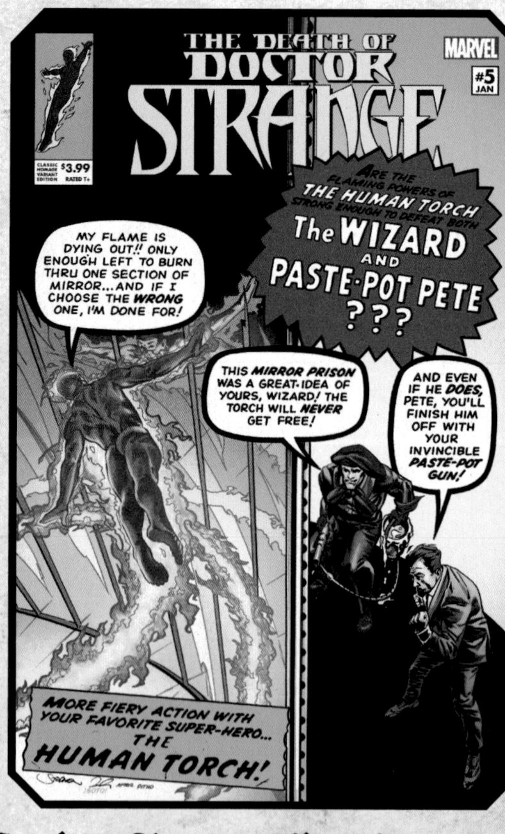

THE DEATH OF
DOCTOR
STRANGE
MARVEL
#5 JAN
$3.99 RATED T+
ARE THE FLAMING POWERS OF THE HUMAN TORCH STRONG ENOUGH TO DEFEAT BOTH The WIZARD AND PASTE-POT PETE ???
MY FLAME IS DYING OUT!! ONLY ENOUGH LEFT TO BURN THRU ONE SECTION OF MIRROR...AND IF I CHOOSE THE WRONG ONE, I'M DONE FOR!
THIS MIRROR PRISON WAS A GREAT IDEA OF YOURS, WIZARD! THE TORCH WILL NEVER GET FREE!
AND EVEN IF HE DOES, PETE, YOU'LL FINISH HIM OFF WITH YOUR INVINCIBLE PASTE-POT GUN!
MORE FIERY ACTION WITH YOUR FAVORITE SUPER-HERO... THE HUMAN TORCH!

Stephen Mooney & Chris Sotomayor

#5 CLASSIC HOMAGE VARIANT

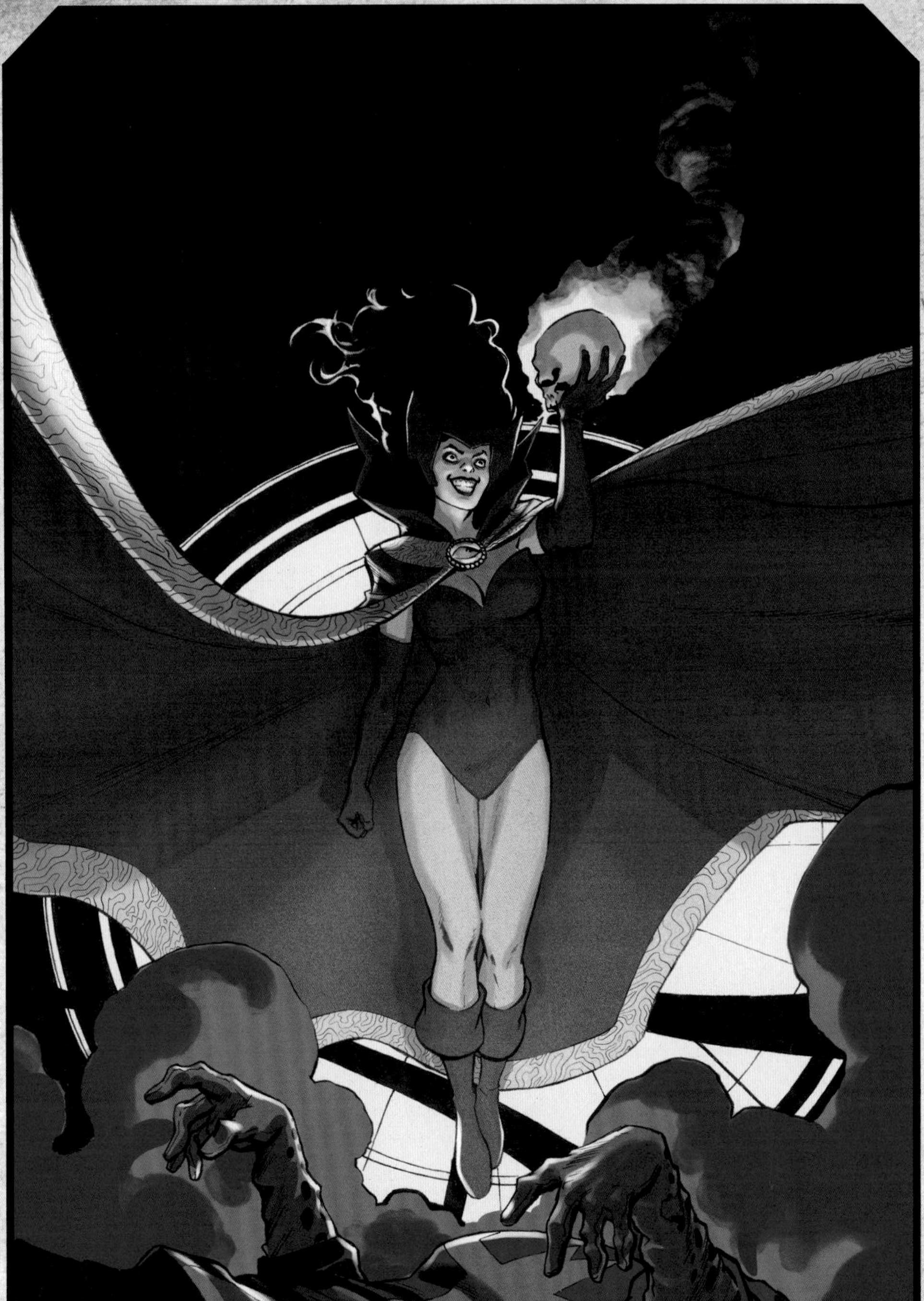

David Lopez
#5 VARIANT

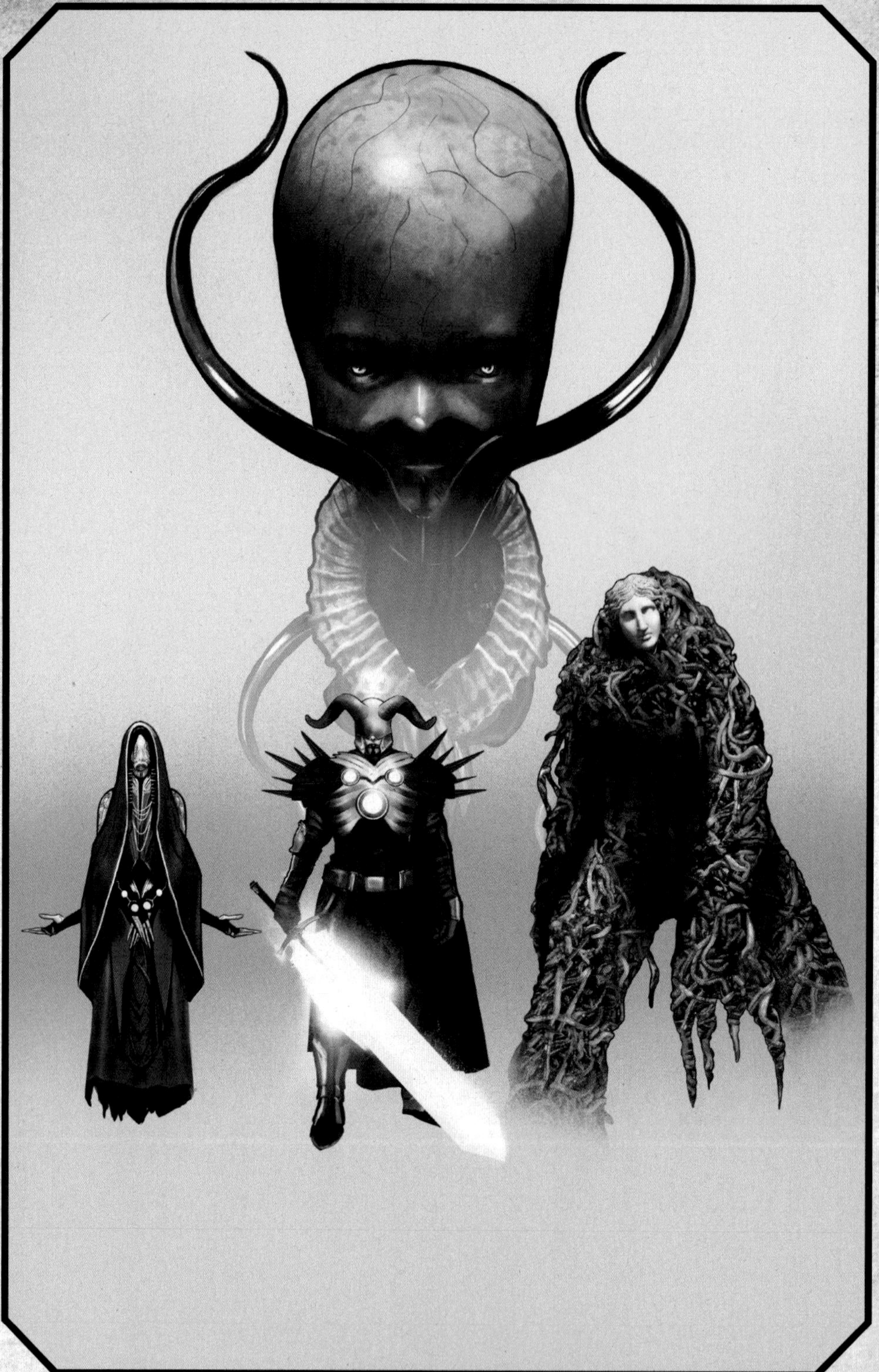

Lee Garbett

CHARACTER DESIGNS

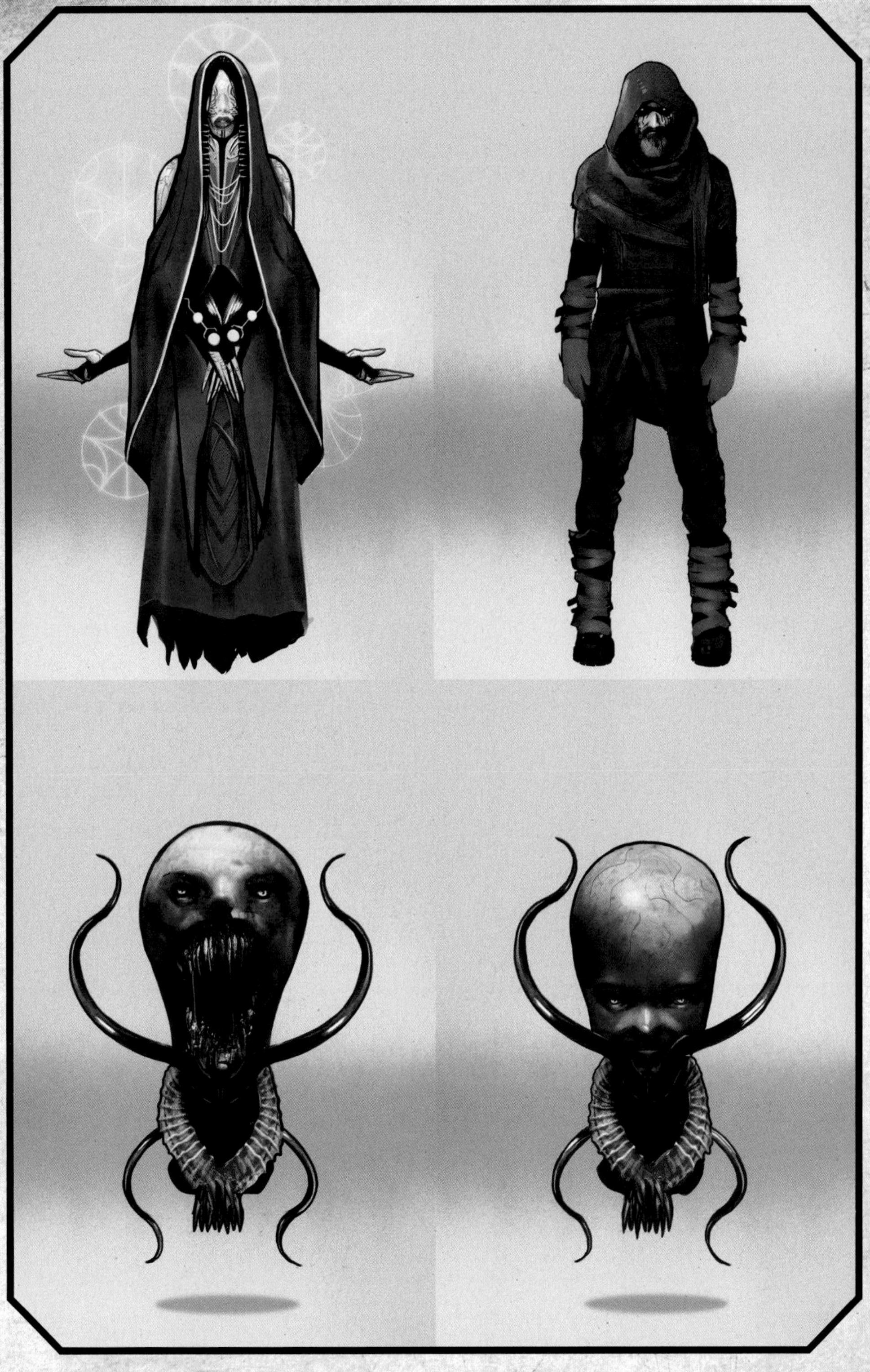

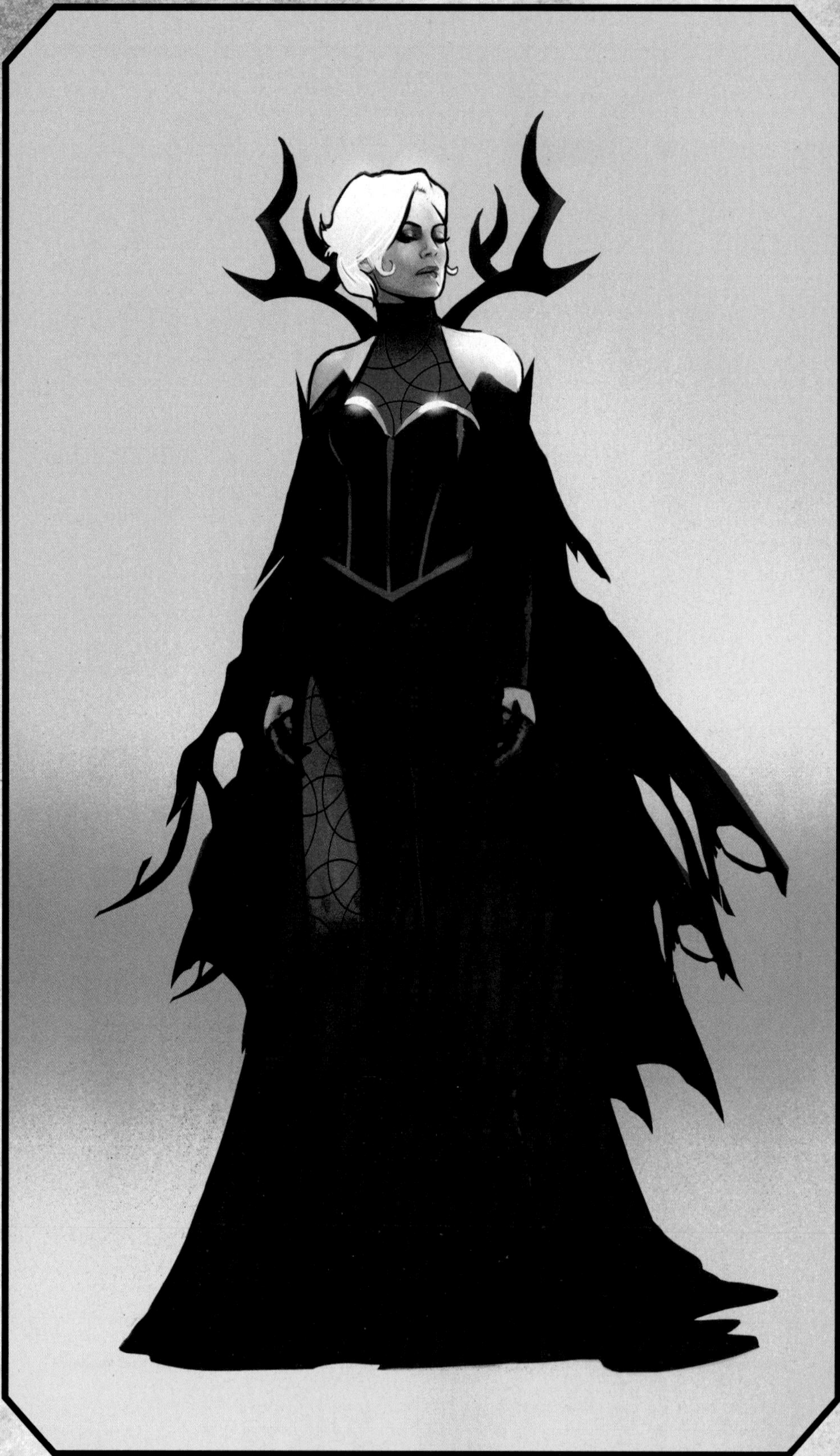

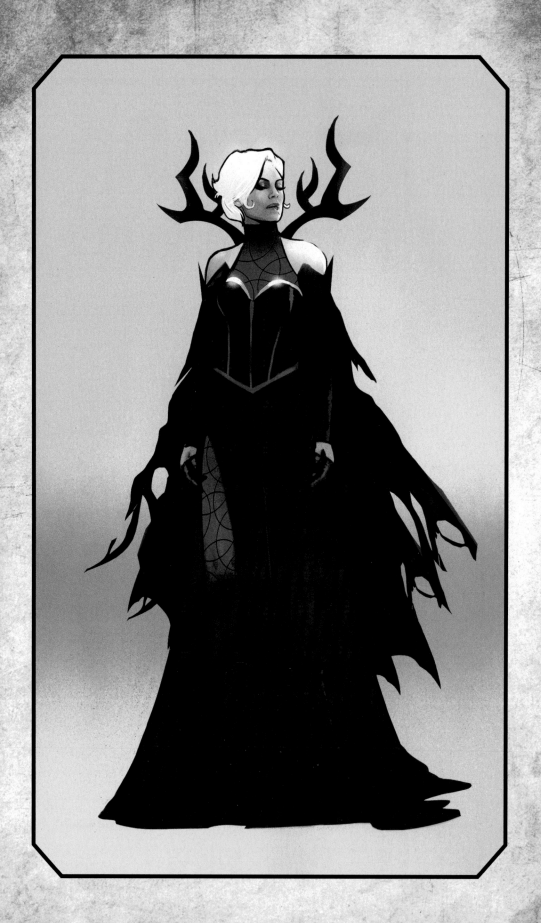